Unfinished Business

Race, Equity, and Diversity in Library and Information Science Education

Edited by
Maurice B. Wheeler

THE SCARECROW PRESS, INC.
Lanham, Maryland • *Toronto* • *Oxford*
2005

SCARECROW PRESS, INC.

Published in the United States of America
by Scarecrow Press, Inc.
A wholly owned subsidiary of
The Rowman & Littlefield Publishing Group, Inc.
4501 Forbes Boulevard, Suite 200, Lanham, Maryland 20706
www.scarecrowpress.com

PO Box 317
Oxford
OX2 9RU, UK

British Library Cataloguing in Publication Information Available

Library of Congress Cataloging-in-Publication Data

Unfinished business : race, equity, and diversity in library and information
    science education / edited by Maurice B. Wheeler.
    p. cm.
    Includes bibliographical references.
    ISBN 0-8108-5045-1 (pbk. : alk. paper)
    1. Library education—United States. 2. Information science—Study and
teaching (Higher)—United States. 3. Minorities in library science—Recruiting—
United States. 4. Library schools—Curricula—United States. 5. Minorities—
Education (Higher)—United States. 6. Multicultural education—
United States. 7. Affirmtive action programs—United States. I. Wheeler,
Maurice B.
Z668.U525 2005
020'.71'073—dc22

2004012515

∞™ The paper used in this publication meets the minimum requirements of
American National Standard for Information Sciences—Permanence of Paper
for Printed Library Materials, ANSI/NISO Z39.48-1992.
Manufactured in the United States of America.

To E. J. Josey—
Library and Information Science's "Drum Major for Justice"

For the past sixty years, Professor E. J. Josey has been a bold, articulate, and outspoken leader for inclusion and equality in library practice, professional association leadership, and library education. No accurate history of the library and information science profession can be written without recognition of the effect of his work and his words. Although he is without peer as a mentor of both students and professionals, his most extraordinary accomplishment is to have mentored an entire profession, encouraging the transition from racial segregation to integration, from mere tolerance to acceptance, and from inclusion to full participation.

Contents

Part II: Student Recruitment

Part III: Faculty and Curriculum Issues

Foreword

The year 2004 marks the fiftieth anniversary of the *Brown v. Board of Education* U.S. Supreme Court decision requiring the desegregation of public schools in America. As the nation pauses to consider the effect of this landmark decision on our collective social and educational evolution, it seems fitting to consider a wide range of educational issues regarding race, equity, and diversity in our own profession. The groundbreaking court decision had a tremendous effect on libraries and librarians. It reshaped laws, policies, and practices and, to some degree, attitudes about education as well as use of public facilities such as libraries.

It seems hard to imagine that in 1991, a new generation of Supreme Court justices quietly began what could be viewed as an incremental reversal of the 1954 decision.[1] In January 2004, the Civil Rights Project at Harvard University released the findings of new research on the re-segregation of American public schools.

> The report finds that in the past decade there has been backward movement for desegregation in U.S. schools, especially for Latino and African American students, and particularly in the South; and, that Asian students are the most integrated and most successful students by far.[2]

Realistically, there is no need for research regarding the re-segregation of library schools. Statistically speaking, there are few, if any, that have ever been truly integrated. Several contributors to this book point to student and faculty demographics that clearly indicate that while library school classrooms are not segregated by policy, they have remained so by negligent recruitment and retention practices. Yet, despite frustrations fueled by enormous political and organizational challenges, there is optimism for the future.

There is a distinct change in the exchange of rhetoric on the topic of diversity, both in the profession and in the nation. As witnessed by the level of support for the University of Michigan's recruitment policies, there is a critical mass of people who at least understand the significance of racial, ethnic, and cultural diversity for education, the professions, and enterprise.[3] The enthusiastic support for the American Library Association's Spectrum Initiative is both exciting and encouraging. Equally exciting are innovative recruitment models being developed at universities through significant support from agencies such as the Institute of Museum and Libraries.

The complexity of issues within the educational process, however, is daunting. For example, when universities finally get faculty excited about teaching new material in new ways that speak to a wide range of students, those who are committed to maintaining the status quo see it as a "call to arms."

In April 2003, the president of the University of Kansas and the Kansas Board of Regents affirmed their support for a faculty member whose extremely popular method of teaching human sexuality had been challenged by Kansas State Senator Susan Wagle. Wagle attempted to address the matter through a budget appropriations bill, causing Governor Kathleen Sebelius to veto the proviso in the bill "as an inappropriate use of legislative powers designed to impinge upon academic freedom in the State of Kansas."[4]

Considering such inappropriate responses to innovation in the classroom, it is not difficult to understand why faculty fight so hard for the right to teach unencumbered by external forces. However, sometimes faculty do need encouragement and support to incorporate diversity, technology, and other new curricula issues into their teaching.

This volume covers a wide range of topics related to diversity in library and information science education, including those mentioned above. The contributors bring an equally wide range of experience and perspectives on diversity. They have been challenged to reflect on the past, consider the present, and reinvigorate the discourse regarding the future.

Indeed, great strides have been made in an effort to provide African Americans, and later other people of color, with equal opportunities for intellectual and professional pursuits. Yet, 141 years after the Emancipation Proclamation, 50 years after *Brown v. Board of Education*, and 40 years after the Civil Rights Act of 1964, the Supreme Court has determined that affirmative action in higher education is still appropriate, and necessary. America has yet to be fully exorcised of its demons of racial bigotry and inequities in education. There is still a great deal of *Unfinished Business*.

Maurice B. Wheeler

NOTES

1. The Supreme Court's *Dowell v. Oklahoma City* (1991) decision "authorized a return to segregated neighborhood schools, through the 2001–2002 school year." The Civil Rights Project, "*Brown* at 50: King's Dream or Plessy's Nightmare?" news release, 17 January 2004. Available at: www.civilrightsproject.harvard.edu/news/pressreleases/brown04.php (accessed 15 January 2004).

2. Gary Orfield and Chungmei Lee, *Brown at 50: King's Dream or Plessy's Nightmare*. Cambridge, MA: Civil Rights Project, Harvard University, 2004. Available at: www.civilrightsproject. harvard.edu/research/reseg04/brown50.pdf (accessed 15 January 2004).

3. Diana Schemo, "300 Groups File Briefs to Support the University of Michigan in Affirmative Action Case," *New York Times*, 18 February 2003.

4. The University of Kansas Office of University Relations, "State Funding of Sexuality Classes," www.ur.ku.edu/News/sw303/index.html#Anchor-veto (accessed 15 January 2004).

I

ENVIRONMENTAL AND EXTERNAL FORCES

1

Brown v. Board of Education and Its Effect on Libraries and Library and Information Science Education:

Mapping and Storytelling a Historical Journey Fifty Years in the Making

Elizabeth Figa and Janet Macpherson

> We come then to the question presented: Does segregation of children in public schools solely on the basis of race, even though the physical facilities and other "tangible" factors may be equal, deprive the children of the minority group of equal educational opportunities? We believe that it does. . . .We conclude that in the field of public education the doctrine of "separate but equal" has no place. Separate educational facilities are inherently unequal.
>
> —Supreme Court Chief Justice Earl Warren, May 17, 1954

What is the effect of *Brown v. Board of Education* on library and information science education? And will mapping and storytelling its historical fifty-year journey (which is still in the making) reveal answers?

The word map comes from the word that the Romans used for napkin, *mappa*, which means signal cloth. Maps reveal information to us on a multitude of levels. Through the eye's lens, the visualization of a landscape as drawn by a cartographer yields the lay of the land, documents indicators of direction, colorizes the texture of landscapes, provides a sense of place and space, reveals dimensions and relationships, and depicts the effect of the advancement of time.

Storytelling, like maps, "is as old as humankind yet as new as this morning's news headlines. We have told stories since the beginning of time. They are the narratives of life, spanning the centuries and connecting the generations. They are the vessels in which we carry our history and traditions, our values and lessons for living, our hopes and dreams."[1]

Mapping and storytelling become metaphors for exploring the terrain and considering stories from the past toward our goal—to reveal the landscape

of *Brown v. Board of Education* (hereafter referred to as *Brown*)—and inspire us to consider its effect on library and information science education.
Conceptualizing and realizing this framework for discussion of the various
dimensions and intricacies of *Brown* was both daunting and stimulating, and
yet, sense-making. There is an incredible body of literature about *Brown* and
the process required narrowing the resources considerably for a chapter-
length discussion.

Once the "here" and "there" were plotted and traversed, what was revealed became allegorical, with abstract ideas suggesting deeper, symbolic,
and parallel meanings of *Brown* as it forms a cultural information system.
The facts and opinions and effect of this case are inextricably connected and
unfold in a story that is still being written. Like the variants of a folktale, the
motifs of *Brown* are dynamic and can be represented in a variety of forms.
Even the most fastidious mapmaker or storyteller is imperfect and never able
to tell the whole truth because of the restrictions imposed by representation.
Our ethnographic survey of this history results in the presentation of our
viewpoints and some important questions we believe should be considered.

Like maps and stories, some people are more comfortable with simple and
straightforward forms. Others want more elaboration and detail, with a leg-
end that provides a sense of the scale of the landscape scale and the rules of
the map. Because maps are wrought from the social milieu, they come with
flaws, prejudices, biases, and problems of imperfection. Still, they help to organize understanding and act to reflect the map-making systems of various
environments, social structures, or entities.[2]

The story that emerges over fifty years about *Brown* is remarkable, disturbing, and laden with serious implications. We do not claim authority on this
topic. We are two library and information scientists with interdisciplinary training who have considered the social construction that is *Brown*. We entered
into a discourse to explore the contemporary milieu as we consider the fiftieth
anniversary of this watershed event in American history. During *Brown*'s
golden anniversary year in 2004, many voices can be heard in national, regional, and local venues with commemorative events, editorial pages splashed
with opinions, retrospective works, celebrations, and even protests. The U.S.
Congress has created the *Brown v. Board of Education* Fiftieth Anniversary
Commission to lead a national observance of the event.[3] With these opportunities, we challenge readers to participate in some way and learn more about
the story of *Brown* and what it means in their life and work.

THE CASE—A BASIC LAY OF THE LAND

Linda Brown was a black third-grader living in Topeka, Kansas, in 1951. She
lived seven blocks from a school—an all-white school—in which she was
not allowed to enroll. Instead, she was required to walk a mile to school

through a dangerous railroad-switching yard with moving trains and over a rough, potholed dirt road. Her parents' failed attempts to change her school venue resulted in their receiving the help of the local branch of the National Association for the Advancement of Colored People (NAACP), a group determined to use the federal courts to challenge the segregation of blacks and whites in public schools.[4]

On May 17, 1954, U.S. Supreme Court Justice Earl Warren delivered the unanimous ruling[5] in the landmark civil rights case *Brown v. Board of Education of Topeka, Kansas,*[6] which determined that state-sanctioned segregation of public schools was a violation of the Fourteenth Amendment and therefore unconstitutional.[7] This historic decision marked the end of the "separate but equal" precedent set by the Supreme Court nearly sixty years earlier in the *Plessy v. Ferguson* decision, which "upheld a Louisiana statute that required segregation of railway carriages"[8] and served as a catalyst for the expanding civil rights movement during the 1950s.[9]

Often characterized as "the most important Supreme Court ruling in our history,"[10] *Brown* also marked the beginning of the modern Supreme Court.[11] Martin's book treats *Brown* as a cultural symbol or metaphor shedding light on American hegemony and the civil rights movement—becoming the landmark decision in which, as Bell states, "the court ordered the end of state-mandated racial segregation of public schools."[12] As the subject of nearly fifty years of interpretation, Bell recalls one of his professors warning that there was more to *Brown* than met the eye.[13] Sarat quotes the editors of the *Yale Law Journal*, arguing that what they said then is no less true today: "No modern case has had a greater impact either on our day-to-day lives or on the structure of government,"[14] despite continuing mixed reviews about *Brown* and its legacy.

Many do not understand that the "case called *Brown* was actually a collection of five cases . . . the Court heard them together because each raised the issue of the constitutionality of racially segregated public school, albeit with slight different facts and circumstances."[15] Balkin argues that *Brown* has become a beloved legal and political icon, the country's national narrative, in our historic quest for democratic ideals. Balkin's fascinating book brings together leading constitutional scholars, each assigned to rewrite the *Brown* opinion—whether as majority opinion, concurrence, or dissent—using only materials available at the time of the decision. It is clear from the text, the arguments, and discussion within its pages that the meaning of *Brown* is still grappled with and that the effect of law on reshaping social change continues to be wildly debated.

PRE-*BROWN*—THE LEGAL LANDSCAPE[16]

There are a number of legal cases that set precedents about issues of race and education prior to *Brown*. Contextualization of these cases into the cultural and legal information system we are examining reveals the variations in decisions in a timeline that, at its core, is about race, power, and the transformation of the lives of a people.

Dred Scott v. Sandford (1857). The Supreme Court held that blacks, enslaved or free, could not be citizens of the United States. Chief Justice Taney, arguing from the original intentions of the framers of the 1787 Constitution, stated that at the time of the adoption of the Constitution, black people were considered a subordinate and inferior class of beings, "with no rights which the white man was bound to respect." Significance: The Supreme Court denied citizenship to black people, setting the stage for their treatment as second-class citizens.

Bureau of Refugees, Freedmen, and Abandoned Lands (1865). The Bureau of Refugees, Freedmen, and Abandoned Lands, also known as the Freedmen's Bureau, was established by an act of Congress on March 3, 1865. Its main mission was to provide relief and help freedmen become self-sufficient in all areas of life. Significance: The first black schools and universities were set up under the direction of the Freedmen's Bureau.

Black Codes (1865). The name given to laws passed by southern governments established during the presidency of Andrew Johnson. These laws imposed severe restrictions on freedmen, such as prohibiting their right to vote, forbidding them to sit on juries, and limiting their right to testify against white men. They were also forbidden from carrying weapons in public places and working in certain occupations. Significance: Segregation begins—public schools were segregated, and blacks were barred from serving on juries and testifying against whites.

Civil Rights Act (1866). The 1866 Civil Rights Act guaranteed blacks the basic economic rights to contract, sue, and own property. Significance: The intention of this law was to protect the civil rights of all persons in the United States, including blacks.

Ratification of the Fourteenth Amendment to the Constitution (1868). The Fourteenth Amendment guaranteed that all persons born or naturalized in the United States are citizens of the United States and of the state in which they reside, and that no state shall abridge the privileges and immunities of citizens, deprive any person of life, liberty, or property without due process of law, nor deny to any person the equal protection of the law. Significance: The Fourteenth Amendment overruled *Dred Scott v. Sandford*.

Slaughterhouse Cases (1873). These cases narrowly defined federal power and emasculated the Fourteenth Amendment by asserting that most of the rights of citizens remain under state control. Significance: Pro-segregation states would come to justify their policies based on the notion that segregation in their public school systems was a states' rights issue.

Civil Rights Act (1875). The Civil Rights Act of 1875 prohibited discrimination in inns, theaters, and other places of public accommodation. Significance: It was the last federal civil rights act passed until 1957.

Civil Rights Cases (1883). The Supreme Court overturned the Civil Rights Act of 1875 in 1883 and declared that the Fourteenth Amendment does not prohibit discrimination by private individuals or businesses. Significance: In overturning the Act of 1875, the Court emphasized what the Fourteenth Amendment does not prohibit, and thus paved the way for segregation in public education.

Jim Crow (1887). The practice of comprehensive racial segregation known as "Jim Crow" emerged and racial separation became entrenched by the late 1880s. Significance: Florida was the first state to enact a statute requiring segregation in places of public accommodation. Eight other states followed Florida's lead by 1892.

Plessy v. Ferguson (1896). Homer A. Plessy challenged an 1890 Louisiana law that required separate train cars for black Americans and white Americans. The Supreme Court held that separate but equal facilities for white and black railroad passengers did not violate the equal protection clause of the Fourteenth Amendment. Significance: *Plessy v. Ferguson* established the "separate but equal" doctrine that would become the constitutional basis for segregation.

Cumming v. Richmond County [Georgia] *Board of Education* (1899). The Supreme Court upheld a local school board's decision to close a free public black school due to fiscal constraints, despite the fact that the district continued to operate two free public white schools.

Berea College v. Commonwealth of Kentucky (1908). The Supreme Court upheld a Kentucky state law forbidding interracial instruction at all schools and colleges in the state.

NAACP founded (1909). A multiracial group of activists answer the "call" to renew the struggle for civil and political liberty and formed the National Negro Committee, which soon became the NAACP. Significance: The NAACP is the oldest civil rights organization in the United States.

Gong Lum v. Rice (1927). The Supreme Court held that a Mississippi school district may require a Chinese-American girl to attend a segregated black school rather than a white school.

State of Missouri ex rel. Gaines v. Canada (1938). The Supreme Court decided in favor of Lloyd Gaines, a black student who had been refused admission to the University of Missouri Law School. The Court held that the state must furnish Gaines "within its borders facilities for legal education substantially equal to those which the State there offered for the persons of the white race, whether or not other Negroes sought the same opportunity." Significance: This case set a precedent for other states to attempt to "equalize" black school facilities, rather than integrate them.

Sipuel v. Board of Regents of University of Oklahoma (1948). A unanimous Supreme Court held that Lois Ada Sipuel could not be denied entrance to a state law school solely because of her race. Significance: The Court ruled unconstitutional denial of entrance to a state law school solely on the basis of race.

Briggs et al. v. Elliott et al. (1949). Thurgood Marshall and NAACP officials met with black residents of Clarendon County, South Carolina. They decided that the NAACP would launch a test case against segregation in public schools if at least twenty plaintiffs could be found. Significance: *Briggs v. Elliott* became one of the cases consolidated by the Supreme Court into *Brown v. Board of Education.*

Sweatt v. Painter (1950). The Supreme Court held that the University of Texas Law School must admit a black student, Herman Sweatt. The University of Texas Law School was far superior in its offerings and resources than the separate black law school, which had been hastily established in a downtown basement. Significance: The Supreme Court held that Texas failed to provide separate but equal education, prefiguring the future opinion in *Brown* that "separate but equal is inherently unequal."

McLaurin v. Oklahoma State Regents (1950). The Supreme Court invalidated the University of Oklahoma's requirement that a black student admitted to a graduate program unavailable to him at the state's black school must sit in separate sections of or in spaces adjacent to the classroom, library, and cafeteria. Significance: The Supreme Court held that these restrictions were unconstitutional because they interfered with the student's "ability to study, to engage in discussions, and exchange views with other students, and, in general, to learn his profession."

Bolling v. Sharpe (1950). The Consolidated Parents Group attempted to enroll a group of black students in the all-white John Philip Sousa Junior High School in Washington, DC. Significance: The *Bolling* case became one of the consolidated *Brown* cases.

Davis et al. v. County School Board (1951). This case was a challenge to Virginia's segregated school system. Significance: This case was another of the cases eventually consolidated as *Brown v. Board of Education.*

Briggs et al. v. Elliott et al. (1951). This South Carolina case went to trial. Marshall and the NAACP presented a vast array of social science evidence showing how segregation harmed black school children, including evidence from sociologist Kenneth Clark's controversial "doll study." Significance: The U.S. District Court denied the Briggs plaintiffs' request to order desegregation of Clarendon County schools, and instead ordered the equalization of black schools.

March Davis v. County School Board (1952). The U.S. District Court found in favor of the school board under the theory of "separate but equal." Significance: The U.S. District Court unanimously rejected the Davis plaintiffs' request to order desegregation of Prince Edward County, Virginia, schools, ordering instead the equalization of black schools.

April Gebhart et al. v. Belton et al.; Gebhart et al. v. Bulah et al.; Belton et al. v. Gebhart et al.; Bulah et al. v. Gebhart et al. (1952). A Delaware court ruled that the plaintiffs were entitled to immediate admission to white public schools. Significance: In the Gebhart cases, the court ruled that the plaintiffs were being denied equal protection of the law and ordered that the eleven children involved be immediately admitted to Delaware's white schools. The board of education appealed the decision.

December 9th–11th (1952). First round of arguments held in *Brown* and its companion cases.

Brown v. Board of Education (1954). The Court overturned *Plessy v. Ferguson*, and declared that racial segregation in public schools violated the equal protection clause of the Fourteenth Amendment.

PRE-*BROWN*—THE GENERAL LANDSCAPE

The timeline of legal cases just reviewed packs a powerful punch; a definitive construction of the panorama of legal issues and themes pressing change in America; changes that gradually affected black American life and radically shook up white culture. As noted earlier, sometimes when people discuss hard topics, such as issues of race, they have greater comfort with the simple and straightforward approach; however, these kinds of discussions are complex and dynamic. The pre-*Brown* landscape paints a necessary temporal stream for remembering an era in our history.

Peterson defines race as "a fluid, social construct devised as a form of social control."[17] Dickeman indicates that institutional racism "refers to all those aspects of the structure and operations of an institution which result in discrimination."[18] Dickeman continues that "it assists us to identify those points at which we can expect racism, and to comprehend the functions it serves; things which we must know if we are to eradicate racism"[19] in libraries. There are many facets that must be explored to understand the issues of race and racial relations in the United States. We believe this understanding of the times before and just after the *Brown* ruling by the U.S. Supreme Court helps to illustrate how this ruling changed the landscape for black libraries, black librarians, and library and information science education.

Prior to the *Brown* ruling, both the North and South were segregated. The schools naturally reflected a society that was divided. In the South, segregation was based on law, whereas in the North segregation was without the sanction of law, but existed nonetheless.[20] At this time, the federal government sponsored assistance for separate schools, segregated public housing, and segregated programs for farmers.[21] "Segregation affected all blacks—rich or poor, educated or uneducated, northern or southern, light-skinned or dark-skinned, foreign born or native born."[22] The "separate but equal" policy was the only public policy that affected all blacks and only blacks in the history of the United States.[23]

Kevin Brown provides a good overall description of what was happening in this country before the *Brown* decision.

At the time the court delivered that opinion, people of African descent were called "Negro" or "colored" in general and were called "nigger," "darkie," and even "black" as an insult. America had not yet experienced the civil rights movement, the black Consciousness movement, or the Afrocentric movement. Segregation and conscious racial discrimination were not only the explicit law of the land in many places, but also standard American business, educational, political, and social practice. To discriminate based on race in merchandising stores, eating facilities, places of entertainment, and hotels and motels was generally accepted as a fact of life. African Americans seldom occupied positions in American businesses and corporations above the most menial levels. Even lower-level management positions were for the most part unobtainable. What in the 1990s is referred to as the "glass ceiling," forty years ago was a firmly implanted, outright concrete barrier. In 1964, only a handful of black students attended and almost no black faculty taught at prestigious white colleges and universities in this country. A black man had not been elected mayor of a major U.S. city in the twentieth century. And there were only four African Americans serving in Congress, none having been elected from the south since 1900. In 1954, many places in the country had separate water fountains, waiting rooms, transportation facilities, rest rooms, schools, hospitals, and cemeteries for whites and blacks.[24]

To further understand the cultural climate, consider that in 1954, the black poverty rate was close to 70 percent. President Truman had desegregated the armed forces, and the black soldiers who had come home from military service wanted jobs and equal opportunity. The Soviet Union was criticizing the treatment of black citizens in the United States. And in 1955, a black teenager was lynched in Mississippi for greeting a white woman.[25]

PRE-*BROWN*—BLACK LIBRARIANS

With the previously described backdrop of the cultural milieu and racial constructs of the pre-*Brown* nineteenth century and early- and mid-twentieth century in the United States, we will now consider the benchmarks and topography concerning black libraries and black librarians. The professional education of black librarians and paraprofessionals was slow to start but not absent from American culture. There were blacks being educated and their needs, desires, and ability to both produce and obtain information was no different from that of whites. There are several firsts worth noting.

In 1900, Edward C. Williams was the first African American to receive a library degree, graduating from the New York State Library School in Albany.[26] Virginia Procter Powell Florence was the first professionally educated female black librarian, graduating from the Carnegie Library School in Pittsburgh in 1923.[27] Eliza Atkins Gleason was the first African American woman to be awarded a PhD degree in librarianship from the University of Chicago in 1940.[28] Annette Hoage Phinazee was the first woman and the first black to earn a doctorate in library science from Columbia University in 1961.[29]

Innovative opportunities were also evolving. For example, from the early 1900s through the early 1930s, the Louisville Free Public Library offered an apprenticeship training program for African Americans.[30] The program came about out of necessity since the Western Colored Branch of Louisville needed "colored library assistants," which were certainly rare during this time period. The obvious solution was for the assistants to be trained by the library itself. In total, twenty-nine local persons and twelve from out of town took courses under the apprenticeship program.[31]

By 1925, only six African Americans were known to have graduated from accredited library schools. Between 1925 and 1939, African Americans were able to attend library school at Hampton University in Virginia.[32] Hampton was chosen as the place to put the library school from four institutions: Fisk, Howard, Tuskegee, and Hampton.[33] As reported by Dumont (1986), Hampton was selected as the site for several reasons. "First, it had a significant book collection in a good library building with a trained staff. Second, Hampton allowed a bi-racial faculty and so it could hire qualified white faculty to teach. Third, Hampton's alumni were placed in black leadership positions throughout the South and could aid in the placement of the library school's graduates."[34] Shiflett presents a slightly different picture of the process of choosing the appropriate place for the first black library school, which has to do with the influence of whites in positions of power. This would be consistent with other decisions made on behalf of blacks that benefited the interests of whites.[35] For instance, in 1930 there were more than 50 black college libraries, but only five were headed by blacks, leaving the influence and decision making in the hands of the whites in charge.[36]

Prior to the establishment of Hampton Institute Library School in Virginia in 1925, professionally trained black librarians were educated at predominantly white institutions.[37] Hampton was founded by a grant from the Carnegie Corporation on the recommendation of the officers of the General Education Board and the American Library Association (ALA). During its years of operation, Hampton graduated 183 black librarians.[38] This number may sound small, but it was not possible to place more than fifteen to twenty black library school graduates each year due to limited opportunities in not only the South but also the North and West.[39]

In 1925, there was only one other accredited library school program in the South besides Hampton—Emory University Library School in Atlanta, Georgia.[40] There was limited contact between Emory and Hampton, or later Atlanta

University, due to the racial situation in the South.[41] During the early-to-middle twentieth century, the development of librarianship as a field for professionally trained blacks happened for the most part through endowments and grants from private organizations, such as the Rosenwald Fund, the General Education Board, and the Carnegie Corporation of New York.[42]

In 1941, the School of Library Science at North Carolina College for Negroes and the Atlanta University School of Library Service were founded. Atlanta University was accredited by the ALA in 1943 and remained the only prominent library school for African Americans until 1975.[43] Similarly, there was no public institution with predominantly black students accredited by the ALA until 1975.[44] Atlanta University received the library collection from the library science program at Hampton Institute when it closed[45] (Stevenson, 1991). North Carolina College for Negroes, now North Carolina Central University, received accreditation from the ALA in 1975 under the leadership of Annette Hoage Phinazee.[46]

Totten indicates by 1950, only 72 of the 1,051 surveyed white colleges and universities employed African American teachers, and they usually held visiting appointments for limited periods of time. By the end of the 1950s, the number of African Americans teaching on a regular, full-time basis in predominantly white colleges and universities had increased to 200 individuals. In 1960, African Americans were 3 percent of all college and university faculty members, most members of historically black institutions.[47]

PRE-*BROWN*—BLACK LIBRARIES

Stories of the development of black libraries form a mosaic depicting colorful personalities, possessing both determination and foresight. There was no single plan, but rather the optimization of opportunities, such as life was for African Americans pre-*Brown*. In 1905, the Louisville Free Public Library established the first separate public library facility in America exclusively for blacks, which was operated and administered entirely by blacks, although supervised from the main library.[48] In 1912, Cincinnati opened a branch for blacks; Little Rock did the same in 1916 and Atlanta opened one in 1921. In 1922, there were only two cities in the South that provided free and unrestricted access to libraries for blacks—Hagerstown, Maryland, and Wheeling, West Virginia.[49]

Musmann reported that in 1913, Rochester Public Library librarian William F. Yustfrom, in an address to the ALA conference, attempted to establish the status of the Negro in the public library sphere by stating that libraries cannot thrive in an environment where people are prevented from learning to read and owning books. He indicated that education must precede the development of library services. The fact that there were so few libraries giving services to blacks, as well as so few blacks seeking library services, was attributed to the attitudes of white people about the education of African Americans. On the extreme edge of the meridian was the idea that education would "spoil a good plow hand" among other perceived threats to the ongoing subordination of black culture.[50]

The first discussion group for library workers among "colored people" took place at the 1921 ALA conference. The first formal round table to explore library work with African Americans was at the 1922 ALA conference held in Detroit. Ernestine Rose, a white librarian working in Harlem at the 135th Street Branch in New York City, prepared and delivered a summary of a questionnaire about library services for African Americans that was distributed to 98 library-related institutions. A report was published in the 1922 *ALA Bulletin* based upon data from the questionnaire responses. Musmann notes the following significant items included in the report: African Americans were not included in the governance of libraries, except for two segregated libraries in Charlotte, North Carolina, and Savannah, Georgia; none of the surveyed libraries employed African Americans educated in a library school, except for the segregated libraries, which only employed black library assistants; only two southern libraries provided unrestricted access to African Americans; and some libraries in the East and Midwest provided access to libraries for African Americans, but not all. Rose expressed her concern about an increase in segregation in the libraries in the northern states, but these concerns were ignored.[51]

During the second meeting of the Work with Negroes Round Table at the ALA convention held in Hot Springs, Arkansas, in 1923, approval was given to allowing segregated facilities, as long as they met the minimum requirements of being well organized and providing relevant services.[52] It was also agreed that individual sections of the country should be allowed to deal with the problems of library service to blacks on their own, with no national focus.[53] In contrast to this policy, the ALA made it quite clear that aid to immigrants, generally European immigrants, was a major organizational goal, and this topic was discussed at annual conferences by the Round Table on Work with the Foreign Born, a committee that was established in 1916 and which continued for thirty years.[54]

In 1930, Louis Shores published the results of a survey that examined the library services available for African Americans in eighty cities. From the results of the survey, Shores was able to divide the cities into five categories, including cities which provided no services to African Americans at all (which included eighteen cities); cities that allowed for limited use of the library facilities (for instance, books could be checked out, but blacks could not remain in the library to read); cities that provided segregated public library services; cities that had segregated branch libraries that were used by blacks but where use of other branches was also allowed; and cities that allowed full use of all library facilities to everyone.[55] Generally, cities located in the South provided no library services to blacks or provided them in segregated facilities, while cities in the East and West provided unrestricted and free access.[56] Even though many of the cities included in Shores' survey offered training programs and some technically allowed blacks to be admitted, no blacks actually matriculated to these training programs.[57]

It was common practice for rural black and white communities to be served by school libraries. In 1933, according to Lee only 20.5 percent of 215 black high schools in South Carolina held a library collection. Sources of funding to provide this type of service were rare. An indication of the inequity of the "separate but equal policy" can be seen in the average books per student in Richland County Library in 1936, which was 2.3 books per white student but less than two-thirds of one book per black student.[58]

The ALA convention in 1936 was held in Richmond, Virginia, where the state laws prohibited blacks and whites from staying in the same hotel or eating meals at the same place.[59] Conventions held in 1937, 1938, and 1939 were held in New Orleans, Kansas City, and Milwaukee respectively. The hotels where these conventions were held were segregated, and thus the African American members who attended were not permitted to stay at the hotels selected by the ALA. While there were members of the ALA who wrote letters asking the ALA to boycott the southern states for future conventions, others felt the treatment of the African American members of the ALA was appropriate because of the customs and practice of not only the South, but of most of the United States.[60]

Various surveys conducted between 1941 and 1953 kept the ALA membership informed about the state of segregation as it related to libraries.[61] Eliza Gleason's survey in 1941 revealed that only four states offered integrated library services for blacks and whites. Emily Miller Danton's 1948 survey showed that segregation was the standard practice, but that there were cases where exceptions were made. Lucretia Parker's 1953 survey indicated that conditions of segregation were improving and that thirty-nine cities in eleven states offered integrated services. Also in 1953, the Southern Regional Council revealed that fifty-nine cities offered full use of their main public libraries by blacks, twenty-four communities allowed limited use of facilities, and eleven allowed full service at one or more branches regardless of race.[62]

A. P. Marshall reminds us that equality is not something that can be had by degrees. "One is either equal or one is not equal. There are no in-betweens."[63] Jones discussed the resourcefulness of black librarians that came from the restricted circumstances under which they operated. Not only were black librarians closely identified and involved with their communities, but the meager library budgets forced skillful book selection based on strong book knowledge and a keen understanding of what was required by patrons. Black librarians couldn't be just librarians. They were much more. As the following description by Jones indicates, black librarians were "part teacher, part social worker, part counselor, whatever was needed to deal with patrons' needs relating to information, reading, research, or library programming. Typically, they have shared their talents and library facilities with the community as a part of their involvement in civic and cultural life."[64]

POST-*BROWN*—THE LEGAL LANDSCAPE[65]

The *Brown* decision was a landmark event. The legal and social obstacles that states and people put in place served as a catalyst for more change, protests, and the violent passions that launched the civil rights movement. There were immediate responses; many were swift, many were unpredictable, and many were predictable. It was clear that the all-white Supreme Court recognized the harmful nature of segregation and that the justices imagined a different kind of American educational landscape. The tidal waves that would erupt to enforce *Brown* would be many and involve even more legislation and more interpretation. The post-*Brown* timeline of legal decisions over the course of the ensuing fifty years reveals its weakness and holes. Still, as the sands of time pass, *Brown* stands steadfast as the core protectorate of equality in educational opportunity. As with the pre-*Brown* era, there are a number of post-*Brown* legal cases and events that are noteworthy.

Lucy v. Adams (1955). A federal district court ordered the admission of Autherine Lucy to the University of Alabama, and the Supreme Court quickly affirmed the decision.

Rosa Parks (1955). In 1955, Rosa Parks refused to give her bus seat to a white passenger and move to the back. Her arrest sparked the 382-day Montgomery bus boycott and the civil rights movement. The Legal Defense Fund (LDF) assisted local counsel in defending Parks.

President Eisenhower (1957). In 1957, President Eisenhower ordered National Guard troops to Little Rock, Arkansas, to escort nine black students to Central High School to enforce *Brown*.

Cooper v. Aaron (1958). This Supreme Court ruling barred Arkansas Governor Orval Faubus from interfering with the desegregation of Little Rock's Central High School. The decision affirmed *Brown* as the law of the land.

Prince Edward County, Virginia (1959). In 1959, Prince Edward County closed all of its public schools rather than desegregate them.

The Civil Rights Movement (1960–1965). With the sit-ins in North Carolina and Tennessee, the Freedom Rides to Alabama and Mississippi, and the voter registration program in the Deep South, the civil rights movement riveted the nation. The LDF acted as the legal arm of the civil rights movement and represented Dr. Martin Luther King Jr., the Southern Christian Leadership

Conference, the Student Nonviolent Coordinating Committee, and a host of locally based movement organizations.

Holmes v. Danner (1961). This case resulted in the admission to the University of Georgia of two African Americans: Charlayne Hunter and Hamilton Holmes.

Meredith v. Fair (1962). James Meredith finally succeeded in becoming the first African American student to be admitted to the University of Mississippi (Ole Miss) through the efforts of a legal team led by LDF attorney Constance Baker Motley.

The Civil Rights Act (1964). Passed by Congress in 1964, the Civil Rights Act banned discrimination in voting, public accommodations, schools, and employment.

Hamm v. City of Rock Hill (1965). The Supreme Court held that the Civil Rights Act of 1964 voided the convictions of all sit-in demonstrators.

Abernathy v. Alabama; Thomas v. Mississippi (1965). The Supreme Court reversed the convictions of Alabama and Mississippi Freedom Riders on the basis of *Boynton v. Virginia*, a 1960 Supreme Court ruling won by LDF that prohibited discrimination in interstate bus stop restaurants.

The Voting Rights Act was passed by Congress (1965).

Thurgood Marshall was appointed to the U.S. Supreme Court (1967), becoming the first African American to sit on the bench.

The Fair Housing Act (1968) was passed by Congress, prohibiting discrimination in the sale and rental of housing.

Green v. County School Board of New Kent County (Virginia) (1968). The Supreme Court held that "freedom of choice" plans were ineffective at producing actual school desegregation and had to be replaced with more effective strategies.

Swann v. Charlotte-Mecklenberg Board of Education (1971). The Supreme Court upheld the use of busing as a means of desegregating public schools.

Keyes v. School District No. 1, Denver (1973). The Supreme Court established legal rules for governing school desegregation cases outside of the South, holding that where deliberate segregation was shown to have affected a substantial part of a school system, the entire district must ordinarily be desegregated.

Adams v. Richardson (1973). A federal appeals court approved a district court order requiring federal education officials to enforce Title VI of the 1964 Civil Rights Act, which bars discrimination by recipients of federal funds, against state universities, public schools, and other institutions that receive federal money.

Milliken v. Bradley (1974). The Supreme Court ruled that in almost all cases a federal court cannot impose an inter-district remedy between a city and its surrounding suburbs to integrate city schools.

Bakke v. Regents of the University of California (1978). The Supreme Court ruled that schools can take race into account in admissions, but cannot use quotas.

Bob Jones University v. U.S.; *Goldboro Christian Schools v. U.S.* (1982). The Supreme Court appointed LDF Board Chair William T. Coleman Jr. as a "friend of the court" and upheld his argument against granting tax exemptions to religious schools that discriminate.

Geier v. Alexander (1982). As part of the settlement of a case requiring desegregation of its public higher education system, Tennessee agreed to identify seventy-five promising black sophomores each year and prepare them for eventual admission to the state's graduate and professional schools. A federal court of appeals approved this settlement in 1986 despite opposition from the Reagan administration.

Oklahoma City v. Dowell (1991).[66] This ruling allowed school districts to be declared "unitary" systems, meaning all schools were part of a common interracial system and had fair treatment after doing what was feasible to eliminate discrimination. This enabled district authorities to do what they wanted as long as it was not intentionally discriminatory, even through it would increase segregation.

United States v. Fordice (1992). The Supreme Court upheld a Fifth Circuit Court ruling that Mississippi had failed to demonstrate conclusively that it was fulfilling its duty to undo the legacy of *de jure* segregation in its higher education system. The Court approved judicially mandated, race-based measures as remedies.

Missouri v. Jenkins (1995). The Supreme Court ruled that some disparities, such as poor achievement among African American students, are beyond the authority of the federal courts to address. This decision reaffirmed the Supreme Court's desire to end federal court supervision of public schools and return control of schools to local authorities.

Hopwood v. Texas (1996). The Fifth Circuit of the Court of Appeals ruled that the affirmative action plans used by Texas universities were unconstitutional; the Supreme Court refused to review the case.

Gratz v. Bollinger; *Grutter v. Bollinger* (2003). The Supreme Court upheld the use of race-aware admissions policies at public colleges and universities to obtain "educational benefits that flow from a diverse student body." In the law school case, *Grutter v. Bollinger*, the Court upheld the University of Michigan's policy by a margin of 5–4, arguing that there was a compelling interest for a diverse student body and that efforts to maintain a significant number of minority students did not constitute an illegal quota. However, in a 6–3 decision, the justices ruled in the *Gratz v. Bollinger* case against Michigan's undergraduate admissions policy, claiming that it gives an overall advantage to minority students. The court did not reject the use of racial preferences to encourage diversity. Rather, it insisted that students be evaluated as individuals, with race being only one of the many factors considered.

POST-*BROWN*—THE GENERAL LANDSCAPE

Josey points out that even though the legal segregation structures were "torn down" with the *Brown* ruling, the old attitudes remained and laws were only as good as an individual's inclination to observe them.[67] This leads to the discussion of what happened with schools, black libraries, and black librarians after the *Brown* ruling. The *Brown* decision called for the desegregation of the schools in America but did nothing to address the desegregation of society as a whole.[68] The law called for a change in attitude in the schools that did not mirror the attitude that prevailed in society. For that change in the schools to take effect, the leaders needed to be accepting, respectful, and interested in justice and equality, but these qualities were missing or had not yet had time to develop.[69]

President Truman recognized, according to Landsberg, that the racial caste system was damaging to the country and felt the *Brown* decision would help unify the country and vindicate the unmet promise of the equal protection clause of the Constitution. In 1952, under Truman's lame-duck administration, an *amicus* brief was filed in favor of school desegregation. While the commitment of the government as to the correctness of *Brown* was not usually questioned, the enforcement commitment had fluctuated, endangering the promise of *Brown*.[70]

Mathews and Prothro's study began with a baseline look at "Black Monday," a pejorative term for the day on which *Brown* became law, a time when seventeen states and the District of Columbia *required* racial segregation in public schools by law. At the time, the eleven states of the South had only token desegregation.[71] Western and border states (Oklahoma to West Virginia) had a range of desegregation, from 26 percent to 62 percent; however, in the South, "the range was from zero percent in Mississippi, Alabama and South Carolina to 1.4 percent in Texas."[72] Mathews and Prothro determined that when the "state and the folk" come into conflict, "the folkways would inevitably become the dominant force," unless politics and policy direct solutions. It took ten years after *Brown* before the Congress passed laws to speed up desegregation and provide some enforcement power.

In 1956, post-*Brown* resistance resulted in Autherine Lucy being prevented from being admitted to the University of Alabama by an uncivilized mob.[73] The federal government failed to follow through on enforcement, leading to a feeling that if enough resistance could be mustered, the federal government would back down on enforcing the rights of blacks. Lucy withdrew from the lawsuit against the University of Alabama due to lack of federal protection, after which Alabama moved quickly to bar the operation of the NAACP in the state.

In 1958, it became necessary to federalize the Arkansas State Guard to accompany nine children to a school in Little Rock. The governor of Arkansas refused to enforce the federal court order to integrate the school. President Eisenhower, at the insistence of William Rogers, the attorney general, ordered the use of federalized troops for homeland security for the first time in the twentieth century. The images of this were captured by television cameras and sent around the world, showing the lack of respect for the law and the status of race relations in the country.[74]

In 1962, James Meredith was to be enrolled in the University of Mississippi in Oxford.[75] Per an agreement between Robert Kennedy, the attorney general of the United States, and Ross Barnett, the governor of Mississippi, Meredith was to be taken onto campus at night, accompanied by federal marshals, with state troopers present for support and to keep the peace on the campus. When Meredith and the marshals arrived, the anti-desegregation protesters were there in force and no state troopers were to be found. At least three newspaper reporters and a French photographer were killed by the protesters. Federal troops were sent by President Kennedy to finally secure the admission of James Meredith. The marshals had to accompany Meredith to class every day, as well as provide 24-hour protection that required them to sleep in his room during the year he attended the University of Mississippi.

The Mississippi Freedom Summer Project has been recognized for the work it did to promote and implement voter registration, alternative schools, and community centers, as documented by Davis and Malone. What is less well known is there were twenty-five Freedom Libraries established in the summer of 1964 in community centers and schools in Mississippi. These Freedom Libraries served civil rights goals in at least two ways: by delivering books for information gathering and entertainment purposes to people who did not have access to them in any other way and by awakening an appreciation for information in people, which would translate into demands for similar services from local libraries.[76]

POST-*BROWN*—LIBRARIES

The integration of libraries didn't come easily to most of the states in the South due to economic and educational problems and blatant segregation.[77] Many libraries remained segregated until well into the 1960s.[78] According to Lee, demonstrations in South Carolina often preceded the granting of privileges to blacks. In 1960, the main library and the black branch library in the city of Greenville were closed to avoid integration after a sit-in demonstration and subsequent filing of a lawsuit against the library. Eventually, the library was reopened as an integrated facility, but new rules included separate tables designated for males and females to prevent the mixing of black and whites of the opposite sex, thus creating another form of segregation. In Sumter, twenty-three blacks were arrested and charged with breach of the peace for refusing to leave the library after requesting and being denied the use of a library book. Nineteen of the twenty-three were convicted and fined $100 or 30 days in jail. It wasn't until the mid-to-late 1960s that blacks in most areas of South Carolina were allowed the same access to libraries as the white majority.

In 1961 at the midwinter meeting, the ALA Council approved an amendment to the Library Bill of Rights, first adopted in 1939.[79] Amendment Five of the Library Bill of Rights states: "A person's right to use a library should not be denied or abridged because of origin, age, background, or views."[80] A 1963 research study entitled *Access to Public Libraries*, prepared for the ALA by International Research Associates, documented racism, both direct and indirect, in library services to African Americans in the United States.[81] The study indicated library services to African Americans were not improving very rapidly. Indeed, many southern state library associations refused to admit African American members. The ALA made few attempts to rectify this situation, which resulted in the continuation of a large population of underserved citizenry. The ALA adopted a policy condemning racial prejudice in its *Statement on Individual Membership, Chapter Status, and Institutional Membership,* at the Miami Beach annual conference in 1962.[82]

In an effort to force an affirmative action by the ALA, E. J. Josey presented a resolution to the ALA conference held in St. Louis, Missouri, in 1964. The resolution prohibited ALA officers and staff members from attending in their official capacity at ALA expense any meetings of state associations that continued to practice segregation.[83] The resolution came as a protest to ALA's decision to honor the Mississippi Library Association for its National Library week activities, even after Mississippi had decided to withdraw from the ALA to maintain separate library associations for its black and white members.[84] Josey's resolution led to the integration of the remaining four state associations, Mississippi, Alabama, Georgia, and Louisiana, that prior to the resolution refused to extend membership to African American librarians.[85]

POST-*BROWN*—LIBRARY SCHOOLS

In February 1966, an ad hoc committee on Opportunities for Negro Students in the Library Profession was established by the ALA Executive Board to recommend steps to identify promising blacks who could be persuaded to enter library schools.[86] As reported by Dumont, a survey was conducted as part of this committee. It was determined that only 4 percent, or 372 out of 9,204, of the students that graduated from accredited library schools between 1962 and 1966 were black. Over half of these graduates were from Atlanta University. Whether it was for lack of opportunity, lack of incentive, failure to qualify, or some other reason, integration was slow to be adopted. It wasn't until the 1970s that opportunities for black students expanded, due in part to Title II-B fellowship funds becoming available.

In 1967, Dr. Charles D. Churchwell was the first black to join the faculty of the University of Houston as assistant director for public services and associate professor. At the time, he was the only black associate director of a university library in the entire country.[87] Churchwell explains the lessons he learned from his successful two-year experience as follows: "Clear direction and leadership must be provided by top administrators. Choose a place where there is a core of mature staff members who are competent and secure. Choose a workplace where a high premium is placed on trust and respect. Choose a workplace where decision-making is decentralized. All these conditions existed in the libraries of the University of Houston and contributed to their successful desegregation and diversification of the workforce."[88]

In the year 2003, library and information sciences programs and schools continue to scholastically and pragmatically explore the issues of educating students for the digital world and traditional roles while addressing in the needs of diverse populations. Discussions over the past decade or so have revolved around several primary themes. The first is the challenge of recruiting faculty and students of diverse backgrounds by identifying the "gatekeepers" to entrée and devising new strategies for "growing our own."[89] Second is supporting special needs and minority students prior to matriculation, while in school, and during the exiting phase.[90] Third is developing multicultural, gender-specific, and social issue-aware curricula, while ensuring academic freedom for faculty.[91] Lastly is facing issues of race that affect both the recruitment and advancement of librarians.[92]

The library and information science profession is also facing a historical crisis of sorts, one that has been a point of discussion on the Association of Library and Information Science Education (ALISE) listserv: the closing of the Clark Atlanta University (CAU) library school. Despite support from faculty, alumni, and the library profession at large, the board of Clark Atlanta University decided on October 17, 2003, to close the School of Library and Information Studies, the only accredited library program in Georgia.[93] The ALISE discussions reveal the passions in general about library school closings, but also the magnitude of losing this historic program. From *Library Journal Online*:

> For all of its 62-year history, the CAU School of Library and Information Studies (SLIS) has been at the center of the struggle to gain equity and diversity in U.S. library service. According to E.J. Josey—who integrated the Georgia Library Association many years ago, founded the black Caucus of the American

Library Association (ALA), and later served as ALA president—the school has graduated a huge percentage of the black leaders in American librarianship, more than any other program.

Lorna Peterson, Library and Information Science professor at the University at Buffalo, NY, says the master's theses and other scholarship from the CAU SLIS are crucial primary source material for the study of library service to black Americans and the impact of black library leaders on the profession. That scholarly tradition was set in motion by Eliza Atkins Gleason, the first dean of the school. Gleason was also the first black woman to get the Ph.D. from the Library School at the University of Chicago. Her dissertation dealt with public library service to black citizens.[94]

THE LEGACY AND THE EFFECT OF *BROWN V. BOARD OF EDUCATION*

What is the legacy of *Brown*? One of our goals—to reveal the landscape of *Brown v. Board of Education*—results in the acknowledgment that the passage of a half-century of time has diminished neither the power of *Brown* nor its effect. It also begs admission that the ruling was not a panacea. Our survey of the scholarship and stories pertaining to *Brown* find they revel in its promise, but also reveal the boundaries and limitations reflective of the ways it has been contested, even as it becomes predictive of battles still to be fought. A complex process has been necessary for the United States to reconstruct in the post-*Brown* era, 1955–1975, or what Martin refers to as the "second Reconstruction."[95] There is no doubt that there will be more political, social, cultural, and economic transformation to fully realize *Brown*'s ideals. We juxtaposed *Brown* with the pre-*Brown* and post-*Brown* legal landscape, general landscape, and the landscape of libraries and library schools to provide a sense of the times in this transformative story.

In 2000, Betsy Hearne wrote a dynamic paper on the nature of storytelling entitled *Once There Was and Will Be: Storytelling the Future.* She says, "Telling stories is a human condition with a history of human continuities. There's a reason, for instance, that so many stories begin with 'One time' or 'Once upon a time' or 'Once there was and was not' or any one of many other opening formulas that give us distance from past time and place. If the events were not set in the past, we wouldn't know what happened. Not to mention the fact that we wouldn't have the necessary perspective on those events to shape a tale, to sculpt the events into a story."[96]

Legacies, like stories, are something handed down from an ancestor or a predecessor. The legacy of *Brown* will be many more stories to be told or written—reflections from the *Brown* participants,[97] memorials to the justices and legal figures involved, tales of the trials and tribulations of the civil rights movement, websites dedicated to varying aspects of the *Brown* legacy, and persons of all professions telling stories to boards, granting agencies, judges, legislators, etc., to foster further change and improvements to fulfill the promise of *Brown*. The stories will tell what there once was—and what will be. Greenhouse considers *Brown* as biography and discusses fictional lives and living fictions, but perhaps her most important idea is that of a "double life story."[98] We treat the concept differently from Greenhouse, but like the idea of considering the "life" story of *Brown* and the "life" story of our nation as affected by *Brown*. We also hope to story-tell the future and pose questions to challenge the library and information science profession about our communities and practices in light of the issues surrounding *Brown* and to consider the life story of our future.

ACHIEVEMENTS AND MISCONCEPTIONS

To further map the plan for our challenges, we reflect on *Brown* as more than a law and more than the story about what happened after the law was passed. Over time there is a certain mythology about *Brown* that is the dream of its promise. In some measure, the promise has been kept. Douglass cites research that confirms a "dramatic increase in acceptance of racial integration among white Americans during the [forty] years since *Brown* . . . however . . . if *Brown* meant the end in this country to racial division and inequality more broadly defined, then the ongoing social, economic, political, and even geographic division between black and white suggests the promise of *Brown* remains unrealized."[99] *Brown* clearly addressed the "separate but equal" doctrine, while it also gave great momentum for change in other areas, resulting in political, educational, and social advances and achievements in the United States. In this way, it exceeded its promise, as it became a foundation for the related legal cases that followed it. *Brown* kept its promise because it was an "instrument of change in many areas of education . . . bilingual, special and gifted and talented education; admissions to higher education."[100] Brown was the catalyst for the liberation that followed in the United States, including the civil rights, anti-Vietnam war, anti-poverty, women's rights, and gay and lesbian rights movements.[101]

Culp in his symposium paper outlines what he considers the three misconceptions about *Brown*. "The most important misconception was that if we changed the law of the land, 'good' people would comply with it." The second assumption is that there is a race-neutral policy that will achieve racial justice. The third assumption is that a single standard of assimilation can be articulated for all American society.[102] Indeed, there are concerns in light of the fact that *Brown* did not end racial segregation and that "[t]en years after *Brown*, voluntary compliance in the South was a failure: 98 percent of blacks attended rigidly segregated schools. In 1997, after thirty years of federal mandates and local initiative, that figure is approximately one-third."[103] There continue to be stories nationwide about disparities in majority Latino and African American schools and among poor white and immigrant communities.

Smith states, "More than ever before, minority students are pursuing undergraduate and graduate degrees at historically white colleges and universities, both public and private. In looking at the bare principle of integration, the ideals of *Brown*, which call for the elimination of statutory segregation, have been met. However, when looking closely at what is occurring and recurring on historically white campuses, it appears the vestiges of segregation continue. Black students at historically white campuses continue to be the victims of racist incidents, and the nature of these occurrences invariably tarnishes the quality of their academic experience."[104] It is a reality that campuses from coast to coast have racially motivated and violent conduct occurring. Population and educational statistics reflect important factors. As table 1.1 illustrates, the population in the United States is transforming, with predictors indicating population stabilization for whites and blacks and growth of the Hispanic and Asian/Pacific Islander populations. How the library and information science profession addresses these changes may be critical to its life story.

Table 1.2 further endorses that the Hispanic population, while predicted to continue to grow significantly, is showing underrepresentation in their numbers of students graduating from college.

Consider also these statistics from the report *A Multiracial Society with Segregated Schools: Are We Losing the Dream*, by Frankenberg, Lee, and Orfield[105]:

1. Public school enrollment in 1968 by race was 2 million Latinos, 34.7 million whites, and 6.3 million blacks. In 2000, those numbers changed to 7.7 million Latinos, a 283 percent change, 28.8 million whites, a 17 percent change, and 8.1 million blacks, a 29 percent change (p. 23).
2. There are six states in which white students enrolled in public school are the minority: California, Hawaii, Louisiana, Mississippi, New Mexico, and Texas. These states make up one-fourth of the public school enrollment in the United States. Of the entire Latino population in the

Table 1.1.   U.S. Resident Population Statistics (Percentage distribution by race)

Year	White	Black	Am. Indian, Eskimo, Aluet	Asian, Pacific Islander	Hispanic Origin
1980	85.9	11.8	0.6	1.6	6.4
1990	83.9	12.3	0.8	3.0	9.0
2000	82.2	12.8	0.9	4.1	11.8
2025	78.5	13.9	1.0	6.5	18.2
2050	74.9	14.7	1.1	9.3	24.3

Source: U.S. Census Bureau, *Statistical Abstract of the United States: 2001*, Table 10. Accessed at: www.census.gov/prod/2002pubs/01statab/pop.pdf.

Table 1.2. Educational Attainment by Race (Percentage college graduate or higher)

Year	Total	White	Black	Asian, Pacific Islander	Hispanic Origin
1970	10.7	11.3	4.4	N/A	4.5
1980	16.2	17.1	8.4	N/A	7.6
1990	21.3	22.0	11.3	39.9	9.2
1995	32	24.0	13.2	N/A	9.3
2000	25.6	26.1	16.5	43.9	10.6

N/A = Not available.
Source: U.S. Census Bureau, *Statistical Abstract of the United States: 2001*, Table 215. Accessed at: www.census.gov/prod/2002pubs/01statab/educ.pdf.

United States, 58 percent attend public schools in these six states. For the black population, it is 21.3 percent, Asian/Pacific Islanders is 48.1 percent, and American Indians/Alaskans is 19.1 percent. Only one in six white students attend public schools in these six states (p. 25).

3. The percentage of white students in public schools where the average black student attends has gone from approximately 32 percent in 1970, to a high of just over 36 percent in 1980, to a low of 30.9 percent in 2000. This means that there are 5.3 percent fewer white students enrolled in public schools where the average black student attends (p. 30). The percentage of white students in public schools where the average Latino attends was almost 45 percent in 1970 and then steadily declined to a low of just less than 30 percent in 2000 (p. 33).

4. In 2000, more than 70 percent of black students and 75 percent of Latino students attended public school in which there was a 50–100 percent minority student population (pp. 31 & 33).

The San Antonio *Express News*[106] states,

Although it's been nearly 50 years since the U.S. Supreme Court struck down the concept of separate but equal education, public schools still need major changes—particularly in funding—before they can ensure a fair education for Hispanic students . . . Seventy-five percent of the 4.5 million students who speak a language other than English can't participate in class because they sit in English-only classrooms . . . In 2000, 40 percent of black students attended schools that were 90 percent to 100 percent black, up from 32 percent in 1988.

These data are a wake-up call to better understand the transformation of American society and the obstacles that impede improvement of educational systems.

LIBRARY AND INFORMATION SCIENCE EDUCATION

The national education population statistics reveal the changing cultural landscape of schools and depict that a majority of African American and

Latino high school students come from school environments where these ethnic groups comprise the majority of the school population. These statistics are telling for what they reveal and for what they do not explain to us directly. The statistical trends in library and information science education map their own story as well. What follows are some selected statistics quoted from the *Association for Library and Information Science Education Statistical Report 2002*,[107] concerning student enrollment in library and information science (LIS) programs:

1. LIS graduates continue to be predominately white (69.9 percent). Blacks are the most represented non-white ethnic group (5.2 percent). Asian or Pacific Islanders represented 3.1 percent of graduates in 2000–2001, followed by Hispanics at 2.6 percent. Native Americans constitute one-half percent of all graduates of the six degree programs.
2. Hispanic representation is lower than that of blacks for each of the six degree fields. Hispanics have their highest representation (4.3 percent) as recipients of the bachelor's degree. Their percentage of graduates drops to 2.6 for the ALA-accredited LS master's and only 1.2 percent for the IS master's. Persons of Hispanic origin constitute 2 percent of post-master's degree recipients, 1.3 percent of "other master's" degree graduates, and a mere 1.2 percent of those receiving the doctoral degree.
3. Black graduates accounted for 11.5 percent of bachelor's degrees awarded in 2000–2001. They were 6.8 percent of graduates of the "other master's" degree programs, and 4.7 percent of both ALA-accredited LS master's and doctoral degree graduates in 2000–2001. The degree in which black graduates have the lowest representation is IS master's, where they accounted for only 2.1 percent of degrees awarded.
4. International students represent a considerable percentage of graduates of three degree programs. They received nearly one-third (32.8 percent) of "other master's" degrees and 29.1 percent of the IS master's degrees awarded in 2000–2001. Their representation as graduates of doctoral programs follows at 20 percent. These figures are in marked contrast to international student graduation figures for the bachelor's degree and ALA-accredited LS master's degree. For these programs, international students represent only 3.4 and 2.3 percent of graduates, respectively.

There is much to be considered in light of these data and some questions to ask of ourselves as library and information sciences professionals about the effect of a changing population, the changing face of America and our campuses, and the ideals of *Brown* as they affect LIS education. With each passing anniversary of the *Brown* decision, analysts revisit the effect and the extent of its achievements and failures. Has the LIS profession done the same?

Have we considered that on both the local level and broadly as a profession, LIS educators have an enormous impact upon society as the teachers of the workforce that develops, organizes, and distributes information? We teach the future scholars and doctoral-level educators in our field as well. Are we asking ourselves how we are meeting the needs of a more diverse professoriat? The LIS profession, like many professions, is redefining its identity and forms of practice in the digital era. The history of library and information science education and the profession is a story that has experienced its own changing dramatic arch since "[t]he American Library Association was organized in 1876 and Melvil Dewey opened the first School of Library Economy at Columbia College (later Columbia University) in 1887."[108]

Dewey conceived the "Library Faith" as the guiding conviction of librarians—that providing good books would produce a positive benefit to society, whose members, presumably, would read them. It was Dewey who wrote in 1876 in the first issue of the ALA's *Library Journal* that "The time has at last come when a librarian may, without assumption, speak of his occupation as a profession."[109] The language conventions of the time perhaps required the pronoun in Dewey's quote to be the male possessive form, his, even if this was Dewey's personal conviction about the dominant gender of this new profession. However, while Dewey has been criticized in library history for his condescension toward women, his library training program embraced the admission of women, and it was Dewey who also said, "To my thinking, a great librarian must have a clear head, a strong hand, and above all, a great heart. Such shall be greatest among librarians; and when I look into the future, I am inclined to think that most of the men who will achieve this greatness will be women."[110]

Andrew Abbot writes of the systems of professions and maps the trajectory of librarianship as a profession, comparing it to that of the medical and legal professions as to the standards that, in his view, comprise a profession. Long an object of discussion, the identity of this profession is not without strife and is deeply grounded in notions of the role of the library.[111] Wiegand discusses his frustrations with twentieth-century American librarianship and the tunnel vision and blind spots that have resulted from the lack of scholarship that critically analyzes the multiple roles that libraries have played. He challenges professional librarians and professional historians to study the library with greater critical analysis to make connections and explore issues such as power, knowledge, race, class, age, and gender. He states that "without a deeper understanding of the American library's past we cannot adequately assess its present and are thus unable to plan its future prudently."[112] Pawley also considers theories of hegemony and class perspectives in LIS curriculm, indicative of a dialogue among scholars that these are critical issues at this time.[113]

Fortunately, we are a profession that willingly talks about hard stuff—our issues (and controversies) do not linger in silence. In the post-*Brown* era, library and information science education has grappled with change, just as our nation did, and we have talked about it. We worked ardently to explore the profession itself, how to meet its needs, new paradigms, and jurisdictional issues.[114]

We contemplated convergent curriculum and the trends, changes, and design, and the core constructs of what we teach.[115] We argued about accreditation, its affiliation with the ALA, and issues such as where accreditation bodies should be situated, the benefits and costs of accreditation, and whether we should even have accreditation at all.[116]

We continued our dialogue about change and the future of the profession, including discussions about current practices, directions, what does not change and what will change, and the opportunities and dangers ahead.[117] We also went digital with talk about web-based teaching and distance education.[118]

We tackled the implications about the meaning of our name(s), thus bringing into the ontology of nomenclature the hermeneutics of the "L" (library) word vs. the "I" (information) word. In some cases, we transformed what we call ourselves, thus affecting our professional identity.[119] We defended our schools, cried about the crisis of library school closings, bid farewell to historic programs at Columbia and Chicago, and discussed surviving and thriving.[120]

What these discussions reveal is optimistic; however, there is a need for more dialogue about the effect of black library school programs post-*Brown*, the effect of integration in library schools, and what changes in the profession can be attributed directly or indirectly to the integration (or desegregation) of library schools. Consider these statistics noted by award-winning civil rights activist Professor Emeritus E. J. Josey of the University of Pittsburgh School of Library and Information Sciences[121]:

1. While the black population has grown from 20 million in 1977 to approximately 33.5 million in 1998, the number of [black] librarians has increased only slightly.
2. In 1999, the percentage of all librarians that are black was 6.5 percent or 12,200 out of 188,000.
3. In the long history of the ALA, 123 years as of 1999, there have been three black presidents. (In 2004, the current president of the ALA is Carla Hayden, an African American.)

It is perhaps both intriguing and poignant to contemplate these numbers and other data in this chapter in light of the recent developments with the closing of Clark Atlanta University School of Library and Information Studies. "Since 1941—a time when career options were limited for African Americans—the School of Library and Information Studies has been a wellspring of professional opportunity for Clark Atlanta graduates. SLIS is one of only two LIS programs at historically black institutions."[122]

Is this closing or any of the other changes in LIS education directly or indirectly related to the integration (or desegregation) of library schools? Are the issues inherent in these dialogues in any way attributable to *Brown*? Is it pushing the envelope to ask if LIS has helped to achieve *Brown*'s agenda? Is it possible that the achievements of *Brown* have resulted in an odd twist of fate in our history, resulting in the closure of a historic library school that for 62 years served black students seeking degrees in library and information science?

LIS educators are situated in world of opportunity. We are part of national, state, and local communities. We are part of an educational community. And within our own programs, we have communities of scholars, teachers, and students with common interests, objectives, and concerns. As is noted in the *Brown* ruling, Anderson reminds us that "Indeed, the major function of American education is to socialize young people into the cultural values of the society, introduce them to the principles of democracy, prepare them for the world of work, and facilitate their upward mobility." The ivory tower and the LIS profession are not exempt from helping to fulfill this mission and certainly the Code of Ethics.[123] The profession so valiantly defends genuinely contributes to the ideals of *Brown*:

    I. We provide the highest level of service to all library users through appropriate and usefully organized resources; equitable service policies; equitable access; and accurate, unbiased, and courteous responses to all requests.

    II. We uphold the principles of intellectual freedom and resist all efforts to censor library resources.

    III. We protect each library user's right to privacy and confidentiality with respect to information sought or received and resources consulted, borrowed, acquired, or transmitted.

    IV. We recognize and respect intellectual property rights.

    V. We treat co-workers and other colleagues with respect, fairness, and good faith, and advocate conditions of employment that safeguard the rights and welfare of all employees of our institutions.

    VI. We do not advance private interests at the expense of library users, colleagues, or our employing institutions.

    VII. We distinguish between our personal convictions and professional duties and do not allow our personal beliefs to interfere with fair representation of the aims of our institutions or the provision of access to their information resources.

    VIII. We strive for excellence in the profession by maintaining and enhancing our own knowledge and skills, by encouraging the professional development of co-workers, and by fostering the aspirations of potential members of the profession.

While the Code of Ethics emphasizes in its opening "equitable service policies" and "equitable access" and "unbiased, and courteous responses," Dumont states that "there appears to be no clearly mandated policy of equal opportunity in library science education; there is only a collection of loosely defined programs. Consequently, measuring and promoting progress for black librarians has been piecemeal: when racial inequalities in one place are dealt with, unseen inequalities emerge in other places."[124] Wright concludes that "if we are educated and work without contact with people who are different we are poorer for that lack of contact and less well prepared to provide adequate library service to a very diverse society."[125] Morton Horwitz considers the dilemmas that remain unresolved by *Brown* in a series of questions:

> Does it stand simply for color blindness—for the principle that it is constitutionally impermissible for the state to take race into account even for benign purposes—or instead does it stand as a barrier only to the use of racial classifications for the purpose of oppressing minorities? Should the principle of *Brown* continue to be directed only at government discrimination—so-called state action—or should it apply to private action as well? Does *Brown* require only that racial minorities be provided equality of opportunity? But what happens when even after all of the formal barriers of exclusion are dropped, the intangible culture of racism or the scars of a history of deprivation continue to produce racially unequal consequences? Is a racially discriminatory program one that is intended to produce unequal results or one that actually produces such results regardless of the intentions or motivations of its creators? Do such programs interfere with the constitutional rights of non-minority members who may be excluded because of minority reference of jobs, housing or admission?[126]

Perhaps there are other broadly stated questions to be asked about *Brown*: Did *Brown* intend the elimination of mandatory racial segregation? Did *Brown* intend the end to racial division and inequality more broadly defined? Is there a movement toward re-segregation of public schools? Are we still separate and unequal?

QUESTIONS TO STIMULATE DISCUSSION OF THE CHALLENGES AND OPPORTUNITIES FOR LIS EDUCATION

In this chapter, we have attempted to depict the landscape surrounding *Brown v. Board of Education*—a grand narrative—that spans from early Americana to the time of this writing. We mapped the lay of the land in a temporal display of both the social and legal territory. Colorful moments in history came forth, as well as the voices and ideas of scholars. There was formed a sense of place from the rail yards of Topeka, Kansas, to the Supreme Court of the United States. Statistics provided dimension to the nature of our changing society. The ethnography highlighted the changing legal, social, educational, and cultural systems for all people of the United States.

What, then, is the effect of *Brown* on library and information science education? And did mapping and storytelling its historical fifty-year journey reveal answers? Perhaps the answers lie in the opportunity of dialogue—within our own communities and within our profession—to continue questioning our goals, our beliefs, what we value, the mission of our organization, and re-determining the precepts and practices we will foster in the future. Our ethnographic survey of this history results in the presentation of the following questions we believe should be considered.

1. How do we encourage mentoring of the youth who use the library and encourage them to consider librarianship as a viable career? How do we "grow" library-interested students into the profession?
2. How do we mentor library assistants to move to the next level of professionalism by completing the necessary credentialing programs?
3. How do we support the interests, culture, and educational experiences of persons of color?
4. How does the university create barriers to persons of color and how can we make changes in systems to make those systems more accessible, useful, and fair to persons of color?
5. How do we recruit more men and persons of color, especially men of color, to the profession? How do we change the perception of the profession to make it more desirable for men and persons of color, especially men of color?
6. How can we develop active recruitment programs that venture into non-traditional places and go beyond the normal or traditional boundaries of our own universities, educational systems, and professional organizations to recruit non-traditional students?
7. How do we foster successful matriculation to LIS programs and eliminate the barriers that prevent persons of color from going into LIS, such as timelines, access and entrée barriers, economic concerns and salaries, and social, political, and cultural barriers?
8. How can university leaders exhibit strong actions indicating support of students of color?
9. Why do some students of color become "invisible"—constructing ways to marginalize their differences and not draw attention to their culture—to fit in? How do we foster students being themselves and prevent invisibility as a method of fitting in?
10. How can universities use a variety of or varying demographics as success measures for culturally diverse faculty and the student population?

11. How can the university and its leadership identify and prevent overt and covert discrimination and react swiftly and concisely in all cases?
12. How do we recruit, train, mentor, promote, and retain a culturally diverse faculty?
13. How do we promote and advance persons of color to senior-level positions at the university?
14. How do we become active participants in the decision-making processes of society, the campus, and the school? How do we encourage students, especially students of color, to do the same?
15. How do we work with police and figures in positions of authority to understand the needs and culture of our students and their safety and security issues?
16. How do we work with the greater campus at large to ensure there is a Greek system that understands the needs and culture of all students?
17. How do we address issues of equity and pay equity, for persons of color? How do we fiscally support persons of color to help ensure their success?
18. How do we develop curricula that reflect the educational needs of all students and support them both personally and professionally?
19. How can we encourage understanding of the legislative process and the effect of the electorate on our campuses, in our communities, and on the state and national level?
20. How can we identify "invisible" or "hidden" resources that can become resources for persons of color?
21. How are the success stories in higher education being highlighted and how do we prevent failures? How to we analyze failures to prevent them in the future?

Martin (1998) states that *Brown* needs to be recognized for "its enormously liberating impact on America and the world" and that it "signifies hope for America's future . . . a better America: a humane, inclusive, free America."[127] How can—how will—library and information science education map its future . . . what story will it write?

> The challenge for the days ahead is for society to secure the values etched in the *Brown* decision on white campuses and encourage all students to share in each others' rich culture without demanding that people of color abandon their own.
>
> —Clay Smith, 1995

NOTES

1. International Stortytelling Center, 2003. www.storytellingcenter.com/about/about .htm (accessed 9 December 2003).

2. Elizabeth Figa, "Mapping Culture: Rural Circuit Medical Librarians' Medical Information Systems," *Library Trends* 47, no. 3 (1999): 349–74.

3. U.S. Department of Education, *Brown v. Board of Education* 50th Anniversary Commission: www.ed.gov/about/bdscomm/list/brownvboard50th/index.html (accessed 9 December 2003).

4. Richard Kluger, *Simple Justice: The History of* Brown v. Board of Education *and Black Americans' Struggle for Equality* (New York: Alfred A. Knopf, 1976).

5. *Brown v. Board of Education of Topeka, Kansas*, 347 U.S. 483 (1954).

6. Daniel M. Berman, *It is SO Ordered: The Supreme Court Rules on School Segregation* (New York: W. W. Norton & Company, Inc., 1966).

7. Donald R. Mathews and James W. Prothro. "State ways Versus Folkways: Critical Factors in Southern Regions to Brown v. Board of Education," in *Essays on the American Constitution*, ed. Gottfried Dietz (Englewood Cliffs, NJ: Prentice-Hall, Inc., 1964), 139–56.

8. Jack M. Balkin, ed., *What* Brown v. Board of Education *Should Have Said: The Nation's Top Legal Experts Rewrite America's Landmark Civil Rights Decision* (New York: New York University Press, 2001), 10.

9. National Archives and Records Administration Digital Classroom: www.archives.gov/digital_classroom/lessons/brown_v_board_documents/brown_v_board.html

10. Waldo E. Martin, Brown V Board of Education: *A Brief History with Documents* (Boston: Bedford/St. Martin's, 1988), vii.

11. Balkin, *What* Brown v. Board of Education *Should Have Said.*

12. Derrick Bell, *"Brown vs. Board of Education* and the Interest Convergence Dilemma," in *Critical Race Theory: The Key Writings that Formed the Movement*, ed. Kimberly Crenshaw, Neil Gotanda, Gary Peller, and Kendall Thomas (New York: The New Press, 1995), 20.

13. Bell, *"Brown vs. Board of Education* and the Interest Convergence Dilemma," 20–29.

14. Austin Sarat, *Race, Law, and Culture: Reflection on* Brown v. Board of Education (New York: Oxford University Press, 1997), 6.

15. Balkin, *What* Brown v. Board of Education *Should Have Said*, 3.

16. National Archives and Records Administration Digital Classroom: www.archives.gov/digital_classroom/lessons/brown_v_board_documents/timeline.html

17. Lorna Peterson, "Alternative Perspectives in Library and Information Science: Issues of Race," *Journal of Education for Library and Information Science* 37, no. 2 (1996): 163.

18. Mildred Dickeman, "Racism in the Library: A Model from the Public Schools," in *Social Responsibilities and Libraries: A Library Journal/School Library Journal Selection*, ed. Patricia Glass Schuman (New York: R. R. Bowker Company, 1976), 97.

19. Dickeman, "Racism in the Library," 96.

20. Lamar P. Miller, "Tracking the Progress of Brown," in Brown V. Board of Education: *The Challenge for Today's Schools*, ed. Ellen Condliffe Lagemann and Lamar P. Miller (New York: Teachers College Press, 1996), 9–13.

21. Brian K. Landsberg, "The Federal Government and the Promise of Brown," in Brown V. Board of Education: *The Challenge for Today's Schools*, ed. Ellen Condliffe Lagemann and Lamar P. Miller (New York: Teachers College Press, 1996), 27–36.

22. Constance Baker Motley, "The Legacy of *Brown v. Board of Education*," in Brown V. Board of Education: *The Challenge for Today's Schools,* ed. Ellen Condliffe Lagemann and Lamar P. Miller (New York: Teachers College Press, 1996), 38.

23. Motley, "The Legacy of *Brown v. Board of Education*," 37–43.

24. Kevin Brown, "Revisiting the Supreme Court's Opinion in *Brown v. Board of Education* from a Multiculturalist Perspective," in Brown V. Board of Education: *The Challenge for Today's Schools,* ed. Ellen Condliffe Lagemann and Lamar P. Miller (New York: Teachers College Press, 1996), 47.

25. Roger Wilkins, "Dream Deferred But Not Defeated," in Brown V. Board of Education: *The Challenge for Today's Schools,* ed. Ellen Condliffe Lagemann and Lamar P. Miller (New York: Teachers College Press, 1996), 14–18.

26. W. V. Jackson, "Some Pioneer Negro Library Workers," *Library Journal* 64, no. 6 (1939): 215–17; and Klaus Musmann, "The Ugly Side of Librarianship: Segregation in Library Services from 1900 to 1950," in *Untold Stories: Civil Rights, Libraries, and Black Librarianship,* ed. John Mark Tucker (Urbana-Champaign, IL: Publications Office, Graduate School of Library and Information Science, 1998), 78–92.

27. Casper Leroy Jordon and E. J. Josey, "A Chronology of Events in Black Librarianship," in *Handbook of Black Librarianship,* ed. E. J. Josey and Marva L. DeLoach (Lanham, MD: The Scarecrow Press, Inc., 2000), 3–18; and E. J. Josey, Foreword to *Educating Black Librarians (Papers from the 50th Anniversary Celebration of the School of Library and Information Sciences, North Carolina Central University)* by Benjamin F. Speller Jr. (Jefferson, NC: McFarland, 1991).

28. Jordon and Josey, "A Chronology of Events," 3–18.

29. Jessie Carney Smith, "Black Women, Civil Rights, & Libraries," in *Untold Stories: Civil Rights, Libraries, and Black Librarianship,* ed. John Mark Tucker (Urbana-Champaign, IL: Publications Office, Graduate School of Library and Information Science, 1998), 141–50.

30. Rosemary Ruhig Dumont, "The Educating of Black Librarians: An Historical Perspective," *Journal of Education for Library and Information Science* 26, no. 4 (1986): 233–48; and Kathryn C. Stevenson, "Annette Lewis Phinazee and the North Carolina Central University School of Library and Information Sciences, 1970–1983," in *Educating Black Librarians (Papers from the 50th Anniversary Celebration of the School of Library and Information Sciences, North Carolina Central University),* ed. Benjamin F. Speller, Jr. (Jefferson, NC: McFarland, 1991), 113–39.

31. Dumont, "The Educating of Black Librarians," 233–48.

32. Musmann, "The Ugly Side of Librarianship."

33. O. Lee Shiflett, "The American Library Association's Quest for a Black Library School," *Journal of Education for Library and Information Science* 35, no. 1 (1994): 68–72.

34. Dumont, "The Educating of Black Librarians," 236–37.

35. Shiflett, "The American Library Association's Quest for a Black Library School," 68–72.

36. Lorna Peterson, "Alternative Perspectives in Library and Information Science: Issues of Race," *Journal of Education for Library and Information Science* 37, no. 2 (1996): 163–74.

37. Casper LeRoy Jordon, "African American Forerunners in Librarianship," in *Handbook of Black Librarianship,* ed. E. J. Josey and Marva L. DeLoach (Lanham, MD: The Scarecrow Press, Inc., 2000).

38. Jerry D. Campbell, "Choosing to Have a Future," *American Libraries* 24, no. 6 (June 1993): 560–63; and Dumont, "The Educating of Black Librarians," 233–48.

39. Dumont, "The Educating of Black Librarians," 233–48.

40. Campbell, "Choosing to Have a Future," 560–63.

41. Dumont, "The Educating of Black Librarians," 233–48.

42. Campbell, "Choosing to Have a Future," 560–63; and Dumont, "The Educating of Black Librarians," 233–48.

43. Musmann, "The Ugly Side of Librarianship," 78–92.

44. Dumont, "The Educating of Black Librarians," 233–48.

45. Stevenson, "Annette Lewis Phinazee."

46. Stevenson, "Annette Lewis Phinazee."

47. Herman L. Totten, "Perspectives on Minority Recruitment of Faculty for Schools of Library and Information Science," *Journal of Education for Library and Information Science* 33, no. 1 (1992): 46–54.

48. Doris Hargrett Clack, "Segregation and the Library," in *Encyclopedia of Library and Information Science: Vol. 27,* ed. Allen Kent, Harold Lancour and Jay E. Daily (New York: Mercel Dekker, Inc., 1979), 184–204; and Jordon and Josey, "A Chronology of Events," 3–18.

49. Clack, "Segregation and the Library," 184–204.

50. Musmann, "The Ugly Side of Librarianship," 78–92; and Jordan and Josey, "A Chronology of Events," 3–18.

51. Musmann, "The Ugly Side of Librarianship," 78–92.

52. Clack, "Segregation and the Library," 184–204.

53. Clack, "Segregation and the Library," 184–204; and Musmann, "The Ugly Side of Librarianship," 78–92.

54. Donna Rae MacCann, "Libraries for Immigrants and 'Minorities': A Study in Contrasts," in *Social Responsibility in Librarianship: Essays on Equality,* ed. Donna Rae MacCann (Jefferson, NC: McFarland & Company, Inc., Publishers, 1989), 97–116.

55. Musmann, "The Ugly Side of Librarianship," 78–92.

56. Clack, "Segregation and the Library, 184–204.

57. Musmann, "The Ugly Side of Librarianship," 78–92.

58. Dan R. Lee, "From Segregation to Integration: Library Services for Blacks in South Carolina, 1923–1962," in *Untold Stories: Civil Rights, Libraries, and Black Librarianship,* ed. John Mark Tucker (Urbana-Champaign, IL: Publications Office, Graduate School of Library and Information Science, 1998), 93–109.

59. Musmann, "The Ugly Side of Librarianship," 78–92; and Peterson, "Alternative Perspectives in Library and Information Science," 163–74.

60. Musmann, "The Ugly Side of Librarianship," 78–92.

61. Clack, "Segregation and the Library," 184–204.

62. Andrea L. Williams, "A History of the Holland Public Library, Wichita Falls, Texas, 1934–1968," in *Untold Stories: Civil Rights, Libraries, and Black Librarianship,* ed. John Mark Tucker (Urbana-Champaign, IL: Publications Office, Graduate School of Library and Information Science, 1998), 62–77.

63. A. P. Marshall, "The Black Librarian's Stride Toward Equality," in *The Black Librarian in the Southeast: Reminiscences, Activities, Challenges,* ed. Annette L. Phinazee (Durham: North Carolina Central University School of Library Science, 1980), 9.

64. Clara S. Jones, "The Black Librarian," in *The Black Librarian in the Southeast: Reminiscences, Activities, Challenges*, ed. Annette L. Phinazee (Durham: North Carolina Central University School of Library Science, 1980), 19.

65. NAACP Legal Defense and Educational Fund, Inc., *Brown v. Board of Education* web site. Available at: www.brownmatters.org/chrono_detailed.html

66. Erica Frankenberg, Chungmei Lee, and Gary Orfield, *A Multiracial Society with Segregated Schools: Are We Losing the Dream?* (Cambridge, MA: The Civil Rights Project, 2003). Available at: www.civilrightsproject.harvard.edu/research/reseg03/AreWeLosingtheDream.pdf.

67. E. J. Josey, "Revisiting the Past, Reclaiming the Present and Shaping the Future," in *The Black Librarian in the Southeast: Reminiscences, Activities, Challenges*, ed. Annette L. Phinazee (Durham: North Carolina Central University School of Library Science, 1980), 247–57.

68. Miller, "Tracking the Progress of Brown," 9–13.

69. Miller, "Tracking the Progress of Brown," 9–13.

70. Brian K. Landsberg, "The Federal Government and the Promise of Brown," in Brown V. Board of Education: *The Challenge for Today's Schools,* ed. Ellen Condliffe Lagemann and Lamar P. Miller (New York: Teachers College Press, 1996), 27–36.

71. Mathews and Prothro, "State ways Versus Folkways," 153.

72. Mathews and Prothro, "State ways Versus Folkways," 153.

73. Motley, "The Legacy of Brown v. Board of Education," 37–43.

74. Motley, "The Legacy of Brown v. Board of Education," 37–43.

75. Motley, "The Legacy of Brown v. Board of Education," 37–43.

76. Donald G. Davis, Jr. and Cheryl Knott Malone, "Reading for Liberation: The Role of Libraries in the 1964 Mississippi Freedom Summer Project," in *Untold Stories: Civil Rights, Libraries, and Black Librarianship,* ed. John Mark Tucker (Urbana-Champaign, IL: Publications Office, Graduate School of Library and Information Science, 1998), 110–25.

77. Lee, "From Segregation to Integration."

78. Musmann, "The Ugly Side of Librarianship," 78–92.

79. Clack, "Segregation and the Library," 184–204.

80. American Library Association Library Bill of Rights. Available at: www.ala.org/Content/NavigationMenu/Our_Association/Offices/Intellectual_Freedom3/Statements_and_Policies/Intellectual_Freedom2/Library_Bill_of_Rights.htm

81. Jordon and Josey, "A Chronology of Events," 9.

82. Davis and Malone, "Reading for Liberation," 110–25.

83. Jordon and Josey, "A Chronology of Events," 9.

84. Edward A. Goedeken, "Civil Rights, Libraries, & African-American Librarianship, 1954–1994: A Bibliographic Essay," in *Untold Stories: Civil Rights, Libraries, and Black Librarianship,* ed. John Mark Tucker (Urbana-Champaign, IL: Publications Office, Graduate School of Library and Information Science, 1998), 188–99.

85. MacCann, "Libraries for Immigrants," 97–116.

86. Dumont, "The Educating of Black Librarians," 233–48.

87. Edward G. Holley, "Racial Integration at the University of Houston: A Personal Perspective, I," in *Untold Stories: Civil Rights, Libraries, and Black Librarianship,* ed. John Mark Tucker (Urbana-Champaign, IL: Publications Office, Graduate School of Library and Information Science, 1998), 127–35.

88. Charles D. Churchwell, "Racial Integration at the University of Houston: A Personal Perspective, II," in *Untold Stories, Civil Rights, Libraries, and Black Librarianship*, ed. John Mark Tucker (Urbana-Champaign, IL: Publications Office, Graduate School of Library and Information Science, 1998), 136–40.

89. Herbert S. White, "Basic Competencies and the Pursuit of Equal Opportunity, Part 2," *Library Journal* 113, No. 15 (1999): 62–63; Totten, "Perspectives on Minority Recruitment," 46–54; and Ismail Abdullahi, "Recruitment and Mentoring of Minority Students," *Journal of Education for Library and Information Science* 33, no. 4 (1992): 307–10; and E. J. Josey, "The Challenges of Cultural Diversity in the Recruitment of Faculty and Students from Diverse Background," *Journal of Education for Library and Information Science* 34, no. 4 (1993): 302–11.

90. Keith C. Wright, "Library Education and Handicapped Individuals," *Journal of Education for Library and Information Science* 21, no. 3 (1981): 183–95; Helene E. Williams, "Black Students in Predominantly White Library Schools," *Journal of Education for Library and Information Sciences* 27, no. 3 (1987): 139–47; Howard F. McGinn, "Building Support for Services for African-American Students: Part 1," *Journal of Education for Library and Information Science* 42, no. 3 (2001): 264–66; and Howard F. McGinn, "Building Support for Services for African-American Students: Part II," *Journal of Education for Library and Information Science* 43, no. 3 (2002): 223–26.

91. Getinet Belay, "Conceptualizing Strategies for Operationalizing Multicultural Curricula," *Journal of Education for Library and Information Science* 33, no. 4 (1992): 295–306; James V. Carmichael and Marilyn L. Shontx, "A 'Despised' 'Semi-Profession': Perceptions of Curricular Content Relating to Gender and Social Issues Among 1993 MLIS/MLS Graduates," *Journal of Education for Library and Information Sciences* 38, no. 2 (1997): 98 –115; Ann Curry, "Intellectual Freedom Lectures and the Dilemma of Offense-Free Teaching," *Journal of Education for Library and Information Science* 38, no. 1 (1997): 43–53; and Yem. S. Fong, "Race, Class, Gender, and Librarianship: Teaching in Ethnic Studies," *Journal of Library Administration* 33, no. 3/4 (2001): 229–40.

92. Peterson, "Alternative Perspectives," 163–74; Rhonda Rios-Kravitz, "Battling the Adobe Ceiling: Barriers to Professional Advancement for Academic Librarians of Color," in *Library Services to Latinos*, ed. Salvador Guereena (Jefferson, NC: McFarland, and Co., 2000), 28–37; and R. E. L. Spencer, "Saying Something about Race: Models for Minority Recruitment," *American Libraries* 33, no. 7 (2002): 54.

93. Norman Oder, "Clark Atlanta University To Close 62-Year-Old LIS School," *Library Journal Online*, 15 November 2003. Available at: www.libraryjournal.com/article/CA332551

94. John Berry, "Not Just Another Library School," *Library Journal Online*, 15 November 2003. Available at: www.libraryjournal.com/article/CA332541

95. Martin, *Brown V Board of Education*, 230.

96. Betsy Hearne, "Once There Was and Will Be: Storytelling the Future," *The Horn Book Magazine*, Nov./Dec. 2000, 712.

97. *Toledo Blade*, "Cheryl Brown Henderson Speaks at Brown Symposium at University of Toledo Law School," 1 November 2003. Available at: www.toledoblade.com/apps/pbcs.dll/article?AID=/20031101/NEWS21/111010140

98. Carol J. Greenhouse, "A Federal Life: Brown and the Nationalization of the Life Story," in *Race, Law, and Culture: Reflections on* Brown v. Board of Education, ed. Austin Sarat (New York: Oxford University Press, 1997), 170–89.

99. Davison M. Douglass, "The Promise of Brown Forty Years Later," in *Symposium:* Brown v Board of Education *After Forty Years: Confronting the Promise, William & Mary Law Review* 36 (1995): 337–44.

100. Beverley Anderson, "Permissive Social and Educational Inequality 40 Years After Brown," *Journal of Negro Education* 63, no. 3 (1994): 445–46.

101. Wilkins, "Dream Deferred But Not Defeated," 14–18.

102. Jerome M. Culp Jr., "Black People in White Face: Assimilation, Culture, and the Brown Case," in *Symposium:* Brown v Board of Education *After Forty Years: Confronting the Promise, William & Mary Law Review* 36 (1995): 665–84.

103. Martin, *Brown V Board of Education,* 231.

104. J. Clay Smith Jr. and Lisa C. Wilson, "Brown on White College Campuses: Forty Years of *Brown v Board of Education,*" in *Symposium:* Brown v Board of Education *After Forty Years: Confronting the Promise, William & Mary Law Review* 36 (1995): 733–50.

105. Frankenberg, Lee, and Orfield, *A Multicultural Society with Segregated Schools.*

106. Diana Reinhart, "Injustices Still Seen 50 Years after Famed Integration Case," *San Antonio News Express,* October 11, 2003.

107. Association for Library and Information Science Education, *Library and Information Science Education Statistical Report 2002.* Available at: www.ils.unc.edu/ALISE/

108. Joanne Ellen Passet, *Cultural Crusaders: Women Librarians in the American West, 1900–1917* (Albuquerque, NM: University of New Mexico Press, 1994), xiii.

109. Paul Dickson, *The Library in America: A Celebration in Words and Pictures* (New York: Facts on File Publications, 1986), 23.

110. Dickson, *The Library in America,* 21.

111. Andrew Abbott, *The System of Professions* (Chicago: University of Chicago Press, 1988).

112. Wayne A. Wiegand, *Core Curriculum: A White Paper,* Background paper prepared for the ALA Congress on Professional Education, April 30–May 1, 1999, 2.

113. Christine Pawley, "Hegemony's Handmaid? The Library and Information Studies Curriculum from a Class Perspective," *Library Quarterly* 68, no. 2 (April 1998): 123–44.

114. Abbott, *The System of Professions*; R. Apostle and B. Raymond, "Librarianship and the Information Paradigm," in *Education of Library and Information Professionals: Present and Future Proposals,* ed. R. K. Gardner (Littleton, CO: Libraries Unlimited, 1987), 17–31; A. Bohannan, "Library Education: Struggling to Meet the Needs of the Profession," *The Journal of Academic Librarianship* 17, no. 4 (1991): 216–19; Laurie J. Bonnice, *Theory and Practice: A White Paper,* Background paper prepared for the ALA Congress on Professional Education, April 30–May 1, 1999; Richard J. Cox and Edie Rasmussen, "Reinventing the Information Professions and the Argument for Specialization in LIS Education: Case Studies in Archives and Information Technology," *Journal of Education for Library and Information Science* 38, no. 4 (1997): 255–67; Blasé Cronin, Michael Stiffer and Dorothy Day, "The Emergent Market for Information Professionals: Educational Opportunities and Implications," *Library Trends* 42, no. 2 (1993): 257–76; Blasé Cronin and E. Davenport, "Conflicts of Jurisdiction: An Exploratory Study of Academic, Professional, and Epistemological Norms in Library and Information Science," *Libra* 46, no. 1 (1996): 1–15; and Tom Wilson, "Professional Education: The Ever Changing Face," *The Library Association Record* 95, no. 4 (1993): 224–25.

115. Robert Grover, Herbert Achleitner, Nancy Thomas, Roger Wyatt, and Faye N. Vowell, "The Wind Beneath Our Wings: Chaos Theory and the Butterfly Effect in Curriculum Design," *Journal of Education for Library and Information Science* 38, no. 4 (1997): 268–82; F. W. Holmes, "Information Systems Curriculum," in *Education for Information Management: Directions for the Future: Record of a Conference Cosponsored by the Information Institute, International Academy at Santa Barbara, and the Association of American Library Schools, May 6–8, 1982,* ed. E. H. Boehm and M. K. Buckland (Santa Barbara, CA: The Academy, 1983), 93–99; L. H. Jeng, "From Cataloging to Organization of Information: A Paradigm for the Core Curriculum," *Journal of Education for Library and Information Science* 34, no. 2 (1993): 113–26; Deanna B. Marcum, "Transforming the Curriculum; Transforming the Profession," *American Libraries,* 28, no. 1 (1997): 35–38; J. Michael Pemberton and Christine Nugent, "Information Studies: Emergent Field, Convergent Curriculum," *Journal of Education for Library and Information Science* 36, no. 2 (1995): 126–38; Carol Tenopir, "I Never Learned about that in Library School: Curriculum Changes in LIS," *Online* 24, no. 2 (2000): 42–46; and Wiegand, *Core Curriculum.*

116. John N. Berry, "Fighting Academe's Corrupted Values: New Tactics for the Defense of Library Schools," *Library Journal* 116, no. 14 (1991): 108; John N. Berry, Lynn Blumenstein and Susan Dimities, "Move Accreditation Apart from ALA?" *Library Journal* 124, no. 10 (1999): 16–17; John N. Berry, "Federating Accreditation," *Library Journal,* 126, no. 8 (2001): 6; Blasé Cronin, "Accreditation: Retool It or Kill It," *Library Journal,* 125, no. 11 (2000): 54; Michael Eisenberg, "LIS Education & Accreditation: A Dean's Perspective," *ALA/COA PRISM* 10, no. 1 (2002); Kathleen de la Peña McCook, *Using Ockham's Razor: Cutting to the Center,* Background paper prepared for the Professional Concerns Committee of the Congress on Professional Education, April 30–May 1, 1999;" Jane Robbins, *Accreditation,* Background paper prepared for the ALA Congress on Professional Education, April 30–May 1, 1999; and F. William Summers, *Accreditation and the American Library Association,* Background Paper Prepared for the ALA Congress on Professional Education, April 30–May 1, 1999.

117. John N. Berry, "Nothing Ever Changes in Library Schools," *Library Journal* 112, no. 19 (1987): 6; Harold Billings, "The Tomorrow Librarian," *Wilson Library Bulletin* 69, no. 5 (1995): 34–37; John M. Budd and Lisa K. Miller, "Teaching for Technology: Current Practice and Future Direction," *Information Technology and Libraries* 18, no. 12 (June): 78–83; Jerry D. Campbell, "Choosing to Have a Future," *American Libraries* 24, no. 6 (1993): 560–63; Bill Crowley and Bill Brace, "A Choice of Futures: Is It Libraries Versus Information?" *American Libraries* 30, no. 4 (1999): 76–79; J. Stephen Downie, "Jumping Off the Disintermediation Bandwagon: Reharmonizing LIS Education for the Realities of the 21st Century," ALISE 1999 National Conference, http://www.lis.uiuc.edu/~jdownie/alise99/ (accessed 12 December 2003); Richard K. Gardner, "Library and Information Science Education: The Present State and Future Prospects," in *Education of Library and Information Professionals* (Littleton, CO: Libraries Unlimited, 1987), 32–53; Gary E. Gorman, "The Future for Library Science Education," *Libri* 49, no. 1 (1999): 1–10; L. Susan Hayes, "Education for the Future," *Information Outlook* 3, no. 1 (1999): 5; Edward G. Holley, "Does Library Education have a Future? After a Century of Hand Wringing, We Should Realize that Library Schools, on the Whole, will not Perish," *American Libraries* 17, no. 9 (1986):

702; Peggy Sullivan, "The Congress on Professional Education: Lessons Learned from Library School, Past and Future," *American Libraries* 30, no. 7 (1999): 14–15; Herbert S. White, "Library Studies or Information Management: What's in a Name?" *Library Journal* 120, no. 7 (1995): 51–52; Herbert S. White, *Librarianship: Quo Vadis? Opportunities and Dangers As We Face the New Millennium* (Greenwood Village, CO: Libraries Unlimited, 2000); and Anne Woodsworth, *The Future of Education for Librarianship: Looking Forward from the Past* (Washington, DC: Council on Library Resources, 1994).

118. Heidi Julien, Jane Robbins, Elisabeth Logan, and Prudence Dalrymple, "Going the Distance: Distance Education in LIS Education," *Journal of Education for Library and Information Science* 42, no. 3 0:32–38; Norman Oder, "LIS Distance Ed Moves Ahead," *Library Journal* 126, no. 16 (2001): 54–56; Lynn Westbrook, "LIS Distance Education: Modes and Plans," *Journal of Education for Library and Information Science* 43, no. 1 (2002): 62–68; and Herbert S. White, "The Changes in Off-Campus Education," *Library Journal* 124, no. 3 (1999): 128–29.

119. Joe Barnes, "What's in a Name? Preserving the Word 'Library'," *West Virginia Libraries* 51, no. 4. (1998): 2; John N. Berry and Susan Dimities, "U. of Wash. SLIS Drops L-Word," *Library Journal* 125, no. 18 (2000): 13; Dorothy M. Broderick, "Turning Library into a Dirty Word: A Rant," *Library Journal* 122, no. 12 (1997): 42–43; Michael K. Buckland, "The Landscape of Information Science: The American Society for Information Science at 62," preprint of article published in *JASIS at 50* special issue of the *Journal of the American Society of Information Science*, 1999, available at: www.sims.berkeley.edu/~buckland/asis62.html; Henry Voos, "The Name's the Thing," *Journal of Education for Library and Information Science* 25, no. 3 (1985): 232–34; Herbert S. White, "Library Studies or Information Management? What's in a Name?" *Library Journal* 120, no. 7 (1995): 51–52; Pauline Wilson, "Taking the Library out of Library Education," *American Libraries* 12, no. 6 (1981): 321–24; and Gene T. Sherron and Marie B. Landry, "Reinventing the Bachelor's Degree: Call It 'Information Studies!'" *Journal of Education for Library and Information Science* 40, no. 1 (1999): 48–56.

120. John N. Berry, "Fighting Academe's Corrupted Values: New Tactics for the Defense of Library Schools," *Library Journal* 116, no. 14 (1991): 108; John N. Berry, "The Two Crises in Library Education," *Library Journal* 118, no. 14 (1993): 102; Gordon Flagg and Thomas M. Gaughan, "Schools Close, but Library Ed Survives at UCLA and Berkeley," *American Libraries* 25, no. 4 (1994): 295; Stephen P. Foster, "Victimization in Library School Closing Rhetoric: A Response to a Library Quarterly Symposium," *Library Quarterly* 63, no. 2 (1993): 199–205; Thomas M. Gaughan, "Columbia Provost's Report Faults SLS and Librarianship," *American Libraries* 21, no. 6 (1990): 479; Beverly Goldberg, "Denver's New MLS Program a Good Sign for Library Ed," *American Libraries* 26, no. 11 (1995): 1095; Charles R. Hildreth and Michael Koenig, "Organizational Realignment of LIS Programs in Academia: From Independent Standalone Units to Incorporated Programs," 2001, http://phoenix.liunet.edu/~hildreth/hildreth-koenig.htm (accessed 14 December 2003); Edward G. Holley, "Does Library Education have a Future?"; Larry J. Ostler, Therin C. Dahlin and J. D. Willardson, *The Closing of American Library Schools: Problems and Opportunities* (Westport, CT: Greenwood Press., 1995); Michael Rogers and Judy Quinn, "Some Library Schools Make Strides while Others Close," *Library Journal* 116, no. 14 (1991): 117–18; Tefko Saracevic, "Closing of Library Schools in North America: What Role Accreditation?"

Libri 44, no. 3 (1994): 190–200; Margaret F. Stieg, "The Closing of Library Schools: Darwinism at the University," *Library Quarterly* 61, no. 3 (1991): 266–72; and Herbert S. White, "Why do 'they' Close Library Schools?" *Library Journal* 117, no. 19 (1992): 51–52.

121. Jordon and Josey, "A Chronology of Events," 3–18.

122. Oder, "Clark Atlanta University To Close 62-Year-Old LIS School."

123. Code of Ethics of the American Library Association, available at: www.ala .org/Content/NavigationMenu/Our_Association/Offices/Intellectual_Freedom3/ Statements_and_Policies/Code_of_Ethics/Code_of_Ethics.htm (accessed 18 November 2003).

124. Dumont, "The Educating of Black Librarians," 244.

125. Wright, "Library Education and Handicapped Individuals," 193.

126. Morton Horwitz, "The Jurisprudence of Brown and the Dilemmas of Liberalism," in *Have we overcome? Race relations since BROWN*, ed. Michael V. Inamorato (Jackson: University Press of Mississippi, 1979), 178.

127. Martin, *Brown v. Board of Education*, 37.

2

Evolving Issues: Racism, Affirmative Action, and Diversity

DeEtta Jones

Diversity is the foundation upon which the United States is built. The introduction of the Spanish explorers and British colonists to the indigenous peoples of the Americas, the influx of 12 million European immigrants through Ellis Island, and the forced migration of Africans to the Caribbean Islands and southern United States are racial and ethnic group interactions pre-dating, then becoming the framework for, the nation's existence. Like the foundation of a house, this framework has slowly shifted over time and appears to lean a bit. Our cultural shift is the result of experience, changing demographics, and acquired knowledge. And though the outcomes are difficult to measure, the effort that we commit to understanding the complexities of race is continual.

RACE

The U.S. Census Bureau collects information on race in compliance with the Office of Management and Budget's guidance for civil rights monitoring and enforcement. The Census Bureau's definition of race "reflects self-identification by people according to the race or races with which they most closely identify. These categories are sociopolitical constructs and should not be interpreted as being scientific or anthropological in nature. Furthermore, the race categories include both racial and national-origin groups."[1] A typical layperson's definition of race, however, may be more straightforward and apparently "scientific": natural and separate divisions within the human species based on visible physical differences (phenotypes). Social scientists, anthropologists, biologists, and academics, on the other hand, fervently debate this definition because it assumes

43

that human differences are based on biology, not culture. Researchers have found that human populations are not clearly demarcated, biologically distinct groups. In fact, evidence from genetics (e.g., DNA) indicates that there is greater variation within "racial groups" (94 percent) than between racial groups (6 percent).[2] Many believe that an attempt to establish lines of division among biological populations is arbitrary and subjective. In growing numbers, supporters of the concept of inclusion argue that "race" does not even exist and that it is merely a social construct—typically used for divisive and often for oppressive purposes. Building on this assumption, a working definition of race should be twofold—with both social and biological influences. It cannot be either social *or* biological, for their interplay and influence cannot be separated. "Race" can be seen as a sociopolitical term used to classify people on the basis of their cultural, behavioral, and geographic ancestry; yet "race" can also be defined as a group of people sharing similar traits (adaptations) that were specialized to the natural pressures of their ancestral environment. This latter "biological" definition of race depends not only upon one's genes, but also significantly upon social and environmental contexts that influence their expression.

The first task in attempting to gain an analytical understanding of race is to deal with the prevailing assumption that race is a biological fact, rather than a social one. To address this issue, we begin with analyses of the biological foundations (or lack thereof) of the concept. By showing how even biologists (e.g., Gould) reject the notion of race on scientific grounds, we open the way toward developing the notion of race as a social construct—one that has changed over time, and varies across societies. We address head-on the epistemological and social obstacles that make it difficult to gain an analytical understanding of race. As a society we have our own folk knowledge of what race is, a lack of knowledge of other societies' racial classifications, and a tendency to look for a guilty party to explain racial inequality. Rather than employing a group-oriented approach to studying race that examines the history of particular groups, the more common United States approach is problem-oriented—which explores mechanisms of racial domination, including prejudice, discrimination, segregation, ghettoization, and violence. These are the lenses through which many U.S. citizens have learned—intellectually and experientially—about race.

An analysis of race and racism must also include a thoughtful examination of class. Causes of poverty are structural and behavioral, as demonstrated in sociological studies by William J. Wilson: "A household in which a family cannot sustain themselves economically cannot possibly harbor hope or optimism, or stimulate eager participation in the full prerogatives of citizenship."[3] Forty-five percent of all black children are born at or below the poverty line. Economists have shown that one-third of the members of the African American community were worse off economically in the mid-1990s than in 1968. Simultaneously—possibly as a result of affirmative action—the size of the black middle class has quadrupled, doubling in the 1980s alone.[4] And though the representation of blacks and other minorities in the middle class is growing, Hernstein and Murray, in their controversial book *The Bell Curve* (1994), argue that general cognitive ability is a major determiner of social status and that variance in general mental ability is largely attributable to genetic factors.[5] Separate from the population growth rate, some minority groups are disproportionately poor and score lower on IQ tests than non-minorities. In his rebuttal of Hernstein and Murray's biology-based argument, Stephen Jay Gould returned to the theme of a "mismeasure of man" with his unyielding refutation of the validity of any single quantitative measure of intelligence as measuring "a real property in the head." In *The Mismeasure of Man,* a review of *The Bell Curve,* Gould insisted that "the book is a manifesto of conservative ideology." He stated, "I have never read anything so feeble, so unlikely, so almost grotesquely inadequate"[6] as the argument in its final chapter. Obviously, the debate about the sociological implications of race continues to be alive and well.

The issues of race and class are jointly addressed by Henry Louis Gates, Jr., and Cornell West in *The Future of the Race,* where they forward the idea of a social construct of race. They argue, "It is only by confronting the twin realities of white racism, on the one hand, and our own failures to seize initiative and break the cycle of poverty, on the other, that we, the remnants of the Talented Tenth [referring to Du Bois' Talented Tenth of African Americans who provide intellectual leadership], will be able to assume a renewed leadership role for, and within, the black community."[7] The notion of breaking the cycle of oppression and discrimination (as applicable to all groups) surfaces again and again in discussions of race, affirmative action, and diversity.

AFFIRMATIVE ACTION

"The Supreme Court of the United States is poised to make a momentous decision that will affect directly or indirectly virtually every feature of our society."[8] For years, pursuing racial understanding and equitable access has been seen as the work of social justice advocates (and, of course, librarians). The issue that was recently under consideration by the Supreme Court—the abandonment of affirmative action in higher education admissions practices—should not be reserved for advocates alone. In his article "The Consequence of Premature Abandonment of Affirmative Action in Medical School Admission," Jordan Cohen, executive director of the American Medical Association, describes why affirmative action programs are so important for medical school admissions. He says that Justice Powell, in the *Regents of the University of California v. Bakke* case (1978), envisioned that race could be considered a "plus factor" in deciding between two equally qualified applicants. However, medical schools put an even higher emphasis on race because of lower GPAs and MCAT scores among underrepresented minorities (URMs). URMs still lag behind whites and Asians in GPAs and MCAT scores, even after socioeconomic adjustment. So race as a factor—irreplaceable by socioeconomic or other factors—is critical in assuring diverse medical school applicants, students, and doctors. Cohen goes on to say that since affirmative action programs began to be used in admissions programs in 1964, URMs in medical schools have gone from 2 percent to 10 percent. URMs, however, represent 23 percent of the United States population.[9]

In essence, reversing the *Bakke* standard (race as one of many characteristics that can be considered) could negatively affect higher education institutions' ability to attract and admit diverse student bodies, and the demographic makeup of professions that require academic credentialing and could accentuate national socioeconomic stratification.

Though an important affirmative decision was made by the Supreme Court, the debate over affirmative action has raged for years. It's been going on long enough for many Americans to sign on as strongly supporting or opposing affirmative action, switch sides in the mid- to late-1990s anti-affirmative action backlash, and now approach the matter from a calmer perspective. Though the core issue in higher education has remained much the same—using race as a factor in making college admissions decisions—new information has surfaced through years of discussion and legal activity and many are coming to different conclusions than earlier in the legislation's history. Affirmative action can be seen as linked to the government's view of race as a social construct rather than a biological fact. It is rooted in the belief that race does not determine ability and that racism has historically hindered American minorities' chances for self-advancement. Opposition to affirmative action does not necessarily imply, however, a belief in the biological determination of race and racial differences. It is often rooted in the American Dream—the belief is that people are created equal, opportunity for advancement is available to all Americans, and all one has to do is take their bite out of the American pie. Opponents of affirmative action might concede that barriers existed at one point, but those (legal) barriers have now been removed, thus creating equal access to individual accomplishment. Supporters of affirmative action, on the other hand, do not believe that hundreds of years of oppression can be remedied without long-term corrective action. A historical overview is useful for understanding the context within which the debate exists.

HISTORICAL OVERVIEW

An exploration of social, legal, and organizational shifts regarding the subjects of race and affirmative action creates a context within which to understand diversity initiatives. More importantly, a timeline designates familiar touchstones and draws a more comprehensive picture, composed of individual, manageable parts. The following timeline highlights major occurrences that have determined the current state of affirmative action in the United States. It describes events that occurred long before the term "affirmative action" was introduced, as well as recent legal rulings and ramifications.

1866: The most basic rights a U.S. citizen has are described in the United States Constitution. This document serves as the one common denominator in all legal decisions informing the ongoing discussion of diversity. In 1866, the Fourteenth Amendment to the Constitution is enacted. It includes a requirement that in all states there shall be "equal protection of the laws" to all citizens. This is significant because it abolishes slavery by requiring recognition of uniform basic human rights in all states, dismantling the institution of slavery in southern states per the precedent set by northern states. It is the most important post–Civil War enactment because it shifted the balance of power from the states, or federalism, to the federal government. 1866 is also the year in which Congress passed the Freedmen's Bureau Act to establish programs for former slaves. These programs were designed to help former slaves begin an emancipated life, including purchasing property, becoming employed for wages, and exercising other citizenship rights.

1870: Harvard University graduates its first black American, 234 years after the university was founded.[10]

1896: The period following the emancipation of slaves is filled with conflict. Ex-slaves, in their quest to establish themselves in freedom, are often met with hostility by whites with no intention of integrating or sharing what they believe to be "theirs." One such instance leads to the 1896 court case known as *Plessy v. Ferguson*, in which the Supreme Court interprets the Fourteenth Amendment as requiring only "separate but equal" public accommodations. The "separate but equal" concept is used to maintain complete racial segregation in public transportation, restaurants, hospitals, schools, and other public facilities.

1941: The United States defense industry grows in preparation for World War II. A. Phillip Randolph, the leader of the Porter's Union, threatens a "million man march" on Washington, DC, unless black men are allowed to work in the defense industry. This threat leads to President Franklin Roosevelt's issuance of an executive order prohibiting discrimination in hiring in the defense industry. This is the first official government action regarding discrimination in the workplace.

1945: The United States armed services issue an affirmative action policy, the GI Bill of Rights, ensuring that ex-soldiers have access to educational and career opportunities upon discharge from the armed services.

1954: In *Brown v. Board of Education*, the U.S. Supreme Court overrules the "separate but equal" doctrine of 1896, thus declaring racially segregated schools unconstitutional. The time between the original "separate but equal" decision (*Plessy v. Ferguson*) and the overturning of that decision (*Brown v. Board of Education*) creates an educational void—displacing the educational and vocational preparedness of entire generations of minorities, explaining "the fact that, in the late 1960s, the unemployment rate of blacks was double that of whites."[11] The effects of this void continue to be felt, as college-educated parents are much more likely to have children who attend college; as poverty, inversely correlated with formal education, is a cyclical phenomenon affecting those families who come from poverty; and as internalized oppression manifests itself in groups as a result of societal marginalization.

1961: President John F. Kennedy issues Executive Order No. 10,925, prohibiting race, religion, color, or national origin discrimination in federal employment. The order requires that the government take "affirmative steps to realize more fully the national policy of nondiscrimination," and establishes the Equal Employment Opportunity Commission to oversee the adherence of this standard in organizations.

1964: Congress passes the Civil Rights Act of 1964. Titles VI, VII, and IX expand guidelines for nondiscrimination in the workplace to include race, color, religion, sex, and national origin.

1965: President Lyndon B. Johnson issues Executive Order No. 11,246, requiring federal contractors to "take Affirmative Action" to ensure nondiscrimination against workers on the basis of race, creed, color, or national origin. This signifies a shift from a more purely passive nondiscrimination to a more active assurance of nondiscrimination.

1969: President Richard Nixon sets goals for hiring racial minority contractors, pushing federal and state governments to negotiate and hire minority-owned contracting companies. His administration later presses colleges to set goals for increasing the number of racial minority students and faculty at their institutions. This is the first use of targeted numeric goals for increasing minority representation.

1972: Congress passes the Equal Employment Opportunity Act, allowing civil lawsuits against companies for discriminatory employment practices. The fear of legal recourse caused by the passage of this act forces companies to more advanced levels of nondiscrimination—beyond a mere statement and into documented, consistent workplace practices. Congress also passes the Educational Amendments Act of 1972. Title IX prohibits sex discrimination in federally funded educational institutions, requiring such institutions to take specific steps to encourage individuals of the previously excluded sex to apply for admission. These "specific steps" are the groundwork for more comprehensive affirmative action programs. At this stage, however, they only take sex into consideration.

1978: In *Regents of the University of California v. Bakke*, the U.S. Supreme Court issues a landmark decision on affirmative action, allowing race to be considered among the many factors affecting university admissions. This decision establishes a precedent for university admissions standards across the United States.

1989: *Richmond v. Croson* represents the Supreme Court's first application of the "strict scrutiny" standard, as the Court rules that city and state officials may not steer contracts toward minority contractors, except to make up for a clear history of discrimination and to advance a compelling state interest. This decision depicts the increasing social and legal pressure to contextually define appropriate use of affirmative action. The progress of affirmative action is, at this stage, focused on making amends where past discrimination can be proven. This is also the year that the Supreme Court shifts the burden of proof from employers to employees, in *Ward's Cove Packing Company v. Atonio*, making it difficult for workers to challenge workplace discrimination. The Court rules that discrimination cannot be proven solely by relying on statistical evidence, imposing further on employees' recourse.

1990: In *Metro Broadcasting v. FCC*, the Supreme Court reaffirms the constitutionality of congressionally adopted race-conscious remedies that achieve important governmental diversity objectives. In this case, expanding minority participation in broadcasting is found to achieve the objective of enhancing diversity. This case is a milestone because the "objective of enhancing diversity" mirrors the values that the workforce and university administrators have held for years and are being fervently challenged today.

The Americans with Disabilities Act of 1990 takes effect, prohibiting employers with fifteen or more employees from discriminating against qualified individuals with disabilities in job application procedures and in hiring, firing, advancement, compensation, job training, and other terms, conditions, and privileges of employment. At the time this chapter was written, people with disabilities were added to the list of people included in affirmative action programs.

1991: Congress passes the Civil Rights Act of 1991 in response to *Ward's Cove* and similar employment discrimination cases. This revised act reinstitutes the legitimacy of using statistical disparity and places the burden of proof back on employers. It further recognizes the discrepancy in requiring employees to investigate their own claims of discrimination against an employer.

1995: The federally appointed Glass Ceiling Commission confirms the existence of a "glass ceiling" that effectively excludes the advancement of women and minorities, and finds that white men occupy 95–97 percent of senior management positions in the United States. Also in 1995, the University of California's Board of Regents votes to end the use of affirmative action initiatives, such as racial consideration, in hiring, admissions, and contracting, throughout the system. This case is a direct challenge to the 1978 *Bakke* decision that set the precedent for allowing race to be one of many factors considered when choosing from a pool of applicants.

1996: The U.S. Court of Appeals for the 5th Circuit reverses and remands the decision of the district court in the *Hopwood v. University of Texas* (1994/1996) law school case. The court challenges that taking race into consideration regarding university admissions, as is the precedent set by *Bakke*, is a violation of the Fourteenth Amendment right to equal protection under the law because additional "points" are given to minority candidates. In response to *Hopwood*, the Texas Legislature passes the Texas Ten Percent Plan, which ensures that the top ten percent of students at all high schools in Texas have guaranteed admission to the University of Texas and Texas A&M system, including the two flagship schools UT-Austin and A&M College Station.

A federal appeals court upholds California's controversial Proposition 209, the first state law to bar thirty years of affirmative action programs.

1998: A ban on the use of affirmative action in admissions at the University of California goes into effect. UC Berkeley has a 61 percent drop in admissions of African American, Latino/a, and Native American students, and UCLA has a 36 percent decline. Voters in Washington pass Initiative 200, banning affirmative action in higher education, public contracting, and hiring.

2000: Many circuit courts throughout the country hear cases regarding affirmative action in higher education, including the 5th Circuit in Texas (*Hopwood*), the 6th Circuit in Michigan (*Grutter and Gratz*), the 9th Circuit in Washington (*Smith*), and the 11th Circuit in Georgia (*Johnson*). The same district court in Michigan makes two different rulings regarding affirmative action in Michigan, with one judge deciding that the University of Michigan's undergraduate affirmative action program was constitutional, while another judge finds the university's law school program unconstitutional.

Florida Republican Gov. Jeb Bush introduces "One Florida," a plan that replaces current affirmative action programs with a system that bans consideration of race and gender in admissions to the state's ten public universities. In exchange, it guarantees admission to a state university for the top 20 percent of each high school graduating class—provided the student has taken the necessary college preparatory courses.

In an effort to promote equal pay, the U.S. Department of Labor promulgates new affirmative action regulations, including an Equal Opportunity Survey, which requires federal contractors to report hiring, termination, promotions, and compensation data by minority status and gender. This is the first time in history that employers have been required to report information regarding compensation by gender and minority status to the federal equal employment agencies.

2001: California enacts a new plan allowing the top 12.5 percent of high school students admission to the University of California system, either for all four years or after two years outside the system, and guaranteeing the top 4 percent of all high school seniors admission to the University of California system.

A split exists at the circuit court level on affirmative action in college admissions. In *Smith v. University of Washington*, the 9th Circuit upholds the university's affirmative action program, although the program could no longer be used after the passage of Initiative 200. On the other hand, 11th Circuit Court of Appeals follows the 5th Circuit in *Hopwood* and declares the University of Georgia's affirmative action program unconstitutional in *Johnson v. Regents of the University of Georgia*.

2002: The Bush administration files legal briefs with the U.S. Supreme Court, siding with the defendant in the *Grutter v. Bollinger* case.

2003: In response to President Bush's statement and the filing of the brief, University of Michigan President Mary Sue Coleman says to the University of Michigan Board of Directors: "Every student we admit is qualified and prepared to do the work. We consider many other factors in addition to academics, including race. Geographic diversity is important, too; so if you come from Michigan's upper peninsula you earn 16 points. A student who is socioeconomically disadvantaged earns 20 points. We look at leadership, at service and extra-curricular activities, at life experiences, among others. Overall, we strive for a student body that is richly diverse in many ways because it enriches each student's learning environment. . . . In making decisions at the Law School, we also carefully review individual experiences and interests in a highly competitive process. Every applicant competes fairly for every seat. There are no numerical targets, and the actual enrollment of underrepresented minorities at the Law School over the past 10 years has ranged from 12.5 to 20 percent. (Our enrollment of students from California has ranged from 11 to 15 percent during that same time; but I don't imagine anyone would think we had a numerical target for Californians!)"[12]

In February 2003, a month after the Bush administration filed a brief with the Supreme Court opposing affirmative action policies at the University of Michigan, more than 300 organizations representing academia, major corporations, labor unions, and nearly 30 of the nation's top former military and civilian defense officials announce that they will file briefs supporting the university. The number of friend-of-the-court briefs challenge the record of 62 briefs filed during the Court's 1978 *Bakke* decision. The variety of organizations filing briefs this time reflects the broad reach of affirmative action policies in the quarter-century since the Supreme Court's landmark *Bakke* ruling.[13]

On April 1, 2003, the Supreme Court began hearing oral arguments supporting and opposing the use of race as even one factor in college and university admissions programs. Opponents describe the use of race as a violation of constitutional rights. Proponents rebutted by comparing the injury of a white person denied admission while an affirmative action program is in place to a white denied admission because she's not an athlete or he's not an alumnus. Both valid arguments; unfortunately neither are addressed by the equal protection clause. Discussions also focused on breaking the cycle of past discrimination, for which legal precedents have been set. According to Justice Steven Breyer, "75 percent of black students below the college level are at schools that are more than 50 percent minority. And 85 percent of those schools are in areas of poverty. . . .The only way to break this cycle is to have a leadership that is diverse. And to have a leadership across the country that is diverse, you have to train a diverse student body for law, for the military, for business, for all the other positions in this country that will allow us to have diverse leadership in a country that is diverse."[14]

On June 23, 3003, in *Grutter v. Bollinger et al.*, the Supreme Court ruled 5–4 in favor of the University of Michigan Law School's use of race in considering admissions. In *Gratz v. Bolinger*, a separate but parallel case, the Supreme Court ruled 6–3 against the University of Michigan's affirmative action policy for undergraduate admissions, which awarded 20 points for blacks, Hispanics, and Native Americans on an admissions rating scale. The majority ruled that the point system violated equal protection provisions of the Constitution and was not "narrowly tailored" to achieve the university's diversity goals.[15]

The cases tested whether a university is allowed to discriminate because it values diversity in its student body, or whether discrimination is only justified to reverse past racial injustice. The Supreme Court does not have responsibility for outlining more acceptable alternatives for achieving the goal of diversity, so universities are responsible for designing programs that fit within constitutional parameters and continuing to settle definitional disputes in the lower courts.

DIVERSITY

In her book chapter "The Definition of Diversity: Two Views. A More Specific Definition," Lorna Peterson describes the transition from affirmative action to diversity as the cumulative result of affirmative action and equal employment opportunity legislation protecting a variety of groups. She said, "Affirmative Action, and the benefits of Equal Employment Opportunity (EEO) laws, was extended to provide opportunity to white women, the disabled, Vietnam Veterans, person over 40 . . . that is, all U.S. citizens are recognized as members of a protected class and entitled to the benefits of EEO law."[16] Peterson's point is well taken. A huge portion of the U.S. population fell into protected class status by the mid-1990s. As legislation was introduced, the pieces began melding together and led to forums on "increasing sensitivity" or "raising awareness." For many diversity educators and social justice activists, the mid-1990s were an exciting time. Grassroots efforts were flourishing on university campuses and within liberal-minded communities around the country. All sorts of models (identity development, cycle of oppression, internalized oppression, Mosaic of Diversity) were created and people examined, many for the first time, how we are different and how we are the same at group and individual levels.

Diversity awareness was embraced on university campuses, within community groups, and in private companies throughout the country. "Political correctness" governed the activity of people in social and business settings and non-subscribers described their interactions as monitored by the "diversity police." For many, diversity awareness was a time to explore one's own identity and be introduced to other cultures—all the while being reminded to seek common ground. Quite a few of the early-1990s diversity educators subscribed to the view that the only way to approach diversity awareness and sensitivity development was through first being "cleansed" of our "isms"—socialized prejudices that are inevitably embedded in the developmental experiences of every American. This metaphoric "cleansing" was often done in an educational context (like a workshop or seminar) where people were asked to disclose their cultural identification according to categories (race, gender, sexual orientation, etc.) and then be classified as oppressor or oppressed. Then learners were asked to testify about their socialization and how it led them to become a racist/sexist/heterosexist, etc. These testimonials were sometimes expected to preface apologies for discriminatory practices or for privileges enjoyed by the individual or group. Though this style of diversity awareness and sensitivity training was very popular, and embraced at the time, a backlash occurred by 1996.

Contention came from a variety of camps. Some thought that the prevalent style of training was isolating much needed allies—white men in particular. In response, a new type of education became popular, ally building, which focused on building coalitions to overcome oppression of all sorts. Others turned their backs on diversity altogether because they felt personally attacked, marginalized, and victimized by the education process. Some described the diversity "movement" as reverse discrimination.

As the backlash surfaced, so did a new mindset about how the issue of diversity should be examined and used to redefine the U.S. macro-culture. Educational processes shifted from group identification (which is what affirmative action and EEO did—describe legal and social barriers for whole groups) to overlapping individual characteristics that combine to form a multicultural person. These characteristics are a blend of biological (like race, gender, and age) and sociocultural (like ethnicity, class, and geographic background) elements. Discussing our individual differences, rather than focusing on large group oppression, allowed for more expansive conversations than previous approaches. First, it was not tied only to those groups that had been identified in U.S. legislation—of which the gay, lesbian, bisexual, and transgendered community was not a part. Second, it created a framework with access points for a variety of people. For example, the white man, who had previously been demonized for his oppressive roots and socialization, was now able to identify more specifically as a straight Jew of German decent with a learning disability, raised in New York City in a large, middle-class family.

Exploring one's cultural background and expanding the definition of diversity grew in popularity but was met with its own backlash. In the library community, a debate about inclusiveness (or an expansive definition of diversity that may be used to divert attention away from more inflammatory issues, like race) versus equity-focused diversity engagement was most forward thinking. In this context, equity issues represent those groups that have historically been marginalized or denied access to social, professional, and educational opportunities because of their group identification. Peterson urges librarians interested in equity and its achievements to "beware the imprecision of the diversity concepts and re-embrace Affirmative Action."[17]

On April 1, 2003, thousands of college students and advocates met on the steps of the Supreme Court in support of affirmative action. That evening, opening arguments began and, judging from the justice's comments, we had come full circle.

In organizational settings, businesses and institutions of higher education evolved from "sensitivity training," to "managing diversity" (that is, building work environments that were non-discriminatory, responsive to a diverse customer base, and comfortable for women and people from underrepresented groups), to systemic organizational change. Duke University's diversity statement describes the evolution of the concept and their rationale for focusing on systemic change: "The expectation is that systems change is more fundamental and long lasting than individual behavior change alone. . . . Systemic responses include: changes in hiring, staff development and retention processes, changes in conflict management approaches, as well as changes in reward and recognition systems."[18]

CONCLUSION

During the 1965 civil revolt in the Watts area of Los Angeles, commentators and other outsiders referred to it as "riots," but to insiders it was an "uprising." This is an important distinction. The battle over affirmative action and equitable participation in U.S. society will not end with the Supreme Court's most recent decision, but it is the most tangible battleground available. Despite the outcome, race relations in the United States still have a long way to go before the oppressive marks of the past are reconciled. Nationally, the Hispanic segment of the U.S. population is now the largest minority group and the fastest growing. The United States has to deal with issues of equitable pay, treatment of migrant workers, and the present effects of the genocide of American Indians. By 2025, the minority populations in four states (California, New Mexico, Texas, and Hawaii) will be the majority.[19]

What needs to be done? Well, one sociological theory that suggests that the only time humans will truly unite, as a human race, is in the event that Earth is attacked by extraterrestrial beings. The next best thing, at least at a national level, is to find a common U.S. enemy and divert our collective attention away from micro-cultural distinctions within the same macro-culture and toward *them*. The September 11, 2001, attacks on the World Trade Center and Pentagon replaced the lukewarm "tolerance of diversity" with a new national sentiment—"others" must be held in suspicion, our very existence depends on the identification and elimination of "them." In this author's opinion, we now have the opportunity to behave differently than in the past, to learn from past mistakes. Instead of repeating the marginalizing behaviors of the U.S. past—rooted in ignorance, fear, and intolerance—we can choose to be informed and act as bridges during this time of turbulent international relations. Breaking the cycle of oppression may begin with us.

NOTES

1. U.S. Census Bureau. "State and County Quick Facts 2003," http://quickfacts.census.gov/qfd/meta/long_68172.htm (accessed 15 October 2003).

2. Conrad P. Kottak, *Anthropology: The Exploration of Human Diversity* (New York: The McGraw-Hill Companies, 2000).

3. Henry Louis Gates, Jr. and Cornell West, *The Future of the Race* (New York: Vintage Books, 1996), xiii.

4. Gates and West, *The Future of the Race*, xi–xii.

5. Richard J. Herrnstein and Charles Murray, *The Bell Curve: Intelligence and Class Structure in American Life* (New York: The Free Press, 1994).

6. Steven J. Gould, "Curveball," *The New Yorker*, November 1994, 372; and *The Mismeasurement of Man*, (New York: Norton Press, 1996).

7. Gates and West, *The Future of the Race*, xv.

8. Jordan J. Cohen, "The Consequences of Premature Abandonment of Affirmative Action in Medical School Admissions," *Journal of the American Medical Association* 289 (2003): 1143.

9. Cohen, "The Consequences of Premature Abandonment," 1143–49.

10. Gates and West, *The Future of the Race*, xi.

11. Hugh Davis Graham, "The Origins of Affirmative Action: Civil Rights and the Regulatory State," in *The Annals of The American Academy of Political and Social Sciences*, ed. H. Orlans and J. O'Neill (London: Sage, 1992), 57–58.

12. Mary Sue Coleman, "President Mary Sue Coleman Responds to Bush Administration Announcement on Affirmative Action," *University of Michigan New Service*, 15 January 2003.

13. Diana J. Schemo, "300 Groups File Briefs to Support the University of Michigan in an Affirmative Action Case," *New York Times*, 18 February 2003.

14. "The Supreme Court; Excerpts From Arguments Before the Supreme Court on Affirmative Action," *New York Times*, 2 April 2003.

15. Nina Totenberg and Juan Williams, "Split Ruling on Affirmative Action: High Court Rules on Race as Factor in University Admissions," National Public Radio. www.npr.org/news/specials/Michigan/ (accessed 23 June 2003).

16. Lorna Peterson, "The Definition of Diversity: Two Views: A More Specific Definition," in *Managing Multiculturalism and Diversity in the Library: Principles and Issues for Administrators,* ed. Mark Winston (New York: The Haworth Press, 1999), 20.

17. *Managing Multiculturalism and Diversity in the Library: Principles and Issues for Administrators,* ed. Mark Winston (New York: The Haworth Press, 1999).

18. Duke University, Office for Institutional Equity, 2003. www.duke.edu/web/equity/ (accessed 11 October 2003).

19. FedStats, U.S. Census Bureau Definition of Race. www.fedstats.gov/qf/meta/long_68185.htm (accessed 11 October 2003).

3

In Union There Is Strength: Library and Information Science Educators and Librarians' Associations of Color

Cora P. Dunkley and Kathleen de la Peña McCook

Recruiting and retaining new librarians of color is a challenge that both the library profession and the faculty of schools of library and information science must face together. In this chapter, we summarize the historical connection among members of the associations of color of the ALA and faculties of schools of library and information science. We also present the wisdom of faculty who have been active advocates for the recruitment and mentoring of new librarians of color. We feel that our collaboration on this article reflects the mode of interaction that is necessary for this work to go forward. Cora P. Dunkley is a member of the Black Caucus of the American Library Association (BCALA) and began teaching in LIS in the fall of 2002. Kathleen de la Peña McCook is a member of National Association to Promote Library and Information Services to Latinos and the Spanish-Speaking (REFORMA) and began teaching LIS in 1976.

HISTORICAL ISSUES OF ASSOCIATIONS AND COMMITMENT

The "librarians' associations of color" affiliated with the ALA are (in order of their founding): the Black Caucus of the American Library Association (BCALA), 1970; REFORMA,1971; American Indian Library Association (AILA, 1979); Asian/Pacific American Librarians Association (APALA,1980); and the Chinese American Librarians Association (CALA,1983). Each association has a proud history of advocacy and diligent efforts to enhance service to and inclusion of people of color—often born of the indifference and lack of attention on the part of the ALA.[1] In 1981, the ALA established a Committee on Minority Concerns (CMC) to provide a forum for debating, discussing, and resolving problems and issues of concern that affect librarians of color and culturally diverse groups within the ALA, ALA affiliates, and the profession.[2]

One of the first tasks of the CMC, in collaboration with the ethnic affiliates, came about with the release of the 1983 report of the National Commission on Libraries and Information Science (NCLIS) Task Force on Libraries and Information Services to Cultural Minorities, which was based on concern that the 1979 White House Conference on Libraries and Information Services had not adequately addressed the information needs of cultural minorities.[3] In 1984, ALA President E. J. Josey (1984–1985) charged the ALA President's Committee on Library Service to Minorities to review the NCLIS report and develop an ALA action document to suggest specific measures and activities.

The president's committee, co-chaired by Elizabeth Martinez and Binnie Tate Wilkin, with Jean Coleman, director of the ALA Office of Library Outreach Services, as ALA Liaison, submitted the report *Equity at Issue: Library Services to the Nation's Major Minority Groups*, in 1985. The report declared, "The major overall finding was that a disparity exists and continues to grow between the provision of library services for minority and poor communities compared to that provided for white and affluent communities. This inequity is most reprehensible in communities where the white population is actually the numerical minority."[4]

Josey's Committee on Library Service to Minorities marked the first major collaboration of members of ALA's ethnic affiliates and representatives of the CMC. A number of the recommendations in *Equity at Issue* related to education for librarianship:

- Committee on Accreditation (COA) to request minority recruitment policies and procedures of all ALA-accredited schools.
- COA to request information from ALA accredited schools on courses focused on services and materials for cultural minorities.
- Letter to National Council of Accreditation of Teacher Education urging the standard requirements for accreditation include a basic understanding of multicultural, multiethnic society.[5]

Monitoring of the recommendations in *Equity at Issue* included the 1990 publication *Addressing Ethnic and Cultural Diversity: A Report on Activities of the American Library Association, 1986–1989*, by Sibyl E. Moses.[6] This report provided documentation about the activities and programs of ALA that responded to the recommendations in *Equity at Issue*. While few related directly to education, all reflected on education in a larger sense. Progress would be difficult without a body of new professionals sensitized and aware of the need to deliver services in the context of cultural awareness. Some of the most substantive work relating to education was generated by the ALA Office for Library Personnel Resources, under the direction of Margaret Myers, which conducted several studies emphasizing the need to recruit more librarians of color.[7]

Evidence of the influence *of Equity at Issue* may also be seen in the *Standards for Accreditation of Master's Programs in Library and Information Studies*, adopted by the Council of the American Library Association in 1992:

- Program objectives need to reflect . . . the role of library and information services in a rapidly changing multicultural, multiethnic, multilingual society, including the role of serving the needs of underserved groups (Standard I).
- The curriculum responds to the needs of a rapidly changing multicultural, multiethnic, multilingual society, including the needs of underserved groups (Standard II).
- The school has policies to recruit and retain faculty from multicultural, multiethnic, and multilingual backgrounds. Explicit and equitable faculty personnel policies and procedures are published, accessible, and implemented (Standard III).
- The school has policies to recruit and retain a multicultural, multiethnic, and multilingual student body from a variety of backgrounds (Standard IV).[8]

The inclusion of language in the *Standards for Accreditation* that reflects the need to consider issues of cultural diversity is a manifestation of the ongoing work on policy issues by faculty and other members of the LIS profession drawing strength and inspiration from the ongoing work of the ethnic caucuses.

It has been mainly within the ALA that the heart of efforts to develop a responsive profession has emerged. Faculty energies for work on issues relating to diversity have primarily been in collaboration with the ALA. The creation in 1998 of the Office for Diversity within ALA intensified this connection. The Office for Diversity is an active liaison with the membership that consults, facilitates, and trains on diversity issues that affect the profession, the workplace, and the quality of services and information delivery, such as recruitment, retention, personal/professional leadership, organizational change, capacity building, and skill building for effective communication within library organizations and with library users. The Office for Diversity serves as a key resource and link to the professional issues that speak to diversity as a fundamental value and key action area of the association.[9]

The scope of concern for diversity has been broadened by the ALA's creation of a Council Committee on Diversity, which provides a forum to research, monitor, discuss, and address national diversity issues and trends. The Office for Diversity oversees the SPECTRUM Scholarship program and has engaged a number of LIS faculty in the annual SPECTRUM Leadership Institute, drawing, in the main, from faculty connections to the associations of color to which they belong. The role of faculty of color in mentoring and supporting students of color has long been a special commitment made with heartfelt intentions to provide broader opportunities. Cora P. Dunkley conducted short interviews to understand the wellspring of this commitment so that new faculty can stand on the shoulders of these pathfinders.

WISDOM OF FACULTY ADVOCATES

According to the *2003 ALISE Statistical Report,* the number of faculty of color teaching in accredited LIS programs is 20 percent. Student enrollment for minorities is 13.3 percent. Neither percentage shows proportionate representation of racial/ethnic groups in the overall number of full-time LIS faculty and LIS student enrollment when compared to the U.S. population at large.[10] All racial/ethnic groups are underrepresented in the student population, and LIS faculty, like many science disciplines, show a disproportionate representation of Asian faculty. What could be a major factor that may prove helpful in increasing these numbers? Some answers may be found through discussion with faculty involved in the librarians' associations of color.

In an effort to understand the importance of being active in professional organizations from the standpoint of a new faculty member of color, several faculty advocates of color who are actively involved in their professional organizations were contacted and asked to respond to five questions. A few introductory statements about these faculty are provided, followed by their comments on each question.

Edward Erazo is an adjunct faculty member at the east coast site of the School of Library and Information Science, University of South Florida (USF). He has been very active in REFORMA and has served as its president. Today, he sits on several ALA committees and as councilor-at-large. He is co-author of the *Library Trends* article, "Latinos and Librarianship."

Dr. Rhonda Harris Taylor is associate professor at the School of Library and Information Studies, University of Oklahoma. She is editor of the American Indian Library Association's *American Indian Librarians Newsletter,* a position she has held since 1996. Dr. Taylor is also area co-chair of libraries, archives, and museums and popular culture for 2002–2003.

Dr. Ling Hwey Jeng is director of the School of Library and Information Studies at Texas Woman's University. She has served as president of the Chinese American Librarians Association. Currently, she is executive director of the Asian/Pacific American Librarians Association and editor of "Visible College," a column in the *Journal of Education for Library and Information Science* "that serves as a forum for exchanging ideas and innovations related to LIS education."

1. Faculty have many demands on their time . . . teaching, research, advising, etc. Why do you think it is important to spend time being active in your professional organization, namely REFORMA, the American Indian Library Association, and the Asian/Pacific American Library Association, respectively?

   Mr. Erazo: We do always seem to have lots of projects, classes, and meetings on the calendar, but it is important to make time for those important activities in our professional lives. REFORMA is one of those. Although I only teach one or two classes per year as an adjunct for USF, I never fail to tell my students about REFORMA and the work that the association does. I also encourage them to join as a way to find out about the organization. Admittedly, today, I am more involved in ALA in my work as councilor-at-large and on committees. There was a time when I spent a great deal of time working with REFORMA and I loved the experience. It is a good thing to bring that experience to the classroom to my students. It might give them the idea that they, too, can become involved in REFORMA and serve our diverse communities.

   Dr. Taylor: Why, because the needs that were articulated as the purpose for the creation of the *American Indian Libraries Newsletter* still exist. These included the need to implement and improve library services to Native Americans, the importance of raising awareness about the need for meeting the information needs of Native Americans, and the need to recruit Native Americans into the profession.

   Dr. Jeng: Service is part of our job. We are evaluated on service we provide. Beyond a requirement, diversity is an issue I care about and I believe I can make a difference.

2. Why is it important to mentor students of color through work with REFORMA, the American Indian Library Association, and the Asian/Pacific American Library Association?

   Mr. Erazo: As I mentioned, there are so few faculty members of color in library and information science schools, it is important to make the most of introducing students to REFORMA and the work they do. It can provide both an education and a network for their professional future. It also shows the growing importance of serving people of color in libraries across our country. Librarians of color provide role models for students of color, and organizations like REFORMA provide the opportunity to get involved with our diverse communities.

   Dr. Taylor: The future of every profession is dependent on its ability to recruit the next generation. And, it's a shortsighted profession that does not see the value of being inclusive in these recruitment efforts, especially in this country, in this time period.

   Dr. Jeng: Students of color need role models and they especially need faculty members who are of color. Most times people with similar backgrounds understand each other better.

3. Do you think the library profession is changing in terms of its inclusiveness to new librarians of color? Do you think the SPECTRUM Initiative has made a difference?

   Mr. Erazo: I have worked in west Texas, southern New Mexico, and south Florida for all of my library career, and I can tell you I have seen firsthand the talented scholarship recipients that have participated in the SPECTRUM Initiative. I think it attracted among the very best and the brightest, who might have chosen other fields if it were not for the financial assistance available through the SPECTRUM Initiative. For those already in graduate programs, it made it possible to finish sooner and with less of a financial obligation. The SPECTRUM Initiative also provided the recipients with a network of fellow scholarship recipients and other librarians of color to jump-start their careers once they completed their degrees.

   Dr. Taylor: Yes. Yes.

   Dr. Jeng: Absolutely! The entire profession has been changing and diversity has been an issue for some time. The change in the growth of population is taking place and the library profession needs to deal with the changes. SPECTRUM has made a big, a huge difference. This program has proven that minority recruitment, when done right, can have a major impact on the profession . . . almost as a role model of how to do recruitment right.

4. What do you consider to be some factors that contribute to such low percentages of librarians of color?

   Mr. Erazo: First of all, librarianship is not a profession that comes to the mind of most people considering career alternatives. It is because they do not know the wide variety of things that librarians do. Unfortunately, we still suffer from an image problem. So just being a librarian, let alone earning a graduate degree to become a librarian, is not something that appeals to many. The related issue is low salaries. Financially speaking, it is a tough sell to people considering career alternatives. Starting salaries are too low. Lastly, you see so few librarians of color that it is hard for many to even imagine ever working as a librarian.

   Dr. Taylor: They are the factors that have been articulated by many others: a lack of role models; the requirement of a master's degree without, oftentimes, a salary scale that matches the requirement; stereotypical images of what the library profession is and what librarians do; more opportunities for students of color to pursue other graduate careers, often ones that offer better pay, and still not enough of a collective pool of students of color to meet the recruiting efforts of all these various professions.

Dr. Jeng: Some say minorities will go into other professions that pay better, to make more money, and lack of recruitment efforts on the part of library schools.

5. Are there some recommendations you would offer to new faculty members of color in library and information science education?

Mr. Erazo: Network with not only librarians of color, but with all librarians at local, state, regional, and national levels. Contribute professionally in these arenas increasingly as you are able. It is good for our colleagues to see us out there working. Tell your students why you became a librarian and tell them about the various ethnic ALA-affiliated library associations. Encourage them to get involved in serving diverse populations in their communities. Find a mentor or two (Kathleen de la Peña McCook has graciously mentored me and others over the years). Work hard, but also take it only one day at a time. You can only do so much at one time. Lastly, enjoy your teaching and research and service. It is a delightful life. Also, remind yourself of how lucky you are to have chosen LIS education and librarianship as your career!

Dr. Taylor: First, remember why you chose to enter this profession. Second, find support systems where you can—often that's not necessarily within your own organization or even in this profession, but there are many individuals and groups that will be supportive—be proactive in seeking them out. Third, be a role model to those individuals who will follow you. Fourth, recruit. Fifth, remember the source of your heart.

Dr. Jeng: To learn the system, make sure you understand the written and unwritten rules of the tenure promotion process, ask for advice from anyone, look for a mentor you will feel comfortable with, don't be discouraged, just do it!

In analyzing the interview responses, the participants seem to agree that: 1) It is the duty of librarians of color to be active in their professional organizations and to inform the profession of the importance of diversity in librarianship; 2) faculty of color, mentoring students of color, fosters the growth of librarians of color; 3) the SPECTRUM Initiative was a major factor that prompted a change in terms of the profession's inclusion of librarians of color; 4) low salaries often cause students of color to seek other professions that offer better pay; and 5) new faculty of color should seek a mentor(s), network with other librarians and other professionals, and understand and work diligently to meet the demands of the tenure promotion process.

As a new faculty member in library education (six months), I have already developed a base of support from Mr. Edward Erazo, Dr. Rhonda Harris Taylor, and Dr. Ling Hewy Jeng. First, they were willing to be interviewed for this article and indicated their willingness to assist me with future endeavors.

That was encouraging for a faculty member seeking to publish her first major writing. Second, they are individuals who have a history of being active in their professional organizations. They expressed the importance of being involved and indicated that much support for new faculty comes from being associated with one's professional organization. Third, they are individuals of color, so they have a better understanding of my position as a faculty member of African American heritage. Finally, they indicated that to make this experience, including the tenure process, a positive one, I must get to know the people with whom I work, seek a mentor(s) among them, network on all levels and with other professions, be an active participant in professional organizations, be a role models for others, be a recruiter, and work hard to contribute to this worthy profession. As a new faculty member of color and as a result of this experience, I am of the opinion that seeking support from persons who play a major role in their professional organizations will assist in building a strong foundation in library education. New faculty members need to know these individuals!

CONCLUSION

Universities mandate that faculty demonstrate a rigorous scholarly productivity. Some may say that this mandate makes it difficult for faculty of color to stay connected to associations like BCALA or REFORMA, as "service" is not so valued by universities as research. We feel that the mandate for research can be accomplished by remaining informed by the ideals of cultural diversity. But what must come first is the process of recognizing the strength that can be gained from being rooted in our respective heritages and then making use of this strength to frame research questions with a new way of inquiring.

In the essay "This Trend Called Diversity," ALA's first diversity officer, Sandra Ríos Balderrama, wrote, "In working toward true diversity, we work without the familiar construct of a mainstream."[11] Faculty of color will establish new constructs for librarianship, as their academic roots are far more inclusive of the information and cultural needs of all people than the traditional canon.

NOTE FROM THE AUTHORS

The opportunity to work together on this project has been a manifestation of the concerns we have summarized. Reviewing the long efforts to define and develop a commitment to diversity in librarianship provided us—Cora and Kathleen—with the chance to reflect on the importance of collaboration.

APPENDIX

**Librarians Associations of Color Affiliated
with the American Library Association**

American Indian Library Association (AILA), Est. 1979; www.nativeculture
.com/lisamitten/aila.html

Asian/Pacific American Librarians Association (APALA), Est. 1980; www.uic
.edu/depts/lib/projects/resources/apala

Black Caucus of the American Library Association (BCALA), Est. 1970; www
.bcala.org

Chinese American Librarians Association (CALA), Est. 1983; www.cala-web
.org

The National Association to Promote Library and Information Service to
Latinos and the Spanish Speaking (REFORMA), Est. 1971; www.reforma
.org

NOTES

1. Kathleen de la Peña McCook, ed., "Ethnic Diversity in Library and Information Science," *Library Trends* 49, no. 1 (Summer 2000). See articles by Alma Dawson (BCALA); Kenneth A. Yamashita (APALA); Mengxiong Liu (CALA); Salvador Güereña and Edward Erazo (REFORMA); and Lostee Patterson (AILA) for historical background on the respective histories of librarians associations of color. See also appendix for websites of these associations.

2. Kathleen de la Peña McCook, "Rocks in the Whirlpool: Equity and the American Library Association," *Equity of Access* 2002. www.ala.org/work/equity.html (accessed 11 December 2002).

3. National Commission on Libraries and Information Science. *Task Force on Library and Information Services to Cultural Minorities.* (Washington, DC.: NCLIS, 1983).

4. American Library Association. President's Commission on Library Service to Minorities. *Equity at Issue: Library Services to the Nation's Four Major Minority Groups.* (Chicago: American Library Association, 1986).

5. American Library Association, *Equity at Issue*, 18.

6. Sibyl E. Moses, *Addressing Ethnic and Cultural Diversity: A Report on Activities of the American Library Association, 1986–1989* (Chicago: ALA, OLOS: 1990).

7. Notably *Librarians for the New Millennium* (1988) and *Occupational Entry* (1989), as noted in Moses, *Addressing Ethnic and Cultural Diversity,* p. 32.

8. American Library Association. "Standards for Accreditation of Master's Programs in Library and Information Studies 1992." www.ala.org/alaorg/oa/standard.html (accessed 11 December 2002).

9. American Library Association. Office for Diversity. www.ala.org/diversity/ (accessed 11 December 2002).

10. Evelyn H. Daniels and Jerry D. Saye, eds., *Library and Information Science Education Statistical Report 2002* (Reston, VA: Association for Library and Information Science Education, 2002).

11. Sandra Ríos Balderrama, "This Trend Called Diversity," In *Ethnic Diversity in Library and Information Science,* ed. Kathleen de la Peña McCook, *Library Trends* 49, no. 1 (Summer 2000): 194.

4

The ALA Spectrum Initiative:
A Student's View

Trina Holloway

Like most people, prior to becoming more familiar with the profession, I thought working in a library would be boring. I hadn't given much thought to what went on in libraries beyond what could be observed by the public. Therefore, even though I hate to admit it, I too thought that librarians spent their days reading and shelving books. Unfortunately, I had even bought into the stereotype of an older white woman with a bun "hushing" patrons. It came as shock to me to discover that a person needed a graduate degree to become a librarian. I soon discovered that there is far more to being a librarian than I initially thought.

Upon gradation from college I was able to obtain a position in an academic library as a library assistant. After working several years in the library and being mentored by my former supervisor, I decided to pursue a career in librarianship. After realizing all the great things librarians have to offer, I knew this was the career for me.

My next decision was where to pursue my graduate education. I decided to attend Clark Atlanta University in Atlanta, Georgia. Not only is it the only accredited library school in Georgia, it is a private, historically black college. Although cost was a major concern for me, I was still determined to attend, even if it meant taking only one course per semester. While conducting research on scholarships, I discovered a scholarship offered through the ALA's Spectrum Initiative. I met the requirements, so I decided to apply. I was selected as a 2001 recipient and awarded a $5,000 scholarship. Many library programs commit to providing additional financial support to Spectrum Scholars, and Clark Atlanta University was one of the accredited library schools that offered additional financial assistance. This was a great help in financing my education, but the real value of the Spectrum Initiative has been the experience and exposure to the profession that I gained. The Spectrum Initiative is more than a program offering financial assistance. It also offers career guidance, mentoring, and an opportunity to meet others and grow from their experiences. The promotion of diversity in the profession is a strong component, and the activities provide avenues to make others aware of the importance of diversity in the profession.

THE SPECTRUM INITIATIVE

The ALA's Spectrum Initiative is currently administered by the ALA Office for Diversity. In January of 1997, former ALA Executive Director Elizabeth Martinez submitted a report to ALA's Executive Board proposing that $1.5 million of the association's unallocated funds be used to establish a three-year scholarship initiative to double the number of librarians of color.

According to the United States Bureau of Labor Statistics figures for 2001, 85 percent of librarians are white. Many people feel that the professionals who work in libraries should to some degree reflect the communities that are being served. The library should be a place where patrons can come and see a variety of people, especially those who look like them.[1] The initiative promotes this position by offering people of color support in entering the profession.

Betty Turock, an ALA Executive Board member, became a strong supporter of the initiative and helped move it on through the approval process. Dr. Turock also established a Presidential Fundraising Task Force for the Spectrum Initiative during her ALA presidency, and her family has supported a Spectrum scholarship named in her honor for the past four years. The first fifty scholarships were awarded in 1998. The association committed resources to fund fifty annual scholarships of $5,000 each for the first four years of the initiative. Today, the Spectrum Initiative continues through the efforts of the Presidential Fundraising Task Force and the generous support of divisions, affiliates, organizations, members, and individuals.[2]

The scholarships are open to African American, Latino/Hispanic, Asian/Pacific Islander, and Native American/Alaskan Native students. The goal of the initiative is to recruit, support, and instill leadership skills in library school students of color. The initial plans were for the program to last for three years. However, because of concerted fundraising efforts, the program still exists. As of 2002, ALA has awarded 227 Spectrum scholarships.

BECOMING A SCHOLAR

Being selected as a Spectrum Scholar was very exciting for me. I knew that the program's selection criteria were based not only on the application and supplemental materials, but also on an assessment of the applicant's leadership potential, academic excellence, and commitment to completing the masters program.[3] I felt very honored to be selected. There were many benefits, in addition to the financial support. The complementary subscription to *American Libraries* was a bonus, as was the information shared and interactions with fellow scholars as a member of the listserv.

The listserv was of great value because it became a place where scholars could vent their frustrations. Some scholars discussed situations they faced as a person of color in their school or job. Other scholars gave suggestions and advice, as well as encouragement and support, to help them handle their situation. This was beneficial to me, because it reminded me that not everyone is open to diversity and I must be willing to stand up and support diversity.

The highlight of being a Spectrum Scholar was the Spectrum Leadership Institute. During this leadership institute, I got the opportunity to meet my fellow scholars and librarians dedicated to promoting diversity in the profession and to obtain skills that would be most useful in my career pursuits. It was useful to be able to discuss in person topics or ideas that may be difficult to articulate in an e-mail. I established relationships and friendships during that time that will hopefully last throughout my career.

LIBRARY SCHOOL EXPERIENCE

One of the terms for accepting the scholarship from the Spectrum Initiative is the willingness to complete a masters program in library and information science. My first semester at Clark Atlanta University was the summer of 2001. Ten years had passed since the last time I was a student. Such a long time away from the discipline of studying required quite an adjustment. Needless to say, I was out of practice, so I decided to take it slowly and enroll in only one class. It was the right decision.

Once I got into the flow of things, I found a lot of the reading actually applied to my current position as a library assistant. I was learning why things were done in a certain way on my job. It was a good feeling to get better insight into why libraries operated in a certain way.

I survived my first semester of library school and I was confident that I would be able to complete the master's program. During the fall semester, I felt I could handle two classes. Again, it took some time organizing my schedule to do the reading and assignments, but I was able to manage. Thus far, my learning experience has been wonderful. I have learned so much over the course of my studies. One of the advantages I have is that I work in an academic library, and I am able to apply my working experiences with course materials.

My studies have been time-consuming and I have had to make adjustments and sacrifice some things, but I know that in the end my dedication and determination will pay off. I will have earned a Master's of Library Science and will be able to continue my professional career and help broaden the minds of others regarding what librarians do and what they have to offer.

THE FUTURE

For 2002, the number of Spectrum scholarships was reduced to 27. The initial endowment was planned to finance a short-term initiative. In order to have a fiscally healthy endowment that will support the Spectrum program for many years, the annual number of scholarships will temporarily stay below fifty to help support the future of the program. A Spectrum Advisory Committee is being created as a subcommittee of the ALA's Committee on Diversity to help with future fundraising and administrative support of the initiative.[4]

While the initiative is doing its part, we who are currently enrolled in accredited library programs, as well as those already a part of the profession, must also do our part. Diversity can only be promoted if we see the importance of it and are willing to become active in spreading the word—not only about diversity, but about the profession as a whole. For many years, concerned librarians have offered ideas and made suggestions of how to address the low number of students of color in library schools.[5] E. J. Josey believes we have to make students attending library school aware that what they are doing "is an investment in their future." It is also an investment in the communities they will serve. We must spread the word.[6]

The Spectrum Initiative has had a great effect on the profession. Martinez and others saw a need and developed a plan. Through Spectrum, ALA has made an investment in its future.

CONCLUSION

Promoting diversity in any profession is important. It is especially important in the library profession, which serves users from many different backgrounds. The Spectrum Initiative helped me to realize how important it is to promote diversity and that it does not take money on my part to assist. I can start contributing by mentoring young people of color and making them aware of what librarians do and how important they are in the communities in which they serve. As a future librarian, I will be dedicated to recruiting highly motivated young people who will not only bring diversity to the profession but who will be willing to make a difference. Thanks to the Spectrum

Initiative for opening my eyes and mind to opportunities and the accompanying obligations.

NOTES

1. American Library Association, Office for Diversity 2003. www.ala.org/ala/diversity/diversity.htm (accessed 12 July 2003).

2. Wendy Prellwitz, program officer, Office for Diversity & Spectrum Initiative, e-mail correspondence, January 2003.

3. The Spectrum Initiative, 2002, www.ala.org/spectrum/ (accessed 19 June 2002).

4. Prellwitz, e-mail correspondence, January 2003.

5. Kathleen de la Peña McCook and Paula Geist, "Diversity Deferred: Where Are The Minority Librarians?" *Library Journal* 118, no. 18 (1993): 35.

6. Melody M. McDowell, "Help Wanted at Our Libraries," *Black Issues Book Review* 3, no. 2 (2001): 78–79.

5

Affirmative Action: The Role of the LIS Dean

Em Claire Knowles

All Americans should embrace a personal commitment to go beyond the requirements of legislated affirmative action to create a variety of inclusive opportunities in higher education and the professions for all underrepresented racial and ethnic group members. This chapter examines what can be done in conjunction with affirmative action to achieve this goal in the United States. Further, it will focus on strategies that deans of library and information science (LIS) programs can use to encourage African Americans and members of other traditionally underrepresented ethnic and racial groups to enter the field of LIS so that their equivalent representation in the U.S. population is reached.[1] I will also review the problems and solutions for LIS programs in light of the recent ruling of the U.S. Supreme Court on affirmative action.

As an assistant dean responsible for general student administrative services, publications, grants, and other projects as assigned, I have served three deans in a private graduate school of library and information science. It has been my responsibility to provide guidance to these deans to establish their agenda in the area of diversity or recruitment and retention of students from traditionally underrepresented ethnic and racial groups, as well as offer strategies for the diversity agenda in other areas of the school.

According to the U.S. Census, many librarians began to reach retirement age in the late 1990s. With the healthy economy of that time, many of these librarians took the opportunity to enjoy their retirement while still in good health. An even greater number was expected to retire through 2000.[2] Already, professional opportunities for librarians are opening up all across the nation. Although job opportunities in LIS are on the rise, minority enrollment in LIS graduate schools has not kept pace.[3] The solutions to the problem will not come easily as we tackle the tough task of valuing each other regardless of race, religion, class, gender, sexual orientation, or national origin.

AFFIRMATIVE ACTION STATUS

Affirmative action is simply the action required by the equal opportunity employment law and may or may not be enforced. It was created by lawmakers in response to the civil rights movement. The law has become a part of American behavior, "doing the right thing" in line with the concept of diversity. It encourages people to embrace the idea that acceptance of individual differences will benefit all people. However, there are misconceptions and negative attitudes about quota systems and racial preferences—similar arguments led to concern about how the U.S. Supreme Court would rule in the recent court case on diversity in the University of Michigan Law School's admissions process. An aspect of one decision upheld affirmative action practices in that "it is proper for such establishments to grant minority students an edge in their application for enrollment," but noted "that using race alone for automatically distributing a percentage of the number of points needed to guarantee admission is unconstitutional."[4] In summary, this ruling gives LIS programs a reprieve to pursue creative strategies to recruit students, staff, and faculty into library and information science programs.

Factors related to diversity in LIS programs that have been extensively discussed in the literature are:

1. With the changing demographics in the United States, ethnic minority populations will be in great demand professionally if they can take advantage of appropriate educational opportunities.
2. The increasing numbers of librarians expected to retire in the next decade place prospective ethnic minority librarians in prime positions to serve as the library information professionals needed not only in their respective communities, but also nationally and globally.

The merging of these two concepts is not yet a reality. Nevertheless, the U.S. Supreme Court decision on the University of Michigan Law School's admissions practices provided an opportunity to focus on increasing the number of African Americans and other ethnic minorities entering the LIS profession.

LIS OUTLOOK

Training for LIS professionals at the graduate level is offered at only 56 library and information science programs that are accredited by the ALA. This amounts to almost one program per state, although the programs are not evenly distributed and some states are without any LIS graduate education program. Although most LIS students pursue their education in their home state, a small percentage of LIS candidates venture beyond their home state to obtain their education. Fortunately, states with more than one LIS program also have the highest number of ethnic and racial minorities (e.g., California [2], Florida [2], New York [3], and Texas [3]).[5] Thus, prospective ethnic and racial minority students in those states have more opportunities to pursue professional training in library and information science. However, one would expect these programs to have more influence than is actually the case. The time is ripe for change.

According to the current statistics provided by the Association for Library and Information Science Educators in 2000, graduates of ALA-accredited LIS master's programs were predominantly white (75.4 percent). African Americans were the next highest represented ethnic group (4.6 percent), followed by Asians or Pacific Islanders (3.4 percent), and persons of Hispanic origin (2.8 percent). Native Americans constituted less than one-half percent (0.4 percent) of graduates.[6]

Of the underrepresented ethnic and racial groups listed above, the African American presence and graduation rate was the most visible and demonstrated the most dramatic growth. African Americans accounted for 12.4 percent of graduates receiving post-master's degrees. The presence of African American graduates from LIS bachelor's degree programs is also noteworthy. Overall, they comprised 10.1 percent of all graduates of these programs. Thus, it is only in the bachelor's and post-master's programs that African American graduates come close to matching their representation in the general U.S. population (12–14 percent).[7] Unfortunately, only a small percentage of B.A. recipients continue to the professional level for the master's degree. It is important to find out why this is so, because these are the best candidates to recruit in the LIS field.

LIS GRADUATES REVEAL REASONS FOR THEIR CHOICE

In an effort to assess the likelihood of African Americans attending LIS graduate programs, I sought out recent alumni to hear their reasons for going into this field. This assessment is not a scientific study, but simply random disclosures through an electronic listserv by recent graduates from the western, northeastern, and southern regions of the United States. Their responses tend to correlate with those of various recently published interviews and statements in the library literature by African American students and professionals.[8] These responses do not specify the importance of affirmative action; however, all the respondents asserted that they assumed that they would be treated fairly and valued for what they could bring to the field. Whether they were or not, these librarians did persevere to become library and information professionals.

The respondents stated that 1) they valued the presence of a group of African American students who offered their support and the benefits of their experience; and 2) they appreciated having forums for discussion, such as:

a. a council of African American graduate students willing to discuss various issues on campus;
b. the presence of individual(s) willing to share their personal or curricular issues affecting their studies;
c. African American faculty to teach in the program;
d. alumni support groups with mentoring opportunities; and
e. funding assistance for their academic studies and attendance at professional conferences.[9]

EFFORTS TO INCREASE ENROLLMENT

The impetus for increasing the number of racial and ethnic minority LIS professionals must come from members of the profession, LIS deans and educators, and the professional associations. Although not all library and information professionals are compelled to take up the baton in this race, it is imperative that LIS professionals partner with African American librarians and librarians from other underrepresented racial and ethnic groups to pursue recruits to the profession.

African American LIS professionals have been successful in increasing their numbers by mentoring LIS students, being active alumni in LIS programs to encourage changes in the curriculum, serving as on-site recruiters, serving on alumni committees, helping to raise funds, recruiting personnel, and supporting other resources for students. But African American librarians must become even more active in LIS organizations to promote professional programs and services and to raise private funds that will not be affected by changes in affirmative action policies.

The large constituency of African American LIS students and the active alumni in LIS programs can work together to ask for changes in the curriculum, to serve as on-site recruiters, to serve on alumni committees, to raise funds for scholarships, to serve as specific personal resources to benefit students, and to recruit African American faculty. LIS deans must value this untapped resource because African American librarians have the clout to strengthen LIS efforts by promoting this profession through programming and services and raising private funds specifically for African American students and to stabilize funding. These factors will not be affected by changing attitudes toward affirmative action.

BECOME THE DIVERSITY LEADER

Library and information science education cannot be developed in a vacuum but must reflect current changes in the services and programs aimed at multicultural constituents. The dean can facilitate the success of these changes. The dean, as chief of the LIS program, is similar to the president on any campus, but in a smaller sphere. The best legacy that any LIS dean can create is to make diversity a part of the fabric of the school.[10] The LIS dean who can set the tone in advancing the diversity agenda as an integral part of the admissions plan and the hiring of faculty and administrators, infusing diversity issues into the curriculum, and incorporating diversity topics into the co-curricular activities that support the LIS program of study. The dean is also positioned to collaborate with African American and other people of nontraditional racial and ethnic groups.

Since the earliest actions to set the tone will contribute to the most lasting expressions, it is critical that early impressions be positive. One tactic that an LIS dean can use as part of her management style is "to include diverse kinds of people in the decision-making process, and mak[e] that process as transparent as possible."[11] The dean must arrange regular meetings with various constituents, such as area employers, alumni, and community leaders. It is imperative that African American and other traditionally underrepresented racial and ethnic groups be a part of these meetings. The dean can build a community to promote ideas and strategies related to the LIS program. It is extremely important that long-time and new people, along with majority and diverse constituents, are included when a LIS dean is trying to develop a team.

Another component in developing collaboration and trust among diverse and majority people is visibility. For example, students look forward to seeing the dean at student events. In my own institution, the LIS dean, when invited, takes part in multicultural presentations, meetings, and Kwanzaa dinners given by diverse students and faculty. Furthermore, it is important to invite students of color to discuss controversial situations and seek solutions. Whenever possible, students' programming should be supported with funding. Also, alumni of color must be tapped as a resource to mentor students and support the school with internships. The variety of opportunities could lead to improved relationships between the LIS dean, the school, and the African American community. These new relationships could also begin to galvanize and encourage African American alumni to become more involved in promoting the field to other people of color.

An LIS dean on the West Coast organized annual diversity summits to bring together LIS alumni of color to discuss ways to increase the number of African American students and other students from nontraditional racial and ethnic groups and to discuss how relevant the curriculum was to diversity and how to get the alumni more involved with the school and students. These summits led to a formalized mentoring program between students and alumni librarians of color, a diversity audit of the curriculum in which each course was reviewed to determine its level of multicultural relevance, the establishment of visiting faculty of color, and more alumni donors of color. Subsequently, this same dean moved to an East Coast LIS program and established similar diversity summits to address issues in the new location. Although some of the issues will be different, this dean has recognized the importance of being visible and available to address the needs of a group that now has increased representation in the library and information science field. The dean can facilitate such changes.

The LIS dean must collaborate with African American LIS leaders and with newcomers in the profession to discern what is needed to attract and retain students. The dean can set the tone in encouraging LIS programs to actively recruit African Americans to undergraduate LIS programs to at least increase the percentage beyond 5–6 percent, which is the current national average.[12] I am certain that all of us could think of other disciplines that have already demonstrated success in this effort.

The LIS dean should be the unofficial "diversity leader," seeking opportunities through meetings with employers, alumni, students, and faculty. Faculty and staff should be active in the recruitment, retention, and teaching of African American students and other minority students. Furthermore, they should allocate funds and offer courses with emphasis on community outreach and services and programs appropriate to diverse communities. The dean's role as diversity leader in the LIS school is pivotal, especially with the recent affirmative action decision and the many efforts occurring through the United States in academic libraries.

NATIONAL EFFORTS TO COLLABORATE WITH LIS PROGRAMS

The ALA's Spectrum Initiative Scholarship and leadership program has been a major force for funding underrepresented racial and ethnic group LIS students, providing a venue for them to expand networking and become involved in professional organizations, to get involved and give back to their communities, and to help others as they have been generously helped.[13] The establishment of the Spectrum Initiative Scholarships, first awarded in 1998 to fifty LIS students from underrepresented ethnic and racial groups, has highlighted the LIS field for students of color. Furthermore, this program has produced a critical mass of students, approximately 250, and also a plan for LIS programs, ethnic and racial professional organizations, and other national information organizations (the Association of American Law Librarians, Special Libraries Association, etc.) to support and strengthen this program.

Due to its broad nature, the Spectrum Initiative encompasses national publicity, a recruitment network, leadership seminars, and mentoring for the Spectrum Initiative scholarship recipients. The national campaign to recruit students for the Spectrum Initiative has included publicity that has significantly increased recognition of library and information science as a practicable career option for African Americans.[14] Many LIS programs that have developed parity fiscal matches, and professional associations that also provide internships to Spectrum Scholars. Finally, Spectrum Scholarship students are graduating and becoming leaders in the field.

The numbers of African Americans who find placement is a positive and more visible sign of success as a group, but it is still not to the level of African Americans' percentage in the profession. The reprieve of the affirmative action ruling has worked successfully in favor of African Americans, but supporters cannot depend on it as the only avenue for admission to the profession. African American library professionals must work diligently and form alliances with other ethnic minority groups and others who believe in this cause. For the benefit of the profession and our communities, LIS deans and educators must continue to demonstrate to African Americans and other members of underrepresented groups that a career in library and information science is possible and integral to the development of minority communities and is relevant to access to information across all racial and ethnic lines. Without our continued presence as information providers, the LIS field may be discounted as no longer a viable profession for African Americans.

RECOMMENDATIONS

At a time when affirmative action has so recently been challenged, one need only consider the level of educational attainment in higher education of all people of underrepresented racial and ethnic groups to conclude that equity has yet to be achieved. The educational trends for African Americans, Latinos, Asian and Pacific Americans, and American Indians are of critical concern. Although this chapter has focused on African Americans, much of this information can be related to other groups. The following is a set of recommendations to address some of the issues raised. The recommendations are not in order of priority and LIS deans and others can take the lead for implementation.

- Support for affirmative action

  Although there was a reprieve with the 2003 Supreme Court decision for the University of Michigan's graduate admissions process, racial discrimination and other biases still exist. Affirmative action policies and programs in the education system still are needed to remedy unequal treatment in American society and institutions, including the education system. Institutions should revisit their policies and programs on a regular basis to consider new directions. For example, some institutions have begun to set goals related to quotas for targeting diverse populations in their institutions. A diverse student body, faculty, staff, and administration benefit all members of the higher education community, as well as society.

- Change the school climate

  The campus should be a positive, thoughtful, and understanding environment for students, faculty, and staff, regardless of their numbers in the program. Every effort should be made to include multicultural experiences in faculty and staff development. Underrepresented racial and ethnic group members should be included in devising these experiences.

- Curriculum infusion

  The experiences, roles, and resources of multicultural populations should be a part of the curriculum in the LIS program. Both singular courses in multicultural resources and the integration of all courses with the discussion, presentation, or experiences of information seeking needs of diverse populations. All LIS students must be prepared for a multicultural and global world. The LIS faculty must ensure that everyone's story is included properly and treated within their mission and programmatic planning.

- Doctoral student recruitment and retention

  Strong recruitment and retention programs should be designed at LIS doctoral degree-granting institutions to encourage applicants from underrepresented racial and ethnic groups to pursue doctorates. Master's programs should identify and mentor prospective diverse students. All doctoral programs should provide the necessary support to their diverse students, including faculty mentors, fellowships, research and publication opportunities, and other aid, to ensure their successful completion of the degree.

- Open the LIS employment pipeline

  Strong faculty, staff, and administrative recruitment activities should be developed in LIS programs to ensure an open employment pipeline. Attention should be given to diverse faculty at the junior level. Close scrutiny is necessary to identify structural, attitudinal, and programmatic barriers that may account for poor hiring and tenure rates of diverse LIS faculty and administrators.

One high priority is to appoint deans from underrepresented racial and ethnic groups. National higher education and library organizations should concentrate efforts in the development and mentorship of diverse leaders, and strong leadership training programs should be developed and supported.

- Foster research on affirmative action and its effect on library education

   More data and better qualitative and quantitative research on affirmative action and its effect on the library profession should be collected and supported. Data that can be gathered by the ALA's Office of Diversity and its ethnic affiliates and the national library and education associations should be tapped and will serve to encourage more research to delineate the progress of ethnic librarians in the library and information science profession.[15]

CONCLUSION

The opportunities offered by affirmative action programs in recruiting prospective African American and other underrepresented racial and ethnic LIS professionals are critical, but should not be the only method for increasing the presence of these populations in the profession. Affirmative action is paramount for all people of color to achieve proportional representation in higher education. Yet, without strong encouragement and support, only the unusually motivated and determined students will finish graduate school and be qualified to enter the profession. Acceptance of diversity as a value is a vital concern of librarians seeking to strengthen their library systems to serve the entire community. The directive established by the ALA to identify diversity as a key area for action has mobilized the profession and library schools to focus on this effort.

LIS deans and educators must persist to keep the momentum in recruiting, retaining, and supporting increased numbers of African Americans in the LIS profession. It is the combined responsibility of current LIS professionals and educators. All of us, regardless of race or ethnic group, must take a stand in striving to increase the presence of underrepresented ethnic and racial groups in LIS. Affirmative action programs may be debated, but it is up to us as citizens to do what we can to see that the policies are enforced and to make them work. Although affirmative action cannot be counted on, neither can it be discounted to achieve empowerment of African Americans and members of underrepresented racial and ethnic groups as LIS professionals.

The role of the dean can be quite influential in setting the tone for the implementation of successful efforts for diversity to occur in the LIS program. This effort can begin with a personal embracing of and commitment to diversity and by rewarding diversity efforts in student recruitment, faculty development and retention, curriculum development, alumni participation, and fundraising. Furthermore, diversity efforts must be creative in light of affirmative action policies, and everyone in the LIS program must take a part for their success. Anything short of full participation, no matter how well meaning the small steps, will be judged ineffectual. This is the challenge.

Note of appreciation: I wish to extend my gratitude to Dean Michèle V. Cloonan, Dale Deletis, Alisa M. Libby, and the faculty of the Simmons Graduate School of Library and Information Science for their assistance and commitment to implementing diversity throughout the school, with or without affirmative action.

NOTES

1. U.S. Census Bureau, *Statistical Report, 2000* (Washington, DC: U.S. Government Printing Office, 2001).

2. Mary Jo Lynch, "Reaching 65: Lots of Librarians Will Be There Soon," *American Libraries* 33, no. 3 (2002): 55–56.

3. Association for Library and Information Science Education, *Statistical Report 2000* (Reston, VA: Association for Library and Information Science Education, 2002), 63.

4. "Bush Applauds Supreme Court Decision on Affirmative Action," http:usinfo .state.gov/usa/diversity.html (accessed 17 December 2003).

5. Laurie Andriot, *LIS Education Directory, 2001* (Fredericksburg, VA: Lakeside Reference, 2001).

6. Association for Library and Information Science Education, *Statistical Report 2000*, 60–65.

7. Association for Library and Information Science Education, *Statistical Report 2000*.

8. Teresa Y. Neely and Khafre K. Abif, *In Our Voices: The Changing Face of Librarianship* (Lanham, MD: Scarecrow Press, 1996).

9. An informal electronic listserv discussion taken at my own LIS program in Simmons College during Spring 2003. However, these comments are generally discussed in past discourse over the years by African American students in library and information science programs.

10. Leo I. Higdon, Jr., "Make the Team," *The Chronicle of Higher Education*, 5 December 2003, C1 & C4.

11. Kathleen de la Peña McCook, ed., *Library Trends* 49, no. 1 (2000):1–5.

12. Association for Library and Information Science Education. *Statistical Report 2000*, 60–65.

13. Tracie D. Hall, *Report on the Spectrum Initiative Scholarship Program* (Chicago: American Library Association, Office for Diversity, 2003).

14. McCook, *Library Trends*, 1–5.

15. Deborah J. Carter and Reginald Wilson, *Minorities in Higher Education* (Washington, DC: American Council of Education, 1997).

6

Race-Based Financial Aid: An Overview

Susan Webreck Alman, Marva J. Bryant, and Anne Steffans

Not until the late 1950s and early 1960s with the National Science Foundation's agenda, the National Student Loan program, and the National Defense Education Act's amended provisions were the first federal steps taken toward making loans and financial aid accessible for students of color. In 1964, programs such as the Basic Education Opportunity Grants Program and the Equal Education Opportunity Program continued to make financial aid available to minority students wishing to pursue higher education. While these programs did not specifically support the pursuit of master's or doctoral degrees in library and information science, they were generally organized to assist youth pursuing their undergraduate degrees.

In 1965, Congress initiated the Higher Education Act (HEA), and, under Title II-B of the act, specific attention was aimed and resources allotted to students of color pursuing careers in the library sciences and those programs and institutions that encouraged and actively supported the recruitment and education of those students. The availability of federal money contributed to an influx of minorities (mostly African Americans) into American institutions of higher education, and, partly as a result, the mid-1970s saw a dramatic increase in the number of minority graduates from American colleges and universities. However, too few of these students pursued degrees in library and information science, and men and women of color remained severely underrepresented behind reference desks across the nation throughout the latter quarter of the twentieth century.

Cognizant of the need to recruit individuals of color into the field, to consistently support those individuals throughout the duration of their careers, and believing that efforts made by the ALA were not enough to resolve these issues, E. J. Josey invited African American members of ALA to meet during the association's 1970 mid-winter conference to organize a plan and take definitive steps toward redefining librarianship. In 1971, the Black Caucus of the American Library Association (BCALA) was established, with Virginia Lacy Jones as its head, to provide opportunities for professional black librarians to gain greater control of the direction of their careers. Also in 1971, the National Association to Promote Library and Information Service to Latinos and the Spanish Speaking (REFORMA) was established with the commitment to promote library and information services to Latinos and Spanish-speaking people in the United States. Further affiliates of the ALA—the Asian/Pacific American Librarians Association, the Chinese American Librarians Association, and the American Indian Library Association—have since been established, each with the central objective of recruiting and supporting library science students from their communities, in particular through scholarships.

In support of other graduate studies, the Graduate and Professional Opportunities Program (G*POP) was conceived in 1976 with an amendment to Title IX of the HEA. G*POP proffered money to female and minority graduate and professional students for up to three years in fields in which their numbers were markedly low. Throughout its duration, the program awarded hundreds of fellowships to African Americans; Hispanic, Asian, and Native Americans; and Caucasian women for the pursuit of master's and doctoral degrees in engineering, mathematics, the physical and life sciences, and the social sciences. Older and more widely known programs, such as those of the National Science Foundation and the National Defense Education Act (which has remerged in similar shape and form with the National Security Education Act of 1991), made provisions for students of color to pursue degrees in the physical and natural sciences, the study of foreign languages, and area studies.

By 1991, the HEA II-B Graduate Library Fellowship Program was regarded as having been especially successful in terms of recruitment, degree attainment, and post-studies employment status—particularly for minorities who fared as well, if not slightly better, than non-minority fellows during the 1980s and early 1990s. However, in 1996 the Museum and Library Services Act replaced HEA Title II-B as the primary guide for library education and services in America. Authorized by the Museum and Library Services Act, the Institute of Museum and Library Services continues to award grants to students of color and those organizations and institutions that primarily serve and represent minority communities.

Non-federal recruitment and support initiatives continue to definitively assist students of color to break into the library and information science professions. Those students of color, however, continue to be sorely underrepresented. In 1998, the ALA Office for Research and Statistics (ORS) estimated that 87 percent of public and academic librarians were white. The ORS report, *Racial and Ethnic Diversity Among Librarians: A Status Report*, documents the numbers that mirror the racial and ethnic makeup of the pool of professional American librarians. Although there are certain limitations in the way these data were collected, table 6.1 indicates the low numbers of professional librarians who are members of underrepresented groups.

The vast majority of Americans continue to be served at their neighborhood libraries by a librarian who is not a part of their community. In response to the increasing urgency of the problem, the ALA established the Spectrum Initiative in 1997. The initiative has recruited and funded library students in anticipation of diversifying American academic, public, school, and special libraries. The Spectrum Initiative's "Library Careers Are as Diverse as You!" poster campaign, featuring "non-typical" Asian, African American, and Latino librarians, has sought to remake the image of librarians into that of urbane and cutting-edge professionals of all skin colors, backgrounds, ages, and ideas.

Through the efforts of the Presidential Fundraising Task Force and the support of divisions, affiliates, organizations, and individuals, ALA initiated the effort by providing 50 annual scholarships of $5,000 per year to African American, Latino/Hispanic, Asian/Pacific Islander, and Native American/Alaskan Native librarians and library students. As of 2002, 227 library school students of color have received financial aid through the Spectrum Initiative. ALA efforts to diversify the profession have further broadened in scope to include the Knowledge River program at the University of Arizona, which has been established to especially appeal to Native American and Hispanic communities in the region. Knowledge River has employed Native American and Hispanic library and information professionals who may act as mentors, as well as educators, to their Native American and Hispanic students.

ALA Vice President/President-elect Carla Hayden, who took on her duties in July 2003, is the association's fourth African American president and plans

Table 6.1. Percent of Librarians by Equal Employment Opportunity Commission Category and Sex

	Academic 1998	Public 1998	School 1994
American Indian/Alaskan Native	0.57	0.25	1
Asian/Pacific Islander	4.98	3.93	1
Black	5.87	6.33	6
Hispanic	1.80	2.95	2
White	86.78	86.55	90
Total	100.00	100.00	100
Female	67.99	78.91	92
Male	32.01	21.09	8
Total	100.00	100.00	100

Source: ALA Office for Research and Statistics, *Racial and Ethnic Diversity Among Librarians: A Status Report.*[1]

to continue recruitment and diversification efforts, helping to develop a more representative and responsive library system for the twenty-first century.

THE SOLUTION

There are many academic institutions that have developed internships and fellowships as a way to remedy the situation. In recent years, however, their efforts have increased and intensified. "Since the mid-1980s some academic libraries have established residency programs in an effort to address the dearth of librarians of color."[2] Today, a variety of libraries have established and are working to establish residency, internship, or fellowship programs to continue in their efforts to recruit minorities to the field of library science. The following is a list of programs that are currently in effect. The programs are listed in categories according to the type of program and type of library.

MINORITY FELLOWSHIPS

1. Cornell University
   Minority Fellowship Program
   www.library.cornell.edu/Adminops/minority.html
2. University of Oklahoma
   National Leadership Grant Fellowship
   www.ou.edu/cas/slis/fellowship.htm
3. Kent State University (SLIS) & Ohio State University Libraries
   KSU/OSUL Diversity Student Fellowship
   www.lib.ohio-state.edu/Lib_Info/diversfellow.html
4. University of Pittsburgh
   Highmark Minority Health Link Fellowship
   www2.sis.pitt.edu/~ellen/highfellow.htm
5. University of Pittsburgh
   University Library System/DLIS Minority Fellowship Program
   www.sis.pitt.edu/~lsdept/fellowship.html
6. National Library of Medicine
   Associate Fellowship Program
   www.nlm.nih.gov/about/training/associate/applicinfo.html

MINORITY RESIDENCIES

1. Auburn University
   Minority Residency Program
   www.lib.auburn.edu/diversity.html

2. Georgetown University
   Law Library Residency Program
   www.ll.georgetown.edu/staff/resident/index.cfm
3. Ohio State University Libraries
   Mary P. Key Diversity Residency Program
   www.lib.ohio-state.edu/Lib_Info/residency.html
4. SUNY, Buffalo
   Library Internship/Residency Program
   ublib.buffalo.edu/libraries/units/ugl/res
5. University of Delaware
   Pauline A. Young Residency
   www2.lib.udel.edu/personnel/brochure.htm
6. University of Iowa
   Minority Research Library Residency Program
   www.lib.uiowa.edu/hr/mrlrp.html
7. University of Minnesota Libraries, Twin Cities Campus
   Affirmative Action Residency
   www.lib.umn.edu/about/grants.html#lib
8. University of Notre Dame
   Librarian-in-Residence Program
   www.nd.edu/~adminoff/libinres.htm
9. University of South Florida, Tampa
   Henrietta M. Smith Residency
   www.lib.usf.edu/residency/
10. University of Pittsburgh
    Health Sciences Library & Biomedical Informatics Traineeship
    www.cbmi.upmc.edu/training_program/training.htm
11. University of Tennessee Libraries
    Minority Librarian Residency Program
    Jill Keally, Head, Library Support Services, 1015 Volunteer Blvd.,
    Knoxville, TN 37996-1000, Fax: 865/974-4696

The following are resources that can be used to find out more information about library science residency and fellowship programs.

ONLINE SOURCES

ARL Research Library Residency and Internship Programs Database; www.arl.org/careers/residencies.html

Medical Library Education Section of the Medical Library Association; www.mles.mlanet.org/fellows.html

Black Caucus of the American Library Association: Student Resources; www.bcala.org/resources/student.html

Lisjobs.com: Jobs for Librarians and Information Professionals; www.lisjobs.com/index.htm

BOOKS

Cogell, Raquel V. and Cindy A. Gruwell. *Diversity in Libraries: Academic Residency Programs*. Westport, CT: Greenwood Press, 2001.

ARTICLES

Brewer, Julie. "Implementing Post-Master's Residency Programs." *Leading Ideas* 4 (1998): 2–7. www.arl.org/diversity/leading/issue4/brewer.html.

Brewer, Julie. "Post-Master's Residency Programs: Enhancing the Development of New Professionals and Minority Recruitment in Academic and Research Libraries." *College & Research Libraries* (November 1997): 528–537.

Cawthorne, Jon E., and Teri B. Weil. "Internships/residencies: Exploring the Possibilities for the Future." In *In Our Own Voices: The Changing Face of Librarianship*, edited by Teresa Y. Neely and Khafre K. Abif, 45–71. Lanham, MD: Scarecrow Press, 1996.

DeBeau-Melting, Linda, and Karen M. Beavers. "Positioning for Change: The Diversity Internship as a Good Beginning." In *Diversity and Multiculturalism in Libraries*, edited by Katherine Hoover Hill, 227–242. Greenwich, CT: JAI Press, 1994.

Glass, Betty. "A Time of Transition." *Library Journal* (February 15, 1986): 127–128.

"Guidelines for Practices and Principles in the Design, Operation, and Evaluation of Post-Master's Residency Programs." *Journal of Education for Library and Information Science* (October 1992).

Internship, Residency, and Fellowship Programs in ARL Libraries–(Spec. Kit 188). Washington, DC: Association for Research Libraries, 1992.

Kendrick, Curtis, Jacob Lipkind, Joyce Clinkscales, Amelia Salinero, and Helen Shapiro-Volat. "Minority Internship/Scholarship in Library and Information Science." *College and Research Libraries News* 51 (November 1990): 965–972.

Mahony, Molly. "Preparation for the Future." *Library Journal* (February 1986): 129–130.

"Organizations that Offer Post-Master's Residency Programs." *Library Personnel* 10 (May/June 1996): 6–8.

"Post-Master's Residencies Receive Positive Response." *Library Personnel News* (May-June 1996): 5.

Shoemaker, Sarah. "A Unique Experience." *Library Journal* (February 1986): 125–126.

Trumpeter, Margo C., and Paul Gherman. "A Post-Master's Degree Internship Program." *Library Journal* (June 1980): 1366–1369.

Velez, Cecilia P. "Academic Libraries Meeting the Challenge of Affirmative Action: The University of California at Santa Barbara Experience." *Reforma Newsletter* (Summer 1989): 11–15.

THE FUTURE

It is evident that there is widespread support for race-based financial aid, but the amount of financial aid is not great enough to effect massive changes in attracting people of color to the profession. The commitment to recruitment is the impetus for programs in various national associations.

Maria Vieira Champlin, chair of the REFORMA Mentoring Program, wrote in 2001, "REFORMA has positioned and committed itself to developing library leaders for the new millennium."[3] Initiatives such as REFORMA, Spectrum, the Association of Research Libraries' Diversity Program, and others will result in a diverse population of librarians and a system of libraries that are reflective of, responsive to, and more deeply involved in America's diverse communities. As Champlin wrote, these initiatives are not simply recruiting and training for the short-term. These initiatives are seeking out and committing themselves to training and supporting men and women of color who will become active participants and leaders within the library and information sphere and within the communities that they serve. It is imperative that each entity in the library profession—from individual to institution—seek out men and women of color. Their participation in the profession will affect the lives of future generations and inspire permanent change in this society.

NOTES

1. Mary Jo Lynch, "Racial and Ethnic Diversity Among Librarians: A Status Report," Office for Research and Statistics, *American Library Association*. www.ala.org/alaorg/ors/racethnc.html (accessed 9 April 2003).

2. Raquel V. Cogell and Cindy A. Gruwell, *Diversity in Libraries: Academic Residency Programs* (Westport, CT: Greenwood Press, 2001).

3. Maria Champlin, "Mentoring the Leaders of Tomorrow: Reforma's Response," *Info Career Trends* 2, no.1 (2001).

II

STUDENT RECRUITMENT

7

Minority Student Recruitment in LIS Education: New Profiles for Success

Teresa Y. Neely

The challenge of how to recruit a more diverse workforce to the profession of librarianship remains a topic of concern for some and a thorny recurring issue for others. Retention, a closely related area of interest, is also of critical concern. Retention, however, defined by *Merriam-Webster's Collegiate Dictionary* as "the act of retaining: the state of being retained,"[1] presupposes that the recruitment effort has been successful and that there is at least someone to retain. This chapter will examine the general recruitment literature and recruitment in library literature as it pertains to people of color. It will also address issues, as evident in the literature, that are perceived to be barriers to recruitment in general. More specifically, this chapter will identify and discuss methods and recruitment models that have been employed and suggested by those interested in recruiting diverse peoples to librarianship.

To date, no one solution or method has been proven to be the most effective or successful for recruiting diverse peoples to the profession of librarianship. A variety of methods, suggestions, and things to consider have been suggested with varying degrees of success; however, there is little tangible evidence that any of the suggested methods have, to date, had a significant effect on increasing the number of minorities entering and graduating from ALA-accredited LIS programs.

How do we—individuals, associations, library educators, and others affiliated with the profession of librarianship—convince energetic and talented diverse individuals of all ages and from all walks of life that a career in library and information science is rewarding and fulfilling? How do we convey to them that a career as a librarian will give them as much satisfaction at the end of the day as successfully completing open heart surgery; finding a cure for AIDS, cancer or the common cold, or significantly advancing the research effort; cleaning up the Chesapeake Bay or the Hudson River once and for all of dangerous and damaging pollutants; or starring in a blockbuster movie, being adored by a legion of fans and making $20 million per picture. As I write this, I wonder why I am not doing some of those other things! The truth of the matter is that a career in librarianship is rewarding to those of us who are in it and who chose to be in it. As LIS professionals, we should make a serious, concerted effort to recruit and retain a more diverse workforce for our libraries, nationwide. The popular, professional, and scholarly literature for librarianship continues to extol the importance and benefits of a diverse workforce.[2] This notion is extremely important and even more relevant in libraries and in an era where information, and access to information, is power, and where a more diverse workforce directly affects the diverse clienteles we serve.

BARRIERS TO RECRUITMENT

A review of the relevant literature reveals a number of concerns that have been identified as possible barriers to recruitment. These perceived barriers include the persistent negative image of librarians; low, noncompetitive salaries; and increased competition from related information professions.

Image Consultants

Regrettably, libraries and librarians do not rank high in the eyes of the American public and the profession of librarianship ranks even lower. Although the image of the librarian is not relevant in terms of what we do, it is critically relevant in terms of recruitment. A recent Gallup Poll conducted to find out what career paths adults were advising young people to follow reported on historical survey results that found that 2 percent of those polled would have recommended librarianship to a young lady as a career option in 1950. Other careers receiving 2 percent of the vote included beautician, modeling, and musician. In subsequent polls in 1998 and 2001, librarianship was not even considered an option; and in eight polls about career choices for young men conducted from 1949 to 2001, librarianship was never considered an option.[3] However, it is interesting to see that the profession that received the highest percentages for both genders was the more generic "computers," whatever that means. Along those same lines, librarians do not enjoy the publicly perceived image as a good thing to be and aspire to; nor do librarians themselves, as a whole, do much to improve the public's perception of what I recently heard referred to as the "bun brigade:" a pursed lipped, shushing, sensible-shoes wearing spinster with her glasses on a chain around her neck and a permanent scowl. I am sure many of us would not be hard pressed to name colleagues in the profession who embody and personify that perception.[4]

Unfortunately for the profession, this perception is most evident to the public and society in general in the way librarians are perceived in advertising, television, motion pictures, and print media. Consequently, a 2001 *New York Times* article profiling the ALA campaign for recruitment did little more than introduce another misleading stereotype.[5] Librarians have been depicted in broadcast and print media and movies for more than one hundred years. There are a number of websites devoted to recasting and bolstering the image of the librarian,[6] as well as various articles discussing the image problem. Beth Yeagley found that "librarians . . . are portrayed mostly positively in recent movies. . . . Both physical and professional characteristics are portrayed mostly positively, but filmmakers do need to keep widening the gap between librarians with positive physical characteristics and librarians with negative physical characteristics."[7]

Interestingly enough, research on the image of librarians from a child's perspective does not include the stereotypical negative image. Jennifer Bobrovitz and Rosemary Griebel investigated the image of the professional librarian in Alberta, Canada, by conducting a three-part survey. They surveyed community leaders and library professionals, conducted street interviews, and analyzed the depiction of librarians in elementary children's artwork. The authors found that the artwork "generally portrayed a positive view of libraries and librarians," with only 17 percent representing librarians with the stereotypical glasses and buns. The street interviews reinforced the stereotypical image; however, "[i]ndividuals with positive images and an understanding of the relationship between librarians and technology usually related it to personal experiences with librarians." This finding was also reinforced by the community leaders' survey, where 90 percent reported forming their "impressions of librarians through personal experience. Sixty-five per cent [*sic*] formed these impressions as children."[8] Pamela Jordan found that the "traditional negative image of librarians was not prevalent among the school-aged children in [her] study." In fact, overall, of those sampled, 76.9 percent rated the image of librarians positively.[9]

It is our responsibility as librarians to ensure that we are projecting the right image and educating the public on who we are and what we do. I recently had the opportunity to interview E. J. Josey, professor emeritus, University of Pittsburgh, about his successful recruiting career. For nearly half a century, Josey has been recruiting diverse peoples of all ages and backgrounds to the profession of librarianship, and, in the process, educating them and many others about the work of librarians. In response to a question about his philosophy of recruitment and why he believed recruitment to be so important, Josey noted that "many people think that everybody that works in the library is a librarian and . . . we have to educate the people that we want to recruit about the important jobs in the library. . . . [If] people do not know the great potential that the profession has for them, those of us who are in the field have a responsibility to help educate about the possible opportunities that are available in librarianship."[10]

The Issue of Salary

In addition to being an area of critical concern in general, the status of pay for librarians has been identified as a potential barrier to recruitment and retention for the profession.[11] The latest figures from three salary surveys do not show much improvement in this area. In the 2002 edition of *The Bowker Annual*, the average beginning salary for 2000 LIS graduates is listed at $34,871, representing an increase of 2.63 percent over 1999. Unfortunately, this increase is reportedly nearly 30 percent behind inflation.[12] In the *ALA Survey of Librarian Salaries 2001*, mean salaries for beginning librarians in all academic and public libraries were reported for four geographic regions: North Atlantic, $33,838; Great Lakes and Plains, $32,856; Southeast, $30,314; West and Southwest, $34,147. The mean salary for all regions was $32,891.[13] These salaries are clearly lower than those reported in the *Bowker Annual*; however, they do represent a small increase from those reported in the *ALA Survey of Librarian Salaries 2000*, when the mean beginning librarian's salary was listed at $32,160.[14] It is also interesting to note that the 2002 reported salaries are lower than those reported for 2000.

The 2000–2001 edition of the *ARL Annual Salary Survey*, produced by the Association of Research Libraries (ARL), reports data on salaries for "all professional staff working in ARL libraries." Beginning salaries are listed for each institution, ranging from a high of $40,333 in Ohio to a low of $21,676 in Canada.[15] It is a well known fact that this profession is not one selected for its lucrative qualities; in fact, the literature reveals other reasons as to why librarians are attracted to the field, including good working environments, "cooperation and collegiality, the opportunity to make a difference, intellectual stimulation, variety, and job security."[16]

INCREASED MARKETPLACE COMPETITION

Individuals graduating with a master's degree in LIS have many career options. There is very little statistical or empirical evidence to determine how many master's of library science (MLS) graduates are accepting positions in libraries and how many are accepting positions in related fields; however, there is general concern that LIS education is not graduating enough MLS graduates to replace those who will soon be retiring or leaving the profession in significant numbers. And in the midst of these discussions, is the concern that the flexibility of an MLS degree, which allows graduates the opportunity to enter a number of fields related to librarianship, including information science, editing and publishing, and specialized positions with vendors, significantly decreases the numbers of our ranks and contributes to the need to aggressively recruit. After reviewing the *Library Journal Annual Placement and Salary Survey 1991–1999* and Association for Library and Information Science (ALISE) statistics, Larry Hardesty concluded, "There may indeed be some potential academic/research librarians attracted away to the private sector, but the *Library Journal* survey suggests their number is not large."[17]

BARRIERS TO RECRUITING MINORITIES

In addition to low salaries, the perceived negative image of librarians, and increased competition in the marketplace for MLS graduates, there are additional barriers to recruiting a more diverse student body to our library schools. These barriers include, but are not limited to, the lack of adequate numbers of minority faculty in library and information science education; the lack of diversity in the curriculum; limited financial support; and an overall lack of a concerted effort from the profession, individuals, and associations to commit and follow through on the effort to recruit more diverse individuals to the profession.

Lack of Minority Faculty

The ALISE collects and reports statistics on faculty and students in LIS programs as reported by ALISE members in its publication *Library and Information Science Education Statistical Report*. It is important to note that the ALISE faculty totals include figures for deans and directors, professors, associate professors, assistant professors, instructors, and lecturers.

Between 1980 and 2000, the number of minority faculty remained significantly low but increased steadily overall. Beginning in 1980, the percentage of minority faculty decreased each year from sixty-three faculty members, until 1985, when it remained at a constant of forty-four faculty members each year until 1988. It then increased steadily, reaching an all-time high of 18.27 percent of the total faculty in 2000. The climb from forty-three faculty members in 1983 to 118 in 2000 represents a significant increase in the number of minority faculty in LIS programs in a given year; however, it is still far less than the all-time low of white faculty, which dipped to 81.73 percent in 2000.[18] Overall, the increase appears to be encouraging, but taken in the aggregate, students enrolled in MLS and other degree programs in LIS schools are far more likely to encounter a white professor than a minority one. And the chances for encounters are far smaller depending upon the ethnicity of the faculty member and the geographic location of the LIS program. According to ALISE data, there have never been more than five full-time American Indian faculty members employed in accredited LIS programs in one academic year. The number of Hispanic-American faculty members is also low, but it has enjoyed a small increase over the past five years, reaching a total of nineteen in 2000. As may be expected, African American faculty members represent the largest group of minority faculty, reaching an all-time high of fifty-one faculty members in 1999; Asian and Pacific Islander faculty members reached their all-time high of forty-nine in 2000.[19]

It is commonly known that faculty members play a significant role in the recruitment, retention, and overall success of students in all disciplines. It is also generally known that minority faculty members are not the only ones qualified to recruit, advise, mentor, and assist in the retention of minority students. However, there is empirical evidence that minority students report that the presence of minority faculty members in their academic discipline is a critical factor in their recruitment, retention, and success at all levels.[20] In addition to mentoring and advising minority students and contributing to a more welcoming, inclusive environment, minority faculty members may have more diverse research agendas and may be more likely to develop and incorporate diversity into their courses. The lack of a significant presence of minority faculty members in LIS programs is a continued barrier to minority recruitment to MLS programs.

Lack of Diverse Curriculum

Similar to the importance of minority faculty, the presence of diversity in the curriculum is an important factor for recruiting a more diverse student body. Ideally, diversity should be integrated across the curriculum, within each course offered. However, short of interviewing or surveying each faculty member who teaches a course in the LIS curriculum, it is virtually impossible to determine the level of diversity integration across the curriculum. More typically, the presence of diversity in the LIS curriculum can be identified by reviewing the course offerings available for particular library schools. It must be noted that experimental or infrequently offered courses may bear the same course number depending on the semester, so the course listings available in spring 2003 may not actually reflect the complete offerings of the LIS program.

In 1996, it was reported that a review of the LIS curriculum revealed that two of the fifty institutions for which there was information available offered an African American resources and services course. Five institutions offered a course in multicultural librarianship.[21] This author recently reviewed curriculum offerings of the fifty-six ALA-accredited LIS master's programs by visiting their websites and reviewing course descriptions for the presence of diversity courses. Two of the websites were excluded from review because they were not in English and one was excluded because course listings were not available on the website.[22] The majority of the remaining fifty-three LIS schools had a course listing for special topics that may or may not be offered each semester. A few of these websites listed areas of diversity as the course focus in previous semesters. Nearly 45 percent (twenty-three) had no diversity course listed at all; however, of those that listed a diversity course, 28 percent listed two or more diversity courses. The remaining fifteen programs listed one course. Most of the course offerings were resources and services courses; however, there was some variation in the diversity course offerings. For example, a student attending North Carolina Central University would have the option of taking a course titled *Interpretation of Slavery at Historic Sites* or *Ethnic Materials for Children and Adolescents* and a student attending the University of South Carolina would be able to take *Libraries in Institutions for Ill or Severely Disabled Persons.*

Without historical numbers, it is difficult to discern whether these findings represent an increase in the diversity course offerings or the norm. In any event, students enrolling in MLS programs in 2003 have a more than 50 percent chance of attending a school with a diversity course on the books.

Limited Financial Support

In response to a question about how recruitment differs today from recruitment twenty or thirty years ago, E. J. Josey addressed the issues of financial aid and the role it plays in recruiting minorities.

> Most of the students will need financial support; and most of the students have received student loans for their undergraduate degrees and usually, they don't want to get into more debt to obtain another degree. I don't let financial difficulty or money be a stumbling block. I have always tried to encourage students to think that if they have to get another loan to go to graduate school, this loan would be an investment in their educational future and in their professional future. I never had a problem finding and recruiting the students to the field; however, since the demise of the HEA Title IIB grants, the problem has been finding the money for the students.[23]

For the 2000–2001 academic year, library schools reported that 1,673 MLS students received a total of $4,990,228 in financial aid. This amount represents funding administered by the library school regardless of the source. It does not include funding received directly by the student, such as a Spectrum Initiative Scholarship or other sources. According to ALISE statistics, this amount represents an increase of 5.1 percent over the 1999–2000 year. The amount awarded to MLS students represents 75 percent of the total amount awarded to all LIS students ($6,646,893) for the 2000–2001 academic year.[24]

A 1999 article in the *Journal of Library Administration* discussed diversity initiatives including scholarships for minority students. The article identifies a number of financial support initiatives including the Spectrum Initiative, which has spawned a number of Spectrum Partners—library schools, public libraries, and associations who have "joined forces with ALA in support of the Spectrum Initiative." In addition to this scholarship, the ALA ethnic caucuses all offer some form of financial aid to minority students and other library associations and organizations do as well.[25] The Spectrum Initiative is somewhat unique in that recipients receive the monies directly and have autonomy in the use of the funds. This is especially important to minority graduate students, as tuition remission may not be their only area of financial need. The flexibility to use funds to pay for childcare or transportation could be the deciding factor in enrolling in and completing the MLS degree.

The availability of various types of financial support for all MLS students, and minority students in particular, is a critical issue in recruitment. It is important for library schools to ensure that there is funding available at the local level as well as via library organizations and associations to supplement and support minority graduate student recruitment and retention.

Lack of Concerted Recruitment Effort

In general, there has been an overall lack of a systematic, concerted effort to diversify the profession. A 1999 article reviewing library diversity initiatives concluded, "Until all areas of the profession are united in the effort to achieve parity and to eradicate the evidence of too many years of benign neglect, this profession will find itself moving into the twenty-first century with the population of the nation of one composite, and the library profession serving the nation, another."[26] This same article outlined the diversity initiatives in place at that time; throughout the profession, little has changed since that time. The landscape of diversity and recruitment is still disparate. The majority of the recruitment efforts evident in the literature are in the form of scholarships, advertised by word of mouth, library listservs, on library association and organization websites, and in library publications. The chances of these efforts reaching a wider audience outside of the profession without collaborative additional intervention is slim, and considering the history of collaborative efforts in the profession of librarianship in recruitment efforts, this may never be the case. The ALA is not the only association responsible for diversifying the profession through recruitment; neither are the ALA ethnic caucuses. It is the collective responsibility of every individual, organization, and association committed to diversifying our ranks.

RECRUITMENT: A BROADER VIEW

The profession of librarianship is not the only profession suffering from low enrollments and pending massive retirements. Recent articles in the popular press note the shortages in several critical professions, including nursing and teaching. A recent study by the University of Pennsylvania revealed a "really strong and unequivocal relationship between nurse staffing and mortality."[27] Although the pending librarian shortage does not create a life or death situation, nevertheless it is a critical problem as it directly affects school, college and university, and public libraries, which significantly affect students, parents, and the general public at all levels. In a 1985 article, E. J. Josey commented on the upcoming demographic shifts of this country:

> These facts have serious implications for America's economic planning, the educational system and library and information services. . . . Since [minorities] will constitute a major segment of the workforce and will contribute substantially to the economic well being of the nation, the United States government must be certain that its [minority] population[s] receive a quality education and are guaranteed access to library resources and information. Further, the [minorities] of the country must have the knowledge and skills to use the new technologies in the workplace as well as in every aspect of their lives. The nation cannot afford to ignore the education, training and library needs of its [minorities].[28]

I would submit that at this point in time, we, collectively, cannot afford to ignore the education, training, and library needs of this nation. To do so would negatively affect us all. As a profession, we tend to identify the problems within the profession, conduct the research, crunch the numbers, and publish the findings in library science publications, all the while wringing our hands and lamenting to each other. With the exception of a few recent newspaper articles, very few publications outside of the library literature have even acknowledged that there is a critical shortage of qualified librarians pending. No wonder we find it difficult to recruit. Too few people outside of the profession know who we are, what we do, why we do it, or how we do it. Despite the fact that twice a year we descend en masse on major metropolitan cities in the United States and Canada for the ALA annual and midwinter conferences and less frequently, in smaller but significant numbers, we visit other major cities for ALA-affiliated local and regional library association conferences. We come, we conference, we eat, we drink, we shop, and we leave. These conferences provide a prime opportunity for recruitment, if we take advantage of them.

THE NEED FOR RECRUITMENT TO THE PROFESSION

While the focus of this article is recruiting people of color to the profession, it is worth noting the critical need for large-scale recruitment to the profession as a whole. Stanley Wilder's research profiling aging trends of Association of Research Libraries (ARL) university librarians is revealing and provides the most comprehensive data to support the need for widescale recruitment. Simply put, "as a group, librarians in the US are unusually old and aging rapidly. . . . As a group, ARL university librarians are older than comparable professionals and even older than US librarians in general, and they are aging quickly."[29] Using data from the ARL salary survey, Wilder found that in 1990, 48 percent of the ARL university librarian population was aged 45 or older. By 1998, this figure had increased to 66.1 percent.[30] In terms of racial and ethnic minority groups, more than 50 percent of African American librarians, 62.4 percent of Asian American librarians, and 65.6 percent of Hispanic librarians were aged 45 or older in 1998.[31] Overall in 1998, 23.2 percent of the population studied was age 55 or older.[32] A 2000 survey reported that 40 percent of librarians intended to retire by 2009 and 68 percent by 2014.[33] ALA immediate past President John Berry confirmed these data in early 2002, when he noted that U.S. Census data revealed that "more than one-quarter of all librarians with a master's degree will reach the age of 65 by 2009."[34]

In December 2002, the report of the Association of College and Research Libraries (ACRL) Focus on the Future Task Force announced the top issues facing academic libraries. Although the list of issues was not prioritized, "recruitment, education, and retention of librarians" was first on the list.[35] The report also listed "low pay" and "diversity" as subtopics of recruitment.[36] The focus of a May 2002 white paper produced by the Ad Hoc Task Force on Recruitment and Retention Issues, a subcommittee of the ACRL personnel administrators and staff development officers discussion group, is recruitment to the profession and to academic libraries. The authors identified the following primary factors that signal a critical need for recruitment:

- the aging of the general labor supply and of the library profession, leading to an increasing number of retirements;
- one of the lowest unemployment rates in U.S. history;
- the flat or declining number of master's of library and information science graduates;
- increased competition from other career sectors (e.g., private sector, corporate libraries, technology, and dot-com companies);
- less than competitive salaries; and
- a lingering negative image of the profession.[37]

The theme for the ALISE 2002 conference was "Faculty Recruitment in a New Key." In a 2002 article reporting on the conference, Gordon Flagg noted that "much attention was paid to the overriding concern about recruitment of new librarians, particularly minorities, to the profession."[38]

In response to this pending shortage of new librarians to replace those re-tiring in record numbers, in January 2002 First Lady Laura Bush, former school librarian, announced that the president's fiscal year 2003 budget request would include a proposal for an initiative to recruit and educate a generation of librarians for the twenty-first century.[39] The initiative outlines the need for librarians in the twenty-first century, citing the need to replace the significant number of librarians who are expected to retire in the next ten to twelve years. In addition to replacing retiring librarians, the initiative notes the need to meet the new demands of the profession, the need for librarians in underserved rural areas, the need for librarians with diverse language and cultural skills, and the "need to equip librarians with skills for information technology." It also addresses the effect this initiative to recruit and educate librarians will have on library science faculty and library science education programs. If funded by Congress, this $10 million initiative could potentially significantly affect the profession. In November 2002, the Institute of Museum and Library Services, the organization charged with managing the initiative if funded, released "Recruiting and Educating Librarians for the 21st Century: A Proposed Program of the Institute of Museum and Library Services."[40]

The evidence is clear; librarianship is in a recruitment crisis. However, as John W. Berry has noted, "Our challenge is clearly about recruitment, but it is also about diversifying our workforce."[41] It is evident that there is a critical need to recruit to the profession. It is also evident that the problems with recruiting in general also apply to recruiting people of color to the profession.

STATISTICALLY SPEAKING

This would not be a proper article on recruitment if there weren't some statistics included. Librarians, and most professionals for that matter, are enamored with numbers, percentages, and statistics. We must examine the appropriate data to determine where we are statistically with minority representation in the profession. One method that may be used to illustrate the continued systemic lack of diversity in the profession is to compare the percentage of ethnically diverse individuals in the general population, based on U.S. Census data, to the percentage of ethnically diverse individuals in the library profession. These statistics are used as a basis to support the argument that the library profession should reflect the makeup of the peoples populating North America. A number of researchers have already done the math and the numbers aren't pretty.

In 1996, Deborah Hollis reported that in 1990, according to U.S. Census Bureau information, white librarians made up 85 percent of the total population (200,881) of librarians, while minorities made up the remaining 15 percent.[42]

Preliminary analysis of the 2000 U.S. Census reveals that the U.S. population estimate for 2000 is 281,421,906 people. Seventy-five percent (211,460,626) of those are white, and the remaining 25 percent are minorities. Twelve and one-half percent (35,305,818) are Hispanic or Latino, 12.3 percent (34,658,190) are black or African American, 0.9 percent (2,475,956) are American Indian or Alaskan Native, and 3.6 percent (10,242,998) are Asian.[43] Although the detailed occupational tables for Census 2000 have not yet been released, the 2000 *Statistical Abstract of the United States* reports that in 1999, there were 236,000 persons employed as librarians: 83 percent of those were women, 7.7 percent were African American, and 4.8 percent were Hispanic. The omission of Asian Americans and American Indians or Alaskan Natives is not addressed.[44] In 2000, the total number of librarians was reported as 232,000, with 6.7 percent African American and 6.6 percent Hispanic.[45] In 2001, although the total number of librarians decreased to 203,000, the percentage of black librarians rose to 10.8 percent (21,924). Unfortunately, the number Hispanic librarians decreased to 3 percent (6,090) of the total.[46]

In 1997, Kathleen de la Peña McCook and Kate Lippincott compared U.S. Census data to graduation rates from library and information science programs for 1984–1985 and 1994–1995.[47] A more revealing comparison might be the number of self-identified librarians as reported by the U.S. Census and census population data. Unfortunately, the only detailed occupational tables available to date are for 1990. Prior to and after the 1990 Census, available occupational data for librarianship does not include statistics for American Indians or Asians and Pacific Islanders. Figures from the *Statistical Abstract of the United States* report only occupation data for African Americans, Hispanics, and women.

BY THE NUMBERS

A word to the wise about population and industry/occupation statistics is in order. There is no one source that provides consistent data for population and industry/occupation figures. The author consulted multiple years of the *Statistical Abstract of the United States*, as well as online census data from the U.S. Census website. In many cases, there were discrepancies within the same volume on population figures. Some data are as of April 1 and some as of July 1, and some do not list an "as of date," presumably indicating year-end totals. Data for industries are even more unreliable or just not available. The most complete data for population and industry are from the 1990 Census. These are also the data that most articles on recruitment and retention are based on. Unfortunately, these data are nearly fifteen years old and the data reported in the intervening years are not consistent from year to year. In March 2002, Mary Jo Lynch reported that according to the U.S. 1990 Census,

197,000 people reported being librarians. Subsequently, she discovered that "fewer than half of those 197,000 had the master's degree or higher." Using statistics reported to the National Center for Education Statistics in 1990, she concluded that the most reliable figure is most likely between 87,409 and 97,315, a considerable decrease from the numbers we are currently using, based on the 1990 Census as reported in the detailed occupation tables.[48] The ALA and the ARL both publish annual salary surveys. However the ALA survey is not comprehensive and the *ARL Annual Salary Survey 2000–2001* only includes racial and ethnic data for professionals working in ARL libraries. The report notes that of the ninety-eight libraries reporting, 952 professional minorities were employed, representing 11.7 percent of the total staff in the ARL libraries reporting.[49]

In addition to the inconsistency and unavailability of detailed occupational data, other intervening factors may contribute to the fluctuation in numbers of total librarians in general, and minority librarians in particular, including the effect of affirmative action legislation, which directly affects undergraduate enrollment, and the overall effect of technology on the profession. All things considered, the numbers tell only half the story and should be interpreted as such.

Keeping that in mind, and continuing in the tradition of McCook and Lippincott, table 7.1 shows MLS minority graduation rates in five-year intervals for the past twenty years with population data from the U.S. Census and the *Statistical Abstract of the United States.*

Table 7.1 shows that the total U.S. minority population has increased slowly but steadily over the past twenty years. According to U.S. Census data, in 1999 the minority population reached an all-time high of 29.12 percent for the twenty-year period; however, from 1980 to 2000, the overall increase is only 8.7 percent. It should be noted that ALISE did not begin to report separate totals for the MLS degree until 1994. Overall, the total number of master's degrees awarded has fluctuated considerably for the past twenty years. For the time period reviewed, the most master's degrees (6,861) were awarded in 1988; the least (3,231) three years earlier in 1985. The number of minorities awarded degrees has also fluctuated, with no discerning patterns, reaching an all-time high in 2000, when 625 were awarded. Of the 96,633 degrees awarded from 1980 to 2000, only 7.88 percent (7,624) were awarded to minorities. As has come to be expected, American Indians received the least number of degrees (288) of all minorities. African Americans received the most at 3,272, Asians and Pacific Islanders received 2,200, and Hispanics received 1,864. In terms of a comparison of graduation rates with the U.S. Census distribution, only Asians or Pacific Islanders come close, with matriculation rates close to or in some cases exceeding their representation in the general population. All other minority groups rarely reach half of their representation in the U.S. population. Of note, and rarely addressed,

Table 7.1. U.S. Census Population and MLS Degrees Awarded, 1980–2000

	Total Population	AA	AI	AP	HS	W	Minorities	International
1980 Census Distribution	226,546,000	11.85	.68	1.64	6.45	86.00	20.62	—
1980 Degrees Awarded	4,670	3.64	.32	2.68	.93	68.93	7.77	—
1985 Census Distribution	238,816,000	12.10	—	—	7.09	85.00	19.19	—
1985 degrees Awarded	3,231	2.88	1.9	1.49	.87	75.67	5.47	3.25
1990 Census Distribution	248,709,873	12.06	.79	2.9	28.99	80.29	24.76	—
1990 degrees Awarded	4,393	2.77	.38	2.04	2.61	76.87	7.83	4.67
1995 Census Distribution	262,890,000	12.69	.86	3.57	10.37	83.00	27.49	—
1995 degrees Awarded	4,991	3.59	.14	2.87	4.13	74.41	10.72	2.30
2000 Census Distribution	281,421,906	12.54	.86	3.96	11.53	80.31	28.99	—
2000 Degrees Awarded	4,877	4.43	.29	2.62	5.47	73.32	12.82	2.87

Source: Census distribution data taken from the U.S. Census and the *Statistical Abstract of the United States*, 1981, 1986, 1991, 1996, 2001. Data for degrees awarded taken from the ALISE *Library and Information Science Education Statistical Report*, 1981, 1986, 1991, 1996, 2001. AA = African American, AI = American Indian, AP = Asian or Pacific Islander, HS = Hispanic, W = White.

is the number of international students receiving degrees. As shown in table 7.1, these figures, when available, often account for more than half of those for total minority degrees awarded.

In a follow-up to the 1993 article "Diversity Deferred: Where are the Minority Librarians?"[50] McCook and Lippincott continued the tradition of using statistics from ALISE to illustrate that not enough is being done to improve the recruitment of diverse individuals to the profession. In "Library Schools and Diversity: Who Makes the Grade," the authors wonder if funding the then forthcoming $1.5 million diversity plan (Spectrum Initiative), along with the "Each One–Reach One" strategy outlined by former ALA Office for Library Personnel Resources Director Margaret Myers, "could be used to create diversity among new entrants to our field." The ALISE data presented is used to reveal whether the Spectrum Initiative, with the first group of Spectrum Scholars being awarded scholarships in 1998 and the most recent group in spring 2001, as well as other recruitment efforts, including "Stop Talking, Start Doing," have been successful in increasing the numbers. Table 7.2 reveals data showing that enrollment and graduation rates do not indicate significant increases despite the Spectrum Initiative, which since its inception has awarded 225 scholarships, and other efforts developed to increase minority representation in the profession.

For the years reviewed, it is evident that overall enrollment in LIS programs increased significantly. Between 1980 and 2000, enrollment increased by 5,342, or nearly 60 percent. For the same time period, minority enrollment increased from a low of 6.76 percent in 1985 to a high of 10.71 percent in 1997, before declining. In addition, 1997 was the year before the first group of Spectrum scholarships were awarded, and it is disconcerting to see that enrollments were lower for subsequent years throughout the period reviewed. A closer look at minority degrees awarded after Spectrum reveals that these numbers increased each year, from 8.76 percent in 1997 to 12.82 percent in 2000. In reviewing the degrees awarded within the minority groups since 1997, it is evident that the significant increase in degrees awarded to minorities can be directly attributed to Hispanics. From 1997 to 2000, the number of degrees awarded to Hispanics increased 3.62 percentage points, from 1.85 percent to 5.47 percent.

As expected, enrollment and degrees awarded to white students increased or decreased in proportion to minority enrollments and degrees awarded. And as mentioned previously, it is important to keep in mind that international enrollment and degrees awarded figures are included in the total and represent amounts that are not negligible.

Although we may never have accurate total numbers of minority professionals in LIS, tracking the enrollment figures and graduation rates overtime may provide us with a better picture of how many individuals of color are matriculating.

Table 7.2. ALA MLS Enrollment and Graduation Rates, 1980–2000

	Total	AA	AI	AP	HS	W	Minorities	International
1980 Enrollment	7,875	3.30	.122	.37	1.86	75.04	7.68	—
1980 Degrees Awarded	4,670	3.64	.32	2.68	.93	68.93	7.77	—
1985 Enrollment	7,818	3.61	.16	1.82	1.15	79.00	6.76	—
1985 Degrees Awarded	3,231	2.88	.19	1.49	.87	75.67	5.47	—
1990 Enrollment	10,586	3.15	.02	2.08	2.28	78.35	7.73	—
1990 Degrees Awarded	4,393	2.77	.38	2.04	2.61	76.87	7.83	—
1995 Enrollment	11,826	3.77	.39	2.58	2.85	76.29	9.62	—
1995 Degrees Awarded	4,991	3.59	.14	2.87	4.13	74.41	10.72	—
1997 Enrollment	12,480	4.40	.88	2.49	2.86	78.19	10.71	—
1997 Degrees Awarded	5,068	3.80	.51	2.58	1.85	78.47	8.76	—
1998 Enrollment	12,801	4.60	.34	2.14	2.98	75.63	10.06	2.57
1998 Degrees Awarded	5,024	4.04	.41	2.78	2.18	79.14	9.43	2.44
1999 Enrollment	12,282	4.68	.43	1.92	3.28	76.42	10.34	2.86
1999 Degrees Awarded	5,046	3.98	.39	2.83	2.85	78.55	10.06	1.94
2000 Enrollment	13,217	4.43	.49	2.35	2.67	76.12	9.96	3.14
2000 Degrees Awarded	4,877	4.43	.29	2.62	5.47	73.32	12.82	2.87

Source: Census distribution data taken from the U.S. Census and the *Statistical Abstract of the United States,* 1981, 1986, 1991, 1996, 2001. Data for degrees awarded taken from the ALISE *Library and Information Science Education Statistical Report,* 1981, 1986, 1991, 1996, 2001 AA = African American, AI = American Indian, AP = Asian or Pacific Islander, HS = Hispanic, W = White.

RECRUITING MINORITIES

In a 1989 article in *The Bookmark*, E. J. Josey advocated that the "schools of library and information studies should reaffirm their commitment to increasing minority access to the library and information science profession by adopting a comprehensive program for the recruitment of minorities."[51]

In spite of the barriers mentioned previously, it is possible to recruit minorities to this field. Given the historical precedent and the numbers, it may not be realistic to expect that the numbers will ever be more than they are now; however, the task remains to maintain the current levels and develop and implement practices to continuously recruit.

> Library practitioners must accept the responsibility for identifying minorities and mentoring them into the library and information science profession. Library education must assume the responsibility for recruiting minority students and retaining them throughout the degree program. Once librarians of color become practitioners, then it is the responsibility of seasoned professionals to help retain them for the profession. All of us in this profession have an important role to play in the recruitment and retention effort.[52]

The published literature provides some suggestions and recommendations for recruiting minorities to the profession. Recruiting diverse individuals to the profession is no mystery. However, there is at least one critical area to be taken into consideration when recruiting and advocating for a more diversified librarian workforce.

A key overriding concern is the continuing presence of racism and discrimination in the United States and in the profession. "Race relations and diversity on the national level are significant for the practice of librarianship because higher education in general and academic librarianship in particular, [is] influenced on many levels by such things as politics, federal policies, and the practices of the entertainment industry."[53] One only has to look to the 2002 faux pas of Senator Trent Lott and the fallout surrounding his comments to recognize that as a nation, we are nowhere near ending racism or even acknowledging that it still exists.[54] The profession of librarianship is not immune to racism. In 1997, Evan St. Lifer and Corinne O. Nelson reported that in response to the question: Has awareness of racism in the library profession improved, stayed the same, or gotten worse? 84 percent of whites reported that it had improved, while 54 percent of Latinos, 41 percent of Asians, and 40 percent of blacks reported that it had improved. Consequently, 49 percent of Asians, 41 percent of blacks, and 36 percent of Latinos reported that the awareness of racism had gotten worse. When queried about "the degree to which librarians of color feel racially discriminated against on the job," the authors reported that "four of ten blacks, one-third of Asians, and one-quarter of Latinos polled said they were discriminated against at their library at least occasionally."[55] There is strong empirical evidence that minority librarians experience racial discrimination on a regular basis.[56] Until racism and racial and ethnic discrimination is addressed and eradicated in the profession, it will remain a significant problem and indicator of the ability to recruit and retain a diverse workforce.

In *Stop Talking, Start Doing! Attracting People of Color to the Library Profession*, Gregory L. Reese and Ernestine L. Hawkins outline five myths that must be overcome if we are going to "effectively target . . . ethnic communities" for recruitment:

- minorities are the same as Caucasians;
- minorities are homogeneous;
- libraries and library professionals can effectively utilize mass media to reach all minority populations;
- language isn't important; and
- minorities are interested only in certain careers and services.[57]

Other stereotypes and myths about minorities abound; however, it is important to realize that although all people are created equal, they cannot all be approached and recruited in the same way. Different populations require different strategies.

RECRUITMENT STRATEGIES: OLD MODELS, NEW PROFILES

A number of successful strategies for recruiting minorities to the profession have been proposed over the years, including mentoring, the presence of minority faculty, and financial aid opportunities. Reporting on the 1997 report *Planning for a Diverse Workforce in Library and Information Science*,[58] Kate Lippincott outlined the most successful strategies for LIS programs to recruit minorities:

- faculty from ethnic or minority groups;
- active multicultural participation
  - bilingual advising/Spanish webpage
  - mentoring by minority faculty or professionals
  - LIS faculty active in campus or community diversity activities;
- financial support
  - Title II-B, university scholarships, association scholarship;
- partnerships with specific libraries;
- targeted recruitment strategies
  - advertising in ethnic yellow pages
  - recruiting trips to historically black institutions
  - participation in minority career days; and

- creative delivery of classes
  - where people work
  - evening or weekend classes.[59]

Lippincott also noted the responsibility of national and state library associations and individuals in the recruitment of minorities to the profession. She believes that associations "need to provide leadership in diversity initiatives aimed at recruitment, retention, and promotion" and admonishes that "[a]ll library professionals need to encourage and promote the profession to the minority support staff in their libraries and to minority students in their communities who are making career choices."[60]

In Josey's *The Black Librarian in American Revisited*, Carla Hayden examined black recruitment and offered additional approaches using William Welbourne's 1977 plan as a springboard.[61] She noted that "the recruitment of blacks to librarianship must be viewed in the broader context of the status of blacks in higher education in which the library profession is one important link in the chain." Hayden continues and highlights the problems of recruitment as not having changed in the past few decades. She writes,

> In fact some of the main barriers to recruitment and retention have worsened in the intervening years, primarily the financial ones, which are the main deterrents to black enrollment across the board. Retention is closely linked to recruitment since aspects such as a hostile environment, lack of black faculty members, and few black students enrolled in the program make the prospect to go to certain schools less attractive. Recruitment to librarianship is even more problematic, because of the nature and public perception of the profession among the general populace.[62]

New approaches advocated by Carla Hayden include the use of new methods such as videos; the use of continuing education programs for recruitment; more cooperative arrangements for paraprofessionals in libraries in general; a redefinition of admission requirements for graduate programs; and beginning recruitment efforts earlier in secondary education.[63]

Hayden also points to Ann Knight Randall's seminal chapter in *Librarians in the New Millennium*, where she recommends that action should take place at the institutional and organizational level, noting specifically the lead taken by ALA and also pointing out the responsibility of ALISE as the library education professional organization. "A more formal involvement on the part of ALISE could include major conference programs, consortia, and task forces to seek funding to support intense recruitment efforts. Programs, scholarships, and endowments should be established. Full-time recruiters shared by library schools, perhaps on a regional basis, support for informal networking and referral, and more internship opportunities in different types of libraries are other possibilities."[64]

In *Stop Talking, Start Doing!* the authors offer tried and proven suggestions for attracting and recruiting diverse individuals to other professions, such as advertising and media, teaching, and corporate America. They suggest that the use of such techniques as mentoring (electronic, formal, and informal), designing a quality recruitment video, target marketing, becoming public relations practitioners, "promot[ing] the library profession to the many minority markets," recruiting at the junior and senior high school levels, and proactive recruitment from library schools "can play an important role in recruiting and retaining minorities in the library profession."[65]

As for individual librarians, they suggest role modeling for minority youth, arranging tours of various local libraries, recruiting college students for internships at libraries, letting a young person shadow a librarian during a workday, sponsoring student memberships in professional organizations, and joining or organizing mentorship programs for neighborhood schools.[66]

In terms of targeting specific groups for recruitment, Reese and Hawkins provide information and specific strategies on the best ways to reach diverse individuals on their own terms.

1. African Americans: "If your goal is to successfully provide a service or deliver a message to the African American community, you must *go to* and become *involved in* the African American community. You must take the time to learn the culture and lifestyle of the minority population with which you are attempting to make contact."
2. Asian Americans: "As library professionals, we can reach Asian Americans through news releases more effectively than any other minority group. However, we need to produce news releases and other promotional material in the language of the subgroups (Asian, Indian, Chinese, Hawaiian, Japanese, Korean, Philippine, Vietnamese, etc.). We can also reach Asian Americans through their television programs and sub-carrier radio channels. . . . We can also reach Asian Americans through events and community organizations."
3. Hispanic Americans: "Minority newspapers such as *La Opinion* and radio and television stations such as Telemundo reach many, but direct mail in Spanish reaches them better. . . . Using recruitment strategies or techniques that center around Hispanic values provides relevance and increases the effectiveness of your recruitment or service efforts. Each segment of the Hispanic American population deserves individual attention. Library professionals should understand that a target-specific approach to various segments of the Hispanic American populations is extremely important. They may differ by country of origin, culture, beliefs, and opinions."
4. Native Americans: "We should be aware that Native American people prefer to be identified by their nation's name (Navajo, Menominee,

Seneca). . . . Most Native American people prefer to be recognized as belonging to a particular nation of people rather than a tribe. . . . We must be sensitive to and find ways to distinguish cultural variations when working with people from different nations. . . . Native Americans are often used as icons on commercial products ranging from foods and automobiles to athletic teams. We must clearly understand that representations of the bow and arrow, tomahawks, war bonnets, feathers, and war paint are depictions of a mythical Native American from a long-gone era."[67]

It is unclear if, taken in the aggregate, these recruitment strategies have the potential to have a significant effect on the profession as a whole. However, for library schools, library associations, and organizations these strategies and models can provide a starting place in the uphill task of recruiting a more diverse workforce to the profession.

CONCLUSION

Diversifying the profession of librarianship has been a topic of concern for many years; and I predict it will be for many years to come. However, I may be in the minority in suggesting that minority groups may never represent more than 15 percent of the total librarian population in general and in enrolling and graduating from library schools. Even based on the rapidly increasing minority population in the United States, it is still unrealistic to ever expect the percentage of minority librarians to reach the percentage of minorities in the general population. In other words, a person may self-select to become a member of the librarian profession, but has no choice regarding the part of the general population into which they are born. Thus, there can be no comparing of the percentages from each group, because they were never equal. This may be a reality that we all have to contend with; and, therefore, it may be unrealistic to expect that reaching numbers we feel are adequate will be achieved in our lifetimes. Promoting unrealistic expectations prohibits the ability to acknowledge the gains we have made in this profession, such as the conceiving and implementation of the Spectrum Initiative and the increase in enrollment and degrees awarded.

In 1995, Maurice Wheeler and Jaqueline Hanson wrote that "with few exceptions, minority recruitment into the library and information science profession in the U.S. over the past several years appears to have been no more than a symbolic ritual."[68] Much has changed regarding minority recruitment in the last decade. That said, the number of librarians of color is still not adequate and the methods suggested for recruiting individual racial and ethnic groups to the profession should be taken into consideration by all who are committed to diversifying the profession. It is also worth keeping in mind that not all racial and ethnic groups are homogenous and should not be approached or treated as such, and that the specter of racism is real and should be acknowledged and dealt with accordingly.

NOTES

1. Merriam-Webster OnLine Dictionary, www.m-w.com/dictionary.htm (accessed 25 February 2003).

2. Rene Carayol and David Firth, "Think Different," *Director* (Feb. 2002): 74; Pasi Raatikainen, "Contributions of Multiculturalism to the Competitive Advantage of an Organisation," *Singapore Management Review* 24, no. 1 (2002): 81–88; Margaret Mayo, "Capitalizing on a Diverse Workforce," *Ivey Business Journal* (Sept./Oct. 1999): 20–26; R. Roosevelt Thomas, *Beyond Race and Gender: Unleashing the Power of Your Total Work Force by Managing Diversity* (New York: American Management Association, 1991); William Sonnenschein, *The Diversity Toolkit: How You Can Build and Benefit from a Diverse Workforce* (Chicago: Contemporary Books, 1999); and Taylor Cox, *Cultural Diversity in Organizations: Theory, Research, and Practice* (San Francisco: Berrett-Koehler, 1993).

3. Darren K. Carlson, "Career Advice from Americans on 'Take Our Daughters to Work Day,'" *The Gallup Organization*. www.gallup.com/poll/releases/pr010426b.asp (accessed 25 February 2003).

4. See Dan T. Hutchins, "We Aren't a Stereotype," *Library Journal* 125, no. 2 (2001): 57; and Mark Y. Herring, "And We Wonder about Our Image!" *American Libraries* 31, no. 10 (2000): 33.

5. John W. Fountain, "Librarians Adjust Image in an Effort to Fill Jobs," *New York Times*, 23 Aug. 2001. See also John N. Berry, "Tell 'em what Librarians Do Each Day," *Library Journal* 126, no. 17 (2001): 6; American Library Association's Campaign for America's Libraries @yourlibrary, https://cs.ala.org/@yourlibrary/index.html (accessed 27 Feb. 2003); and Mary Jane Scherdin and Anne K. Beaubien, "Shattering Our Stereotype: Librarian's New Image," *Library Journal* 120, no. 12 (1995): 35–38.

6. Stephen Walker and V. Lonnie Lawson, "The Librarian Stereotype and the Movies," *MC Journal: The Journal of Academic Media Librarianship* 1, no. 1 (1993): 16–28. Available at: http://wings.buffalo.edu/publications/mcjrnl/v1n1/image.html; for links to sites on the image of librarians, see The Internet Public Library, Image of Librarians Resources, www.ipl.org/ref/RR/static/hum45.10.50.html; The Lipstick Librarian, www.lipsticklibrarian.com/; and E. Olsen, *Librarian Avengers* (Ann Arbor, MI: University of Michigan, 2000). http://www.librarianavengers.com/ (accessed 27 Feb. 2003).

7. Beth Yeagley, "Shelving, Stamping and Shushing: Librarians in the Movies," U.S. Ohio, 1999, *ERIC* ED 435392.

8. Jennifer Bobrovitz and Rosemary Griebel, "Still Mousy After All These Years: The Image of the Librarian in the 21st Century," *Feliciter* 47, no. 5 (2001): 260–263.

9. Pamela A. Jordan, "The Librarian Image: A Child's Perspective" (Master's thesis, Kent State University, 1991), ERIC ED 340379.

10. E-mail interview with E. J. Josey, 5 May 2002.

11. John N. Berry, "Serve and Starve? Not Now," *Library Journal* 127, no. 18 (2002): 8; Maurice J. Freedman, "The Campaign for America's Librarians," *American Libraries* 33, no. 7 (2002): 7; Carol A. Brey, "Taking Our Salary Fight to the Streets," *Library Journal* 127, no. 7 (2002): 38–39; John N. Berry, "The Compensation Crisis," *Library Journal* 125, no. 3 (2000): 100; Larry L. Hardesty, "Future of Academic/ Research Librarians: A Period of Transition—to What?" *Portal: Libraries and the Academy* 2, no. 1 (2002): 79–97.

12. Tom Terrell and Vicki L. Gregory, "Placements and Salaries 2000: Plenty of Jobs, Salaries Flat," in *The Bowker Annual: Library and Book Trade Almanac*, ed. Dave Bogart (Medford, NJ: Information Today, Inc., 2002), 382–395.

13. Mary Jo Lynch, *ALA Survey of Librarian Salaries* (Chicago: American Library Association, 2001).

14. Mary Jo Lynch, *ALA Survey of Librarian Salaries* (Chicago: American Library Association, 2000).

15. Martha Kyrillidou and Karen Wetzel, eds., *ARL Annual Salary Survey 2000–2001* (Washington, DC: Association of Research Libraries, 2001).

16. Hardesty, "Future of Academic/Research Librarians," 93.

17. Hardesty, "Future of Academic/Research Librarians," 90.

18. Association for Library and Information Science, *Library and Information Science Education Statistical Report* (State College, PA: ALISE, 1979–2001).

19. ALISE, *Library and Information Science,* 1979–2001.

20. Anita Blossom Burton, "Retention of Black Students at a Predominantly White University: An In-depth Qualitative Approach" (Ed.D. dissertation, University of Massachusetts at Amherst, 1993); Monica E. Randall, *Minority Achievement Report Summary, 1999. Maryland Community Colleges* (Annapolis, MD: Maryland Higher Education Commission, 1999); and Piedad F. Robertson and Ted Frier, "Recruitment and Retention of Minority Faculty," *New Directions for Community Colleges* 22, no. 3 (1994): 65–71.

21. Teresa Y. Neely, "The Jackie Robinson of Library Science," in *In Our Own Voices: The Changing Face of Librarianship,* ed. Teresa Y. Neely and Khafre K. Abif (Lanham, MD: Scarecrow Press, Inc., 1996), 169.

22. Websites for the Université de Montréal (French) and the University of Puerto Rico (Spanish) are not in English; and the author was unable to locate course descriptions for St. John's University.

23. E-mail interview with E. J. Josey, 5 May 2002.

24. Jerry D. Saye and Katherine M. Wisser, "Students," in *ALISE Library and Information Science Statistical Report, 2002.* http://ils.unc.edu/ALISE/2002/Students/ Students01.htm (accessed 28 Feb. 2003).

25. Teresa Y. Neely, "Diversity Initiatives and Programs: The National Approach," *Journal of Library Administration* 27, no. 1/2 (1999): 123–144.

26. Neely, "Diversity Initiatives and Programs," 141.

27. Linda H. Aiken, Sean P. Clarke, Douglas M. Sloane, Julie M. Sochalski, and Jeffrey H. Silber, "Hospital Nurse Staffing and Patient Mortality, Nurse Burnout, and Job Dissatisfaction," *Journal of the American Medical Association* 288, no. 16 (2002): 1987–1994.

28. E. J. Josey, "Library and Information Services for Cultural Minorities: A Commentary and Analysis of a Report to the National Commission on Libraries and Information Science," *Libri* 35, no. 4 (1985): 320–321.

29. Stanley Wilder, "The Changing Profile of Research Library Professional Staff," *ARL A Bimonthly Report on Research Library Issues and Actions from ARL, CNI, and SPARC*, no. 208/209 (Feb./Apr. 2000): 1–5.

30. Wilder, "The Changing Profile," 1.

31. Wilder, "The Changing Profile," 2–3.

32. Wilder, "The Changing Profile," 2.

33. Evan St. Lifer, "The Boomer Brain Drain: The Last of a Generation?" *Library Journal* 125, no. 8 (2000): 38–42.

34. John W. Berry, "President's Message: Addressing the Recruitment and Diversity Crisis," *American Libraries* 33, no. 2 (2002), 7.

35. W. Lee Hisle, "Top Issues Facing Academic Libraries: A Report of the Focus on the Future Task Force," *College and Research Libraries News* (Nov. 2002), 714–715, 730.

36. Andrew Albanese, "ACRL Report: Challenges Aplenty," *Library Journal* 127, no. 20 (2002), 20–22.

37. ALA Ad Hoc Task Force on Recruitment and Retention Issues, "Recruitment, Retention and Restructuring: Human Resources in Academic Libraries: A White Paper." www.ala.org/acrl/recruit-wp.html (accessed 30 May 2002).

38. Gordon Flagg, "Educators Focus on Recruitment at ALISE Conference," *American Libraries* 33, no. 3 (2002), 32–33.

39. Institute of Museum and Library Services, "Recruiting and Educating Librarians for the 21st Century," 19 April 2002. www.imls.gov (accessed 30 May 2002); see also "Laura Bush Unveils Librarian Recruitment Plan at Topeka Gala," *American Libraries* 33, no. 2 (2002), 18.

40. Institute of Museum and Library Services, "Recruiting and Educating Librarians."

41. Berry, "President's Message," 7.

42. Deborah R. Hollis, "On the Ambiguous Side: Experiences in a Predominantly White and Female Profession," in *In Our Own Voices: The Changing Face of Librarianship*, ed. Teresa Y. Neely and Khafre K. Abif (Lanham, MD: Scarecrow Press, Inc.), 139–140.

43. U.S. Census Bureau, "US Summary 2000: Census 2000 Profile" (Washington, DC: U.S. Department of Commerce, July 2002) 2. Available at: www.census.gov/prod/2002pubs/c2kprof00-us.pdf

44. U.S. Census Bureau, *Statistical Abstract of the United States: 2000* (Washington, DC: U.S. Department of Commerce, 2000), 416.

45. U.S. Census Bureau, *Statistical Abstract of the United States: 2001* (Washington, DC: U.S. Department of Commerce, 2001), 380.

46. U.S. Census Bureau, *Statistical Abstract of the United States: 2002* (Washington, DC: U.S. Department of Commerce, 2002), 381.

47. Kathleen de la Peña McCook and Kate Lippincott, "Library Schools and Diversity: Who Makes the Grade?" *Library Journal* 122, no. 7 (1997), 30–32.

48. Mary Jo Lynch, "Reaching 65: Lots of Librarians Will Be There Soon," *American Libraries* 33, no. 3 (2002): 55.

49. Association of Research Libraries, *ARL Annual Salary Survey, 2000–2001* (Washington, DC: ARL, 2001).

50. Kathleen de la Peña McCook and Kate Lippincott, "Diversity Deferred: Where Are the Minority Librarians?" *Library Journal* 118 (Nov. 1993), 35–38.

51. E. J. Josey, "Minority Representation in Library and Information Science Programs," *The Bookmark* 48, no. 1 (1989), 54–57.

52. Camila Alire, "Recruitment and Retention of Librarians of Color," in *Creating the Future: Essays on Librarianship in an Age of Great Change*, ed. Sally Gardner Reed (Jefferson, NC: McFarland & Co., 1996), 134.

53. Teresa Y. Neely, "Diversity in Conflict," *Law Library Journal* 90, no. 4 (1998): 587.

54. David Rogers, "Lott Is Under Fire on All Sides For His Remarks on Thurmond," *Wall Street Journal*, 11 Dec. 2002.

55. Evan St. Lifer and Corinne Nelson, "Unequal Opportunities: Race Does Matter," *Library Journal* 122, no. 18 (1997): 42–46.

56. See Joyce K. Thornton, "African American Female Librarians: A Study of Job Satisfaction," *Journal of Library Administration* 33, no. 1/2 (2001): 156–158; Deborah A. Curry and Glendora Johnson-Cooper, "African American Academic Librarians and the Profession: An Uncomfortable Fit?" (Unpublished manuscript); Cynthia Preston, "Perceptions of Discriminatory Practices and Attitude: A Survey of African American Librarians," *College and Research Libraries* 59 (Sept. 1998): 434–445; Joyce K. Thornton, "Job Satisfaction of Librarians of African Descent Employed in the Association of Research Libraries Academic Libraries," *College and Research Libraries* 60 (May 2000): 217–232.

57. Gregory L. Reese and Ernestine L. Hawkins, *Stop Talking, Start Doing! Attracting People of Color to the Library Profession* (Chicago: ALA, 1999), 34–35.

58. Kathleen de la Peña McCook and Kate Lippincott, "Planning for a Diverse Workforce in Library and Information Science" (Rev. ed., ERIC ED 402). (Tampa, FL: University of South Florida, School of Library and Information Science, Research Group), 948.

59. Kate Lippincott, "Growing a Diverse Workforce in the Library and Information Science Professions," ERIC Digest, ED411873.

60. Lippincott, "Growing a Diverse Workforce."

61. Carla Hayden, "New Approaches to Black Recruitment," in *The Black Librarian in America Revisited*, ed. E. J. Josey (Metuchen, NJ: The Scarecrow Press, Inc., 1994), 55–64; see also James C. Welbourne, Jr., "Black Recruitment: The Issue and an Approach," in *The Black Librarian in America*, ed. E. J. Josey (Metuchen, NJ: The Scarecrow Press, Inc., 1970), 92–97.

62. Hayden, "New Approaches to Black Recruitment," 59.

63. Hayden, "New Approaches to Black Recruitment," 60.

64. Ann Knight Randall, "Minority Recruitment in Librarianship," in *Librarians for the New Millennium*, ed. Willliam E. Moen and Kathleen Hein (Chicago: American Library Association, 1988), 11–25.

65. Reese and Hawkins, *Stop Talking, Start Doing!* 23–80.

66. Reese and Hawkins, *Stop Talking, Start Doing!* 23–80.

67. Reese and Hawkins, *Stop Talking, Start Doing!* 34–41.

68. Maurice B. Wheeler and Jaqueline Hanson, "Improving Diversity: Recruiting Students to the Library Profession," in *Libraries and Student Assistants*, ed. William K. Black (Binghamton, NY: The Haworth Press, Inc., 1995), 137–146.

8

A Web Model of Recruitment for LIS Doctoral Education: Weaving in Diversity[1]

Laurie Bonnici and Kathleen Burnett

Project Athena, a federally funded, multi-institutional effort to recruit new library and information studies (LIS) faculty, is one of several national efforts undertaken since the passage of the Higher Education Act of 1965 to stem the tide of projected shortages of information professionals and the faculty to educate them. Although the emphasis of federally funded programs shifted during the 1990s away from librarianship to educating the information technology workforce, in 2002 following the dot.com bust and the No Child Left Behind Act, the education of professional librarians reemerged as a focus of critical need.[2] Project Athena was funded by the Institute of Museum and Library Services (IMLS) in 2002, following the passage of the No Child Left Behind Act of that same year, but prior to the appropriation that funded the first round of Recruiting and Educating Librarians for the 21st Century grants.

FEDERAL PROGRAMS

Since 1965, federal legislation has provided funding for a number of efforts to address the shortage of adequately trained information professionals, including two that have recognized explicitly the need to increase the number and improve the quality of preparation of LIS faculty. The first, the Higher Education Act of 1965, Title II-B, funded a fellowship program "to alleviate the critical shortage of professionally trained librarians and the serious shortage of graduate library school faculty."[3] Funding for this program was administered by the Department of Education beginning in 1967 through the last call for applications in 1997.[4] In 1996, "legislation to create an Institute of

Museum and Library Services passed Congress and was signed by the President. This legislation reauthorize[d] federal library and museums programs, and move[d] federal library programs from the Department of Education to the Institute."[5] Included in the funding was a small allotment for a competitive program known as the National Leadership Grants. This program focuses on the improvement of library services and only occasionally and incidentally has funded fellowships and scholarships. In 2003, federal awareness of the impending shortage of professionally trained librarians resulted in a new competitive initiative known as Recruiting and Educating Librarians for the 21st Century. The No Child Left Behind Act of 2002 authorized funding for this initiative.[6]

HIGHER EDUCATION ACT OF 1965

The Higher Education Act of 1965, Title II-B, established the Library Career Training Program. The Higher Education Amendments of 1992 changed the program title to Library Education and Human Resource Development Program. Authorization of the Higher Education Act ceased in 1996. Over the course of the three decades that these programs were active, grants were made to more than 91 institutions of higher education totaling more than $46 million and more than 5,000 students were trained.[7] The priorities for funding of fellowships shifted several times, as did the rules and regulations under which the funding was administered. During the period 1985–1987, for example, the first two of four objectives emphasized recruitment of minorities: "Increase opportunities for members of underrepresented groups to obtain training in librarianship," and "Increase opportunities for professional advancement for members of underrepresented groups by providing training beyond the master's degree level." None of the six priorities in effect after 1987 reference minority participation at all.[8] The six priorities established in 1987 included one that specifically targeted doctoral education: "To increase excellence in library education by encouraging study in librarianship and related fields at the doctoral level," but this priority was not selected for funding until 1990.[9] The Higher Education Amendments of 1992 simplified the goals and objectives of the program for its remaining four years to "assist[ing] institutions of higher education and library organizations to: train persons in the principles and practices of librarianship and information science (including new techniques of information transfer and communication technology), and to recruit, educate, train, and retain minorities in the library and information professions."

Studies[10] that have reviewed these programs present strong evidence of success in meeting the stated goals and objectives. During seven years covered by the Owens report, for example, "88 doctoral, 17 post-master's and 223 master's fellowships were awarded. The amount of federal funds awarded to the 48 institutions of higher education covered in this seven-year study was $3,399,300."[11] Ninety-three percent of the fellows had either received—or it was reported by their institution that they would receive—the degree for which funding had been awarded. The success rate for doctoral students was not unexpectedly somewhat lower at 87 percent. There was no significant difference in completion rates by gender, and the success rate of minority fellows (93 percent) was slightly higher than that of non-minority fellows (92 percent). Fifty-two percent of the total awards between 1985 and 1991 were made to minorities, including 59 percent of master's, 50 percent of post-master's, and 33 percent of doctoral awards. Eleven percent of all fellows either withdrew or no information was available for them.

Nonetheless, the fellowship program was neither transferred to the IMLS when that agency was authorized by the Museum and Library Services Act of 1996, nor was there any language specific to the establishment of a similar program in either this act or the Museum and Library Services Conforming and Technical Amendments of 1997. Between 1997 and 2002, the remaining federal funding for fellowships and scholarships in information-related fields that existed was primarily targeted at preparation for the information technology workforce and administered by the National Science Foundation.

NO CHILD LEFT BEHIND ACT OF 2002

This situation changed with the signing of the No Child Left Behind Act in January 2002. The act emphasized the need to recruit and educate the next generation of professional librarians and led to the establishment of a new federally funded program administered by the IMLS entitled Recruiting and Educating Librarians for the 21st Century. Four priorities were established for this program: 1) Recruit and educate the next generation of librarians; 2) Develop faculty to educate the next generation of library professionals; 3) Enable pre-professional library staff to make the transition to librarianship, especially in locations where recruitment is historically difficult; and 4) Provide the library community with information needed to support successful recruitment and education of the next generation of librarians. Review of the first round of proposals was in process at the time this chapter was written, with expected announcement of awards in mid-October 2003.

ANTICIPATING NATIONAL PRIORITIES

Following the passage of the No Child Left Behind Act, but prior to the establishment of the Recruiting and Educating Librarians for the 21st Century program, faculty at the Florida State University School of Information Studies proposed a comprehensive plan to recruit, educate, and prepare LIS doctoral students to assume responsibility for educating future generations of librarians. The anticipated results of the project include: 1) Demonstration of a self-sustaining web recruitment model; 2) Doctoral education and training of six potential LIS faculty at three top-ranked LIS schools and support for education and training of twelve potential LIS faculty at the PhD-granting institution of their choice; 3) Development of an adaptable, sustainable course to prepare LIS doctoral students for faculty roles; and 4) Compilation of a standard set of resources and instruments to be adopted nationally to evaluate outcomes of LIS doctoral recruitment and education.

Implementation of this plan began in September 2002 as Project Athena (Spinning the Web of our Future). Anticipating the establishment of the Recruiting and Educating Librarians for the 21st Century grant program and the establishment of the national priorities mentioned above, the principal investigators recognized that a new generation of LIS faculty must be recruited to LIS doctoral programs if the number of students to be educated was to increase significantly. A mere 4 percent of students who earn the professional master's degree in library and information science pursue doctoral studies. Thus the number of new faculty available to replace their retiring colleagues at any time is low, a fact that has been recognized since the passage of the Higher Education Act of 1965. This, coupled with the national push to increase enrollments, as well as projected increases in retirement levels due to the graying of the professorate, makes the situation at the beginning of the twenty-first century an alarming one. A review of the status of the LIS faculty job market in recent years points out the magnitude of the problem. Unfilled faculty positions increased from forty-two to fifty-five between 1996 and 2000.[12] The seriousness of this shortfall was further emphasized by the job–posting to job–candidate ratios for 1998–2001 at the ALISE annual conference. In 2000 and 2001, that ratio was greater than 2:1. In response to these alarming trends, ALISE President Prudence Dalrymple (2001–2002) selected recruiting, training, and supporting the next generation of LIS faculty as the theme for the 2002 ALISE national conference. At the 2002 ALISE conference, fifty of the fifty-three member LIS schools posted one or more job vacancies, while only thirty-five applicants filed resumes expressing interest in obtaining a faculty position.[13] Clearly recruitment of the next generation of LIS faculty was a priority of national importance before the No Child Left Behind Act was signed. The announcement of a $10 million initiative for 2003 to recruit a new generation of librarians raised the priority to a higher level of concern.

DESIGNING A RECRUITMENT MODEL FOR NATIONAL EFFECT

Recognizing that the scope of the challenge confronting LIS doctoral education extended well beyond individual institutions and that meeting this challenge would require inter-institutional cooperation rather than competition, the principal investigators of Project Athena focused on the development of a comprehensive recruitment model aimed at benefiting all LIS doctoral degree-granting programs in the United States. The model serves two purposes. The first purpose is to provide and demonstrate strategies and techniques that can be replicated to ensure that a sufficient number of new students will be recruited to LIS doctoral programs to provide an adequate and sustainable pool of faculty candidates. The second purpose is to ensure that these strategies and techniques are deployed in such a manner that the diversity of that pool is dramatically improved, and once this is accomplished, that this improvement can be sustained. This latter purpose is essential to the health of a profession that strives to serve an increasingly diverse and underserved population. The recruitment model is therefore based on a web-like design that acknowledges the importance of personal connections in making choices regarding education and employment goals. To ensure that this "network" or "web" recruitment model will have lasting national effect, it is necessary that its benefits extend very quickly to all LIS PhD-granting institutions. To this end, the deliverables of Project Athena are designed to be flexible, easily adopted, and self-sustaining.[14]

PROJECT ATHENA: SPINNING THE RECRUITMENT WEB

The first of the four components of Project Athena is the self-sustaining web recruitment model. The model consists of a web of institutions that focuses on establishing cooperative relationships between institutions and institution-types.

To establish a foundation for national effect of the recruitment model and to ensure a continual flow of new doctoral students sufficient to meet the needs for LIS faculty in the next decade and beyond, the principal investigators invited two other leading doctoral degree-granting institutions at the University of Illinois and the University of Washington to work collaboratively with six doctoral fellows for each of the three years of the grant period. Each of the six fellows will work with one non-doctoral degree-granting LIS school (sponsor school) to recruit promising students and alumni to enter LIS doctoral programs. The first new student recruited by each doctoral fellow to be fully admitted to the LIS doctoral program of their choice in the second and third years of the funding cycle will receive a $1,000 scholarship.

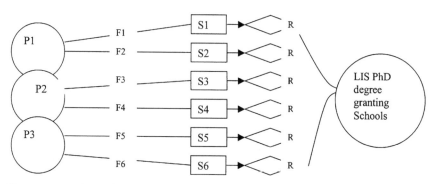

Figure 8.1. Project Athena, Year 1

Considering the participation of the three partnering institutions, the six sponsor schools, and at least one potential doctoral student recruit per fellow attending one of the LIS doctoral degree-granting schools, 33 percent of the LIS schools in the United States will potentially be involved by the second year. As the recruitment process continues through the second year, the potential involvement escalates. There are no restrictive factors that exclude any LIS school from participating in the recruitment process.[15] This approach ensures the project's national effect, sustainability, and adaptability.

WEAVING THE THREADS OF DIVERSITY

A diverse professoriate is essential to assuring diversity among practicing librarians, since faculty often serve as role models for students seeking the professional degrees, as well as those preparing to become faculty themselves. A project sponsored by the Pew Charitable Trusts surveyed 3,956 students enrolled in the third year or beyond of doctoral study. Students included a representative sample from twenty-seven universities, representing eleven arts and sciences disciplines. The sample population consisted of the following demographic representation:

African American	5.3 percent
Asian American	4.4 percent
Hispanic	3.9 percent
Native American	0.8 percent

The Pew Study statistics show an underrepresentation of minority populations preparing to serve as future faculty at major universities.[16] For this reason, the co-principal investigators of Project Athena made recruitment of minorities a major goal in implementation of the recruitment model.

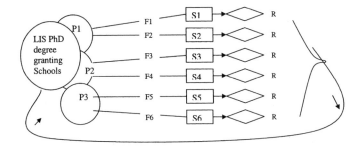

Figure 8.2. Project Athena, Year 2

Recruitment criteria and factors were derived from the ALA's criteria for recruiting Spectrum Scholars[17] and Winston's factors that cause individuals to accept recruitment into the library field.[18] The criteria and factors were modified to establish the basis for the Project Athena LIS faculty recruitment model. Project Athena factors emphasize role modeling, personal contact, and financial support. The Project Athena criteria are used to select doctoral fellows, balancing personal characteristics with potential for scholarship and scholarly and professional performance records (see tables 8.1 and 8.2).

Applying this model of recruitment, the three Project Athena partner schools have recruited the first-year round of doctoral fellows. Four of the six first-year Project Athena doctoral fellows are minorities. This number represents 8 percent of the newly enrolled students for fall 2003 in the three partner schools' doctoral programs.[19]

Following the model's outline, these doctoral fellows, along with faculty at the Project Athena sponsor schools, will apply the same criteria and factors to potential doctoral recruits. Sustaining this process forms the model web of recruitment as illustrated in figure 8.3.

Doctoral fellows serve as the nucleus of energy for continued recruitment of a diverse doctoral student population. Attrition through graduation will extend the diversity to the LIS professoriate. Future generations of librarians are educated by the professoriate.

PROJECT EVALUATION AND ASSESSMENT

Project Athena will be evaluated on several levels. The recruitment model will be evaluated using both process-based and outcomes-based evaluative measures. Process-based evaluation measures will be used to discern the

Table 8.1.   Recruitment Criteria

Spectrum's Criteria	*Project Athena Criteria*
1. Motivation	Motivation to pursue doctoral study
2. Energy	Energy
3. An open mind	An open mind
4. Commitment to diversity	Commitment to diversity
5. Commitment to learning more about diversity	Commitment to role-modeling
6. An awareness of how diversity impacts the design and delivery of library and information service	An awareness of how diversity impacts the design and delivery of LIS education
7. Commitment to librarianship	Commitment to pursuing a faculty position
8. A spirit of service	A spirit of service
9. Constructive critique of issues	Constructive critique of issues
10. Willingness to engage in dialogue and discourse	Willingness to engage in dialogue and discourse
11. Ability to relate to groups other than your own	Ability to relate to groups other than your own
12. Professionalism	Professionalism
13. Professional references	Scholarly and professional references
14. A completed application and official transcripts	Acceptance to the doctoral program of the student's choice
15. An understanding that the Spectrum Initiative is recruitment, scholarship, leadership development, and giving back what you can	An understanding that commitment to the Athena Project and LIS education is recruitment, scholarship, leadership development, and giving back what you can

strengths and weaknesses of the model as the project unfolds, so that iterative improvements can be implemented as needed. The data sets compiled for the goals-based evaluation will be examined incrementally (annually) to measure change through ongoing processes. Focus group interviews will be conducted with the doctoral fellows and faculty of the partnering and sponsor institutions regarding the perceived effectiveness of the recruitment model at the end of the each year. The questions will be tailored to examine the effectiveness of the web model for increasing doctoral enrollment. During the second year, Project Athena participants will work with IMLS to identify and design outcomes-based evaluative measures to be implemented at

Table 8.2.   Recruitment Factors

Winston's Factors	*Project Athena Factors*
1. Personal desire to enter the profession of librarianship	Personal desire to further commitment to LIS
2. Information provided by role models and/or influence on to consider librarianship as a profession	Information provided by role models (doctoral fellows, sponsor faculty, co-PIs) and/or individuals influence of role models on individuals to consider doctoral study w/ goal of faculty employment
3. The availability of financial aid or scholarships	6 3-year doctoral fellowships; 6 $1000 scholarships to be awarded each year for two years to the first new doctoral recruit by each doctoral fellowship
4. Paraprofessional or student assistant library positions held by individuals which, in turn, motivated them to consider the profession	Professional experience post-graduation held by individuals which, in turn, motivated them to consider faculty employment
5. Appreciation for the work in which librarians are engaged, which has encouraged them to consider the information profession as a career	Appreciation of and performance in scholarly graduate-level work, which has encouraged them to consider pursuing doctoral work and a faculty position
6. Appreciation of the environment of library work	Appreciation of the academic environment
7. Interest in entering a service position	Interest in entering a faculty position
8. Availability of professional positions in the field of library education and information science	Availability of faculty positions in LIS
9. Image of the profession	Image of academic life
10. Salaries paid to library and information professionals	Salaries paid to LIS faculty

the end of the project to assess its diffusion beyond the project participants. In this assessment, the principal investigators will be looking for indicators that the web of recruitment has extended beyond the initial web of institutions to LIS education (e.g., increased enrollment and/or increased minority enrollment at schools other than the original partner schools).

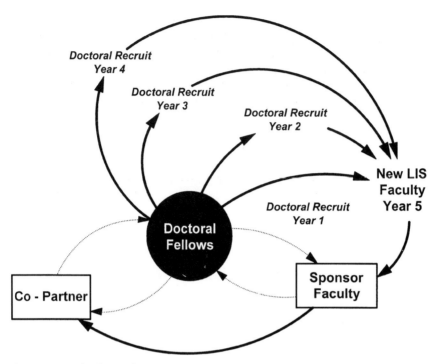

Figure 8.3. Web of Recruitment

THE WEB WEAVES ON

A compilation of assessment resources, instruments, and data analysis tools developed and refined for future use in the evaluation of LIS PhD recruitment and education will be made accessible to all doctoral degree-granting institutions at the completion of the project through the establishment of a Project Athena Center for Outcomes Assessment of LIS PhD Education website. The website will be maintained and technical, data collection, and data analysis support provided for at least five years following the conclusion of the grant award.

In sum, Project Athena addresses government-established national priorities focused on meeting the goal of ensuring that a sufficient number of new librarians are prepared to meet the nation's information needs. Special initiatives to support service-based outcomes, such as the No Child Left Behind Act, are rare in times of economic recession. This act recognizes the importance of librarianship as a navigator and equalizer in the information economy. The nationally recognized need to increase the supply of well-prepared librarians ensures that the demand for Project Athena deliverables will be high, because this supply cannot be increased without a commensurate increase in the faculty to prepare them. Today, as for the past forty years, the LIS educational community is trapped in an endless loop of a need to recruit new doctoral students to become faculty to educate the next generation of librarians. The Project Athena Web Recruitment Model offers hope that simple strategies and techniques, when strategically deployed, may break this endless cycle, resulting in a better served and better informed citizenry.

NOTES

1. The authors wish to acknowledge the support of the Institute of Museum and Library Services. Jane B. Robbins and Judith Mulholland (Florida State University) serve as additional co-PIs (co-principal investigators) with Project Athena. Harry Bruce (University of Washington) and Linda Smith (University of Illinois, Urbana-Champaign) serve as partner school coordinators.

2. Library Science is also included as a "graduate assistance area of national need" and LIS programs may apply for funding of fellowships through the Department of Education's GAANN fellowship program.

3. Janice Owens, *Learning and Earning Analysis of HEA Title II-B, Graduate Library Fellowship Program recipients, fiscal years 1985–91* (Washington, DC: U.S. Department of Education, National Institute on Postsecondary Education, Libraries and Lifelong Learning), iv.

4. *The Bowker Annual Library and Book Trade Almanac* (Medford, NJ: Information Today, 1998).

5. Museum and Library Services Act 2003, /www.imls.gov/about/abt_1996.htm (accessed 17 September 2003).

6. The discussion in this chapter is limited to federally funded programs. Other initiatives of national scope include ALA's Spectrum Scholarships, begun in 1997.

7. U.S. Dept. of Education, 1996.

8. U.S. Dept. of Education, 1996, 4.

9. U.S. Dept. of Education, 1996, 4.

10. William D. Ford, "Federal Library Programs: Past, Present and Future," *Library Journal* 104, no. 16 (1979): 1768–72.

11. U.S. Dept. of Education, 1996, 3.

12. These numbers reflect the number of positions that were advertised but not filled at the end of each recruiting year.

13. Data are unavailable for the 2003 ALISE Conference job placement activities. As of November 2003, 21 open positions have been posted to the ALISE jobs website and Jesse listserv.

14. Prior to the start of the project, the co-PIs met with a wide cross-section of the LIS education community to solicit their input into the project design. Meetings with LIS educators and practitioners to formalize this feedback loop are planned at regular intervals throughout the project cycle.

15. The partner institutions have agreed to work with any non-doctoral-granting LIS school willing to fund the full travel costs in the recruitment effort. In these cases, the doctoral fellow or scholarship holder will receive the same training and opportunities

and will provide the same services on behalf of Project Athena. Other PhD-granting institutions are aware of the project and many have agreed to supplement scholarship awards with tuition waivers or by matching the scholarship in subsequent years.

16. Chris M. Golde and Timothy M. Dore, *At Cross Purposes: What the Experiences of Today's Doctoral Students Reveal about Doctoral Education* (Philadelphia, PA: The Pew Charitable Trusts, 2001). Available at: www.phd-survey.org

17. American Library Association. Committee on Diversity. *Spectrum Report 1997–2000* (Chicago: American Library Association, 2001).

18. Mark D. Winston, "The Role of Recruitment in Achieving Goals Related to Diversity in Academic Libraries," *College & Research Libraries* 59, no. 3 (1998): 240–247.

19. A study is currently in progress to collect data for all LIS schools with doctoral programs to determine 2003 new student enrollment for doctoral programs. Data collection will allow for an analysis of national level impact for minority recruitment.

9

Creating Opportunities and Opening Doors: Recruiting and Mentoring Students of Color

Loriene Roy

This chapter explores the meaning of mentoring, its organization, and effect. It describes students' need for mentoring and provides advice for both mentees and mentors. It also describes the particular pressures students of color face, underscoring their need for mentors. The article closes with recommendations that faculty engage in promoting mentoring through research, in teaching, and through personal engagement.

WHAT IS MENTORING?

A mentor is "a person who takes an exceptionally strong interest in the professional development of the mentee."[1] Mentoring is a topic of concern across disciplines. January is now celebrated as National Mentoring Month, an event organized by the Harvard Mentoring Project and MENTOR/National Mentoring Partnership to promote mentoring among the general population.[2]

Mentoring is commonly discussed in the context of library and information science (LIS), especially in human resources management and professional education. LIS professions use mentoring as an intervention to fill the gaps in professional education and on-the-job training. Evidence of professional interest in mentoring can be seen in the programs of recent professional conferences, such as the program sponsored by the Association for Library Service to Children, "Pardon Me for Being a Manager IV: Growing Your Own: Mentoring as Recruiting," at the 2002 ALA Annual Conference.[3]

There are also a number of professionally supported mentoring opportunities within ALA and its divisions and units. The Association of College & Research Libraries (ACRL) has a mentoring program for new members, as well as a College Library Directors Mentor Program.[4] The New Members Round Table has a Standing Mentoring Committee that organizes a variety of services for new professionals, including an annual orientation program at the ALA annual conference, a "Students-to-ALA" experience that provides housing and registration support for students in ALA-accredited programs to participate in an annual ALA conference, and a mentor/mentee matching service.[5] Regional mentors of color have been available to ALA Spectrum Scholars.[6] The International Relations Office of ALA recruits experienced conference-goers to mentor international librarians planning to attend the ALA annual conference.[7] The Association for Library Collections & Technical Services's Cataloging and Classification Section has organized a program called Education, Training, and Recruitment for Cataloging that includes mentoring.[8] New members to the Reference and User Services Association's Collection Development & Evaluation Section can request a mentor.[9] ACRL, the American Association for School Librarians, and the Public Library Association all participate in National Job Shadow Day, inviting young people to accompany information professionals in the workplace.[10]

Other information service organizations are also involved in mentoring arrangements. In 2002, the Association for Library and Information Science Education began a mentoring program pairing doctoral students and new faculty with more experienced faculty members.[11] The Special Libraries Association honors an association member who has been an exceptional mentor to students or practitioners with the Rose L. Vormelker Award.[12] A key goal of the Department of Information Studies at UCLA's federally funded PRAXIS (Practice, Reflection, Advocacy, Excellence, Inquiry, Solutions) program is to organize a support team for eight pre-doctoral students of color.[13] These supporters include faculty advisers, peer doctoral student advisors, and formal mentoring by faculty members of color in other library and information science schools.

A number of publications feature prominent librarians and the role of mentoring in their professional development.[14] Sheldon conducted in-depth interviews with sixty public library leaders "to gain an understanding of the qualities [they] held in common."[15] She asked five questions in her interviews:

1. What are your strengths and weaknesses?
2. Was there any particular experience or event in your life that influenced your management philosophy or style?
3. What were the major decision points in your career, and how do you feel about your choices now?
4. What, if any, has been the influence of mentors in your career?
5. How do you feel about the future of the profession?[16]

Bennis and Nanus had posed the first three questions to ninety business leaders they interviewed for their book *Leaders: The Strategies for Taking Charge*.[17] Sheldon added the final two questions to focus the study more on the field of library and information science.

Sheldon's respondents differentiated between mentors, role models, and the wider contacts of a peer network.[18] Role models were individuals of standing within the field who provided examples of achievement through their own lives but did not have personal contact with the mentee. Sheldon notes that mentoring relationships are useful at various stages of a professional career, from the first job to positions of increasing responsibility.[19] The Council of Graduate Schools distinguishes among advisers, supporters, tutors, masters, sponsors, and those who serve as "models of identity."[20] The University of Michigan's Rackham School of Business recommends that students gather a mentoring team.[21] Students may need several mentors, each of whom might provide different types of guidance—advice on skills attainment, career guidance, and support.[22]

HOW ARE MENTORING PROGRAMS ORGANIZED?

In some ways, professionally organized mentoring programs aim to equalize the "good old boy" and "good old girl" networks, opening opportunities for a larger audience of beneficiaries. The National Mentoring Center identifies types of mentoring programs: school-based, faith-based, community-based, career/vocational, peer mentoring, and e-mentoring.[23] Mentoring may take the form of offering personal advice; providing employment references, current awareness updates about opportunities, or contacts with others; and long-range career planning. The National Mentoring Partnership provides a "Learn to Mentor Toolkit" that includes a variety of useful forms, including a mentor/mentee agreement, personal assessment forms, forms to help identify goals and objectives, and forms to help prioritize activities and solve problems.[24] Communication can take place face-to-face or via a variety of other communication means, especially through e-mail. Even a brief contact may be very influential if it occurs during a critical moment.[25] Mentoring relationships often are not structured and evolve over time. Some endure for long periods and others last until both mentors and mentees are satisfied with the outcome.

Sheldon notes that locating a mentor can be a difficult task.[26] The profession has provided some formal approaches to connecting mentors with protégés. Some of these approaches are integrated into leadership training programs. Since 1994, the Texas Accelerated Library Leaders (TALL), Texans Leadership Development Institute, has brought approximately twenty early-career professionals to a five-day retreat in the Texas hill country each June.[27]

There, they participate in continuing education experiences focusing on leadership. Six mentors are selected to join each year's class of TALL Texans. One attendee described mentorship as one of the most valuable components of the Snowbird Leadership Institute, which was established in 1990 and is attended annually by thirty librarians who are in the first five years of their careers.[28]

ACRL provides a brief online workbook to guide mentors and mentees.[29] The workbook lists responsibilities for mentors and mentees in a twelve-month rolling timeline from March to February.

WHAT MAKES A SUCCESSFUL MENTORING PROGRAM? CAN MENTORING MAKE A DIFFERENCE?

Shreve reports that mutual commitment to the process is the key ingredient for a successful match.[30] Sipe reminds us "the key to creating effective mentoring relationships lies in the development of trust between two strangers."[31] The mentor assumes the initial responsibility for building trust. In her literature review, Sipe identified the three essential characteristics of a successful mentoring program: mentor/mentee screening, orientation and training, and support with supervision.[32]

Child Trends, a nonprofit research organization, identified characteristics of successful mentor/mentee programs. These programs have:

1. Structure and planning (including a mission statement and principles of operation);
2. Pre-match training;
3. Post-match training and support;
4. Supervised matches;
5. Matches based on mentor/mentee interests;
6. Social as well as academic support; and
7. Flexibility based on the needs of the mentee.[33]

Mentoring Australia adds that successful mentoring programs also should be connected to an official organization; be in congruence with Equal Employment Opportunity requirements; be inclusive as to ethnicity, gender, sexual orientation, and culture; and have policies that protect confidentiality.[34]

Grossman and Johnson list three measurements to use in evaluating mentoring programs: participant outcomes; effectiveness of mentor/mentee relationships, and characteristics of mentors and mentees.[35] The Edna McConnell Clark Foundation funded a study of the effect of mentoring on youth development. The researchers evaluated ten mentoring programs, including Big Brothers/Big Sisters and Campus Partners. They found that young mentees had lower rates of absenteeism from school, had more positive attitudes toward school, and behaved better at school. Mentored youth were also more likely to attend college and less likely to use drugs and alcohol. Mentoring also improved the students' relationships with their parents. Mentored students also experienced more peer support and had a more positive attitude toward volunteering to help others. These positive outcomes were more apt to arise when mentoring relationships extended more than twelve months. In fact, young people involved in short-term mentoring arrangements could experience a negative effect. Disadvantaged or at-risk students were more apt to benefit from mentoring arrangements. Mentees paired with same-race mentors were as successful as matches between mentors and mentees of different ethnic backgrounds.[36]

ADVICE FOR MENTEES AND MENTORS

MENTOR/National Mentoring Partnership estimates that half of U.S. youth aged 10 to 18 years seek mentors.[37] Sheldon identified some characteristics of mentees: high intelligence, ambition, strong communication skills, high energy levels, openness, and strong listening skills.[38] Shreve adds that the successful mentee is also assertive and open to learn from the mentoring process.[39]

The National Mentoring Partnership describes the attributes of mentors who are successful. These are individuals who:

1. Have a sincere desire to be involved with a young person;
2. Respect young people;
3. Actively listen;
4. Empathize;
5. See solutions and opportunities; and
6. Are flexible and open.[40]

Sipe further described less effective mentors as those who do not meet regularly with mentees, are authoritative in their approach, and focus on changing the behavior of the mentee rather than on instilling trust and respect.[41]

AOL Time Warner Foundation conducted a national poll of 2,000 adults in 2002 and found that an estimated 57 million adults from 18 to 44 years old indicated that they were willing to mentor others. Almost half of the poll respondents were willing to be an online mentor to a young person. Almost all (99 percent) of those currently involved in mentoring said that they would recommend that others become mentors. Mentors also wanted assistance to provide the best services they could: they desired orientation and training and ongoing access to consultants who could provide advanced help, and two-thirds (67 percent) wished that their employers would compensate their mentoring efforts with paid time off.[42]

Sheldon noted that a person's demeanor and personality influenced his effectiveness as a mentor.[43] The National Mentoring Partnership identifies the three strengths a mentor can bring to the mentee: advice, access, and advocacy.[44] Good mentors show a willingness to commit time to the relationship. Mentors are visible "because they love their work, they believe that what they are doing is important, they are results-oriented, and they achieve remarkable standards of service."[45] Cargill describes attainment in the mentor/mentee relationship:

> The ideal is that mentor and mentee move toward establishing a peer relationship in which there is graceful acceptance of the fact that the protégé may progress further in a career path than the mentor did.[46]

STUDENTS OF COLOR AND THE NEED FOR MENTORING

In choosing to pursue education beyond secondary school, a student of color may select to be forever apart from her family and removed from her culture. This sense of isolation means that the student's immediate family, while they may speak of pride about her accomplishments, may treat her differently. A student might be severing lifelong ties that could result in spending long periods of her life away from her family. She may be the first generation in her family to continue on to college. It is possible that no near relatives made the same choice. A student of color may know no one who furthered their education or who could provide her with support from which she can draw.

In choosing to go to college, a student of color may feel that she is denying her culture. In a survey conducted in 1987 at Northern Arizona University, Cibik and Chambers reported that minority undergraduates felt a loss of their "familiar past."[47] If the student was raised in her tradition, then there may be a fear of acculturation, or losing cultural identity. If cultural ties were not developed, the student may lose the opportunity to establish or extend them. The student may then embark on a lifelong process of separating family history from cultural history.

Horstman described the guilt felt by migrants for escaping the obligation to "share the common burden."[48] If he relocates to attend school, a student of color may experience cultural guilt for those who do not have a similar opportunity.

Once enrolled in an academic program, the student of color is faced with numerous pressures and obstacles. These may range from difficulty with certain evaluation methods to homesickness and adjustments necessitated by relocating.[49] A student may experience a tremendous loneliness for family and a familiar landscape. In moving to an urban setting, he may have to make certain basic decisions—such as those involved in securing accommodations—alone for the first time. The student may need to learn to drive or find driving conditions very different. The first year and first semester is an especially crucial time when students are at high risk of dropping out due to an inability to integrate into the social and academic setting.

Minority students are more apt to go home often to help their families. Other students may feel that they have a choice in returning home periodically; a student of color may feel that there is no choice. He must be there. Cibik and Chambers found that Native American university students indicated that they were more apt to miss class to help their families or to attend events tied to their culture.[50] By entering college, the student of color becomes the role model for others, the role model they may never have had. The student may now find himself in a position where he cannot reveal that he needs support and instead assume the lifelong role of supporting others.

Students of color may find they have very different backgrounds from the majority of other beginning college students. Cibik and Chambers found significant differences between minority and non-minority students.[51] Minority students were typically older and more apt to be married and from a larger family, with four or more children.[52] Non–African American minority students were more apt to be from either a rural area or a small town.[53] Except for Asian students, parents of minority students were more likely to have completed fewer years of education.[54] Among minority students, Native American students had parents with the fewest years of education.[55]

Students of color may face greater economic pressures than non-minority students. Their grades may be consistently lower; there is a higher rate of attrition among some students of color.[56] Cultural differences may explain some of their difficulties. Cibik and Chambers found that Native American university students wanted help in study skills, reading and writing skills, and test-taking skills, yet did not take advantage of such services when they were available.[57] Measures of achievement take the form of merit-based awards, such as grades, based on individual competitiveness, instead of group problem-solving.[58]

Away from home and in school, students of color may have to face overt displays of discrimination, perhaps for the first time in their lives. Removal from their native environments may expose students to new biases. The students may face pressure from others to know everything about their cultures. Or they may be totally ignored by others because of malice, disinterest, or disappointment. For instance, disappointment may arise when they do not fulfill someone's expectation of what an Indian should be. There will be those who will only be interested in students if their cultural ties are strong.

For self-preservation, students may learn to be guarded, to evaluate the motives of individuals interested in their culture, and to become somewhat suspicious.

If there are other students of color, they may be invisible to each other. They may come from greatly different backgrounds: from urban centers or rural areas, be affiliated with different cultural communities, or have different degrees of cultural background. Away from their families, they may redefine themselves culturally, acquiring a more homogenized culture by drawing from other students or the traditions of the peoples in the new locality.

Students may encounter classmates who are similar to those whom Medicine calls "Indians of convenience": individuals with no cultural affiliation who claim ethnic identities to take advantage of affirmative action policies to recruit minority students, especially those with strong academic potential.[59]

If they receive support for their studies in the form of scholarships and/or fellowships, their classmates or faculty may use that status as an excuse to ostracize them. In this sense, financial aid makes students of color even more separate. Some will regard them as unqualified, while to others they are exceptional.

Acceptance of a high-profile award may create a spotlight effect as students realize that others will monitor their progress more closely. Such awards may carry with them responsibilities to be a new generation of spokespeople for other students of color.

If students of color drop out, this may be seen as inevitable. This may be perceived as a desired event, something their families, even at the unspoken level, may have desired. Native students often follow a pattern of "stopping out": frequent and sometimes lengthy leaves punctuate their higher education.[60] When Native students with stop-out evidence in their undergraduate years apply to graduate programs, admissions committees see their records as dubious.

The drop-outs themselves are worthy of study. What is the effect on their families, on their peers, and on students of color who subsequently enroll at the same institution? They may feel the effect of their schooling as they reenter their culture after dropping out or continuing their education. In continuing her education, the Native woman of color may restrict her marital choices.[61] An Anglo woman does not face the probability that her decision to attend college may mean that she may never marry an Anglo man. To a woman of color this may, indeed, be what she accepts by pursuing a college degree.

For the student of color who receives her undergraduate degree, the best option may be to enter a graduate program. In graduate school, the student faces additional pressures and obstacles. The graduate academic environment is more competitive. During advanced studies, success is measured through completion of specified stages of progress: the program of studies or coursework; research tools; foreign language; oral, written, and comprehensive examinations; proposal development; advancement to candidacy; dissertation preparation and defense; and deposit of dissertation.

The student may find herself relocating again to accept targeted funds or study in a desired subject area. Professors may expect more of her, especially if the student is the recipient of targeted financial aid. Professors may reserve mentoring relationships for students more like themselves. If selected as a mentee, the mentor, who fulfills a much desired affiliation with someone experienced in the profession, may ask the student to relinquish cultural affiliation. The mentor or chairperson becomes god.

The student of color interested in a graduate degree may be advised into certain disciplines deemed acceptable, such as education and social services. In enrolling in graduate studies, he or she may have to learn a new discipline. The student also faces the difficulty of becoming trained in appropriate research methods. In testing possible dissertation areas, she may find herself applying newly acquired analytical tools to analyze her own background. While Medicine reported that recent doctoral recipients had a "more positive self-image" if they became involved in issues related to their Native heritage, a focus on her ethnicity may be seen by a Native American woman's faculty as inferior or unacceptable.[62]

Macias interviewed eleven American Indian women enrolled in a graduate social work program and found that they used multi-modal study techniques.[63] While the students felt they did not do well in certain traditional testing situations, such as in answering true/false and multiple-choice questions, they did very well in essay examinations that allowed them to synthesize and analyze.[64] They had the ability to relate and apply what they learned; they were successful at integrating their educational experience with real-world experiences.[65] They also felt they were good listeners and were especially skilled at nonjudgmental listening. Macias also noted some difficulties the Native American graduate students faced: they indicated that they had difficulty adopting the impersonal tone of academic writing and in acquiring the appropriate scholarly vocabulary.[66]

After making the choice to pursue advanced study and earning one or more post-secondary degrees, the student of color may face a lack of employment opportunities. This is especially the case in geographic locations close to her cultural affiliation. She may be pressured to "work for the benefit of the people." For a non-minority student, working for a social group or cause is largely an option and is seen as a choice of self-sacrifice and vision. For a person of color, it may be expected.

Students of color who pursue a career in higher education may find that socialization in academic life is another obstacle. If they accept a tenure-track position, the road to tenure and job security may be an ill-defined one. A new faculty member, especially when she is on a tenure-track, must ask,

"What am I doing today to ensure that I will get tenure?" Typically, to majority faculty members, that means balancing the priorities of research, teaching, and service to the professional community. Where does meeting with students of color come into play? How do students balance involvement in their cultural communities with the demands of employment and studies? Recruiting students of color? Answering the surveys from researchers interviewing minorities in higher education? Participating in advancing social causes? What counts? When? While the student may not have had a mentor, he or she will be sought out to serve as a role model. When does the student say no? How does she balance everything to meet the needs of the professional position, her personal life, the extended family, and her cultural community?

There are advantages to being a person of color in higher education. First is the acceptance from other people of color who respect differences and acknowledge the strength it takes to achieve. Second is the opportunity to change opinions, challenge stereotypes, and to prove that the exception is in fact the rule. Third is the ability to serve as a role model and to provide the opportunity for faculty and students to learn about a non-dominant culture. Finally, there are the advantages when the student steps into a setting with no prior history. Here he can take advantage of being able to carve out a new character and combine this with the daily struggle to preserve what attributes are considered valuable in his ethnic culture.

MENTORING AS A STRATEGY FOR INCREASING REPRESENTATION

There is no one solution to increasing the number of people of color with postsecondary degrees and those employed in higher education. It is clear that more financial aid is needed. Cibik and Chambers note that finances are the greatest barrier to minority undergraduates completing their degrees.[67] Students rely on an educational institution's financial aid package more than any other source of funding for higher education. Minority students may be unaware of campus career planning and placement efforts. Such services are especially needed since minority students seek help at minority student centers first, counseling centers next, then faculty and staff. When Native American college students need help, they may prefer to approach someone who shares a similar background. Cibik and Chambers recommend that every college or university be charged with the responsibility of retaining minority students by maintaining supportive services and initiating new programs that cater to minorities.[68] The same should be true for individual units, such as LIS programs.

Mentoring is not without its disadvantages. Sheldon found that library leaders noted that there were disadvantages in "hooking one's wagon to a 'star'" and following a mentor's model too closely.[69] In this case, the mentor's influence will quickly diminish if he is no longer in a position of power. Harris wrote of "the mentoring trap: a warning for entry-level librarians [that] mentor–protégé relationships may help a select few, but they haven't catapulted enough women or minorities to leading roles."[70]

Mentoring "is simple and makes sense. It relies primarily on volunteers and thus is relatively inexpensive. It is not a government program. And by drawing on individuals' best motives . . . and making links between people, it makes citizens more civilly concerned and engaged."[71]

Nichols noted that mentors can also help protégés begin to view themselves as leaders.[72] Mentors and mentees in ACRL's New Member Mentoring Program identified these benefits of the program: (1) availability of impartial and objective advice; (2) exchange of new ideas; (3) strengthening of professional identity; (4) development of new professional contacts; and (4) retention in the profession and in the organization.[73] Sheldon's leaders indicated that they all had mentors at the beginning of their careers and many of the leaders still were in contact with these early influences. These mentors helped train the library leaders to become mentors in their own right. As Sheldon notes, "mentoring links generations of leaders."[74]

Faculty, especially, have much to gain through mentoring. Their mentees may collaborate on research and service projects or bring their attention to new information, and they may gain personal satisfaction and professional recognition.[75] Mentors may also strengthen their leadership skills.[76]

RECOMMENDATIONS TO LIS FACULTY

Mentoring is a flexible concept that brings opportunities to both mentors and mentees. Yet, with the many responsibilities they face to balance teaching, research, and service, library science educators may view mentoring as the domain of the library administrator. How do we convince faculty of schools of library and information science that mentoring should continue beyond the structure of formalized coursework? This article concludes with suggestions on how to support mentoring through publication and research, teaching, and engagement.

Recommendation One: Support Mentoring Through Publication and Research

Faculty can assist practitioners in documenting and sharing accounts of successful mentoring activities. This includes writing articles featuring mentor and mentee matches. Faculty can also contribute professional biographies. Biographies provide others with role models who educate through their life stories.

Faculty should be encouraged to conduct research on mentoring. They might start by studying and reporting on interdisciplinary mentoring efforts in fields such as education and engineering. Sheldon's study provided evidence that library leaders were supported by mentors. Further studies could identify successful mentors and their strategies. Researchers might also propose and test mentoring models, such as comparing face-to-face mentoring with other means of communication, including electronic mentoring. In spring 2003, the Institute of Museum and Library Services announced grants available for "Recruiting and Educating Librarians for the 21st Century." Federal funding is now available to explore mentoring approaches to increase the number of professional librarians.

Recommendation Two: Mentoring Can Find a Place in the Classroom

Faculty have many opportunities to provide students with course content and direct experience with mentoring. Content on mentoring can be covered not only through traditional pedagogical approaches—assigned readings, class discussion, guest lectures from practitioners, literature reviews, and term papers—but also through providing students with opportunities to mentor each other through peer coaching and involvement in community service learning experiences.

Recommendation Three: Model Mentoring Through Engagement

Many students look to faculty as their first professional role models. Faculty who acknowledge their mentors and engage in mentoring encourage their students to follow their example. Willingness to mentor is evidence that an individual is progressing through a healthy professional life cycle. Mentoring can help the experienced librarian engage in life review, "the reflection on and return to past life experiences in order to think about and reintegrate them into present life circumstances."[77]

CONCLUSION

The positive effect of mentoring has been evident since ancient times. Homer's mentor was an elder who helped groom Telemachus, while his father Odysseus fought the Trojan War and his mother Penelope juggled the demands of her suitors. The field of library and information science acknowledges and respects the potential of the mentor–protégé relationship. Belief in the power of mentoring is a belief in the future of the profession: "The leaders of today have continuing responsibility to ensure that there emerges a continuing wave of new leaders."[78]

NOTES

1. Brooke E. Sheldon, *Leaders in Libraries: Styles and Strategies for Success* (Chicago: ALA, 1991), 52.

2. Harvard School of Public Health Center for Health Communication. "January is National Mentoring Month." http://www.hsph.harvard.edu/chc/mentoringmonth/ (accessed 3 January 2003).

3. American Library Association, ALA Annual Conference Program, Atlanta, GA, 13–19 June, 2002, 127.

4. American Library Association, Association of College & Research Libraries. "ACRL New Member Mentoring Program Workbook." www.ala.org/acrl/mentorwb .html (accessed 3 January 2003); American Library Association, Association of College & Research Libraries, College Libraries Section, "The College Library Directors Mentor Program." www.ala.org/acrl/cls/mentorprogram.html (accessed 3 January 2003).

5. American Library Association, New Members Round Table, Mentoring Committee. www.ala.org/nmrt/hdbk/mentoring.html (accessed 3 January 2003).

6. Christine Watkins, "Can Librarians Play Basketball?" *American Libraries* 30, no. 3 (1999): 58–61.

7. American Library Association, International Relations Office, "Be a Mentor to an International Librarian at ALA Annual Conference in Atlanta." www.ala.org/work/ international/mentor.html (accessed 3 January 2003).

8. ALCTS, Cataloging and Classification Section, "Education, Training, and Recruitment for Cataloging." www.ala.org/alcts/organization/ccs/mentors.html (accessed 3 January 2003).

9. RUSA, "CODES New Member Request for Mentor Form." www.ala.org/rusa/ codes/mentors_request.html (accessed 3 January 2003).

10. Public Library Association, "Recruitment to the Profession." /www.pla.org/ projects/jobshadow.html (accessed 3 January 2003).

11. ALISE Recruitment Committee, "Interested in. … Being Mentored. … Mentoring?," 2002.

12. Special Libraries Association, "2000 Rose Vormelker Award." www.sla.org/ committee/sarc/awards/rose00.html (accessed 3 January 2003).

13. UCLA, School of Information Studies, "Praxis." http://skipper.gseis.ucla .edu/faculty/cchu/praxis/about.htm (accessed 3 January 2003).

14. Frank G. Houdek, "'Meet My Mentor': A Collection of Personal Reminiscences," *Law Library Journal* 91, no. 1 (1999): 177–255; Kathleen de la Peña McCook, ed., *Women of Color in Librarianship: An Oral History* (Chicago: ALA, 1998); Teresa Y. Neely and Khafre K. Abif, eds., *In Our Own Voices: The Changing Face of Librarianship* (Lanham, MD: Scarecrow, 1996).

15. Sheldon, *Leaders in Libraries*, 2.

16. Sheldon, *Leaders in Libraries*, 3.

17. Warren Bennis and Bert Nanus, *Leaders: The Strategies for Taking Charge* (New York: Harper & Row, 1985).

18. Sheldon, *Leaders in Libraries*, 52.

19. Sheldon, *Leaders in Libraries*, 51.

20. M. Zeilditch, "Mentor Roles." Paper resented at the 32nd Annual Meeting of the Western Association of Graduate Schools, Tempe, Arizona, 16–18 March 1990, 11.

21. Rackham, 6.

22. Sheldon, *Leaders in Libraries*, 66.

23. National Mentoring Center. www.nwrel.org/mentoring (accessed 1 January 2003).

24. The National Mentoring Partnership, "Learn to Mentor Tool Kit." www.mentoring.org/training/TMT/Mentor_training.toolkit.pdf (accessed 1 January 2003).

25. Sheldon, *Leaders in Libraries*, 62.

26. Sheldon, *Leaders in Libraries*, 66.

27. June Kahler Berry, "Texas Accelerated Library Leaders; TALL Texans," *Public Libraries* 39, no. 6 (2000): 311, 313.

28. C. Allen Nichols, "Leaders: Born or Bred; Confessions from a Leadership Training Junkie," *Library Journal* 127, no. 13 (2002): 38; Teresa Y. Neely and Mark D. Winston, "Snowbird Leadership Institute: A Survey of the Implications for Leadership in the Profession." www.ala.org/acrl/winston.pdf (accessed 3 January 2003).

29. "ACRL New Member Mentoring Program Workbook."

30. Catherine Shreve, "Making the Right Connection: The Role of Mentoring," *ALA Cognotes,* 1998. www.ala.org/events/dc98/live/cognotes/issue3h.html (accessed 3 January 2003).

31. Cynthia I. Sipe, "Mentoring Adolescents: What Have We Learned?" in *Contemporary Issues in Mentoring*, ed. Jean Baldwin Grossman (Philadelphia: P/PV, 1999), 15.

32. Sipe, "Mentoring Adolescents," 18–19.

33. Susan Jekielek, Kristin A. Moore, and Elizabeth C. Hair. *Mentoring Programs and Youth Development: A Synthesis* (Washington, DC: Child Trends, 2002), vi.

34. Mentoring Australia, "Mentoring: Benchmarks for Effective and Responsible Mentoring Programs." www.mentoring-australia.com/benchmark.htm (accessed 2 January 2003).

35. Jean Baldwin Grossman and Amy Johnson, "Assessing the Effectiveness of Mentoring Programs," in *The Cost of Mentoring* (Washington, DC: Child Trends, 2002): 26.

36. Jekielek et al., *Mentoring Programs,* iv, v, vi.

37. National Mentoring Partnership, "National Poll Finds 57 Million Adult Americans Are Willing to Mentor," press release, October 28, 2002. Available at: http://www.mentoring.org/common/one_report/one_report.adp?OneReportID=45&Menu=&Preload=

38. Sheldon, *Leaders in Libraries,* 59.

39. Shreve, "Making the Right Connection."

40. National Mentoring Partnership, "Qualities of Successful Mentors." www.mentoring.org/training/tmt/tmt23010.adp (accessed 1 January 2003).

41. Sipe, "Learned," 16.

42. National Mentoring Partnership, "National Poll Finds."

43. Sheldon, *Leaders in Libraries*, 65.

44. National Mentoring Partnership, "What Your Mentor Will Do." www.mentoring.org/training/TME/tem21020.adp (accessed 1 January 2003).

45. Sheldon, *Leaders in Libraries*, 66.

46. Jennifer Cargill, "Developing Library Leaders: The Role of Mentorship," *Library Administration and Management* (Winter 1989): 14.

47. Margaret A. Cibik and Stephen L. Chambers, "Similarities and Differences Among Native Americans, Hispanics, Blacks, and Anglos," *NASPA Journal* 28, no. 2 (1991): 133.

48. Dorothy Horstman, *Sing Your Heart Out, Country Boy* (New York: Dutton, 1975), 3–5.

49. Cathaleene J. Macias, "American Indian Academic Success: The Role of Indigenous Learning Strategies," *Journal of American Indian Education* 29 (August 1989): 45.

50. Cibik and Chambers, "Similarities and Differences," 134.

51. Cibik and Chambers, "Similarities and Differences," 129–139.

52. Cibik and Chambers, "Similarities and Differences," 131.

53. Cibik and Chambers, "Similarities and Differences," 131.

54. Cibik and Chambers, "Similarities and Differences," 132.

55. Cibik and Chambers, "Similarities and Differences," 132.

56. Pauline Rindone, "Achievement Motivation and Academic Achievement of Native American Students," *Journal of American Indian Education* 28, no. 1 (1988): 1.

57. Rindone, "Achievement Motivation," 137; Richard Pottinger, "Disjunction to Higher Education: American Indian Students in the Southwest," *Anthropology and Education Quarterly* 20, no. 4 (1989): 326.

58. Gerald E. Gipp and Sandra J. Fox, "Promoting Cultural Relevance in American Indian Education," *Education Digest* 57, no. 3 (1993): 60.

59. Beatrice Medicine, "Native American (Indian) Women: A Call for Research," *Anthropology and Education Quarterly* 19, no. 2 (1988): 90.

60. Judith Davis, "Factors Contributing to Post-Secondary Achievement of American Indians," *Tribal College* 4, no. 2 (1992): 29.

61. Medicine, "Native American (Indian) Women," 88.

62. Medicine, "Native American (Indian) Women," 91.

63. Macias, "American Indian Academic Success," 46.

64. Macias, "American Indian Academic Success," 45–46, 48.

65. Macias, "American Indian Academic Success," 48.

66. Macias, American Indian Academic Success, 48–49.

67. Cibik and Chambers, "Similarities and Differences," 138.

68. Cibik and Chambers, "Similarities and Differences," 131.

69. Sheldon, *Leaders in Libraries*, 51–52.

70. Roma Harris, "The Mentoring Trap; A Warning for Entry-Level Librarians; Mentor–Protégé Relationships May Help a Select Few, but They Haven't Catapulted Women or Minorities to Leading Roles," *Library Journal* 118, no. 17 (1993): 37–39.

71. Jean Baldwin Grossman, "The Practice, Quality and Cost of Mentoring," in *Contemporary Issues in Mentoring,* ed. Jean Baldwin Grossman (Philadelphia, PA: Public/Private Ventures, 2002), 8.

72. Nichols, "Leaders: Born or Bred," 38.

73. Jeffrey S. Bullington and Susanna D. Boylston, "Strengthening the Profession, Assuring Our Future: ACRL's New Member Mentoring Program Pairs Library Leaders with New Professionals," *College and Research Libraries News* 62, no. 4 (2001): 430–432.

74. Sheldon, *Leaders in Libraries*, 55.

75. University of Michigan. The Rackham School of Graduate Studies. *How to Get the Mentoring You Want: A Guide for Graduate Students at a Diverse University,*

2002. http://www.rackham.umich.edu/StudentInfo/Publications/StudentMentoring/
mentoring. pdf

76. Shreve, "Making the Right Connection."

77. Alvin Walker, ed., *Psychological Index Terms*, 7th ed. (Washington, DC: American Psychological Association, 1994), 121.

78. Sheldon, *Leaders in Libraries*, 66.

III

FACULTY AND CURRICULUM ISSUES

10

The Effect of Technology on Library Education and Students at Risk

Linda Schamber

Technology is the single greatest force affecting librarianship. It has dramatically altered professional roles and called into question the structure of libraries themselves. Recruitment to the profession, including recruitment of a multicultural and multiethnic workforce, is at least in part a survival issue. Technology skills are critical to the academic success of students entering library and information science (LIS) master's programs and to the employability and salaries of graduates entering the field.

In this chapter, I describe the effect of technology on librarianship, the technology skills required of new professionals, and the skills that may be lacking in at-risk students. I examine implications for students from historically marginalized groups and suggest strategies for recruiting, retaining, and placing these students in the mainstream of the technological elite. Finally, I explore the bigger picture of social issues and the potential of a fresh and diverse cadre of librarians to contribute to a technology-driven information society.

TRANSFORMING THE FIELD

Technology is changing the nature of librarianship with all the subtlety of a runaway train. To put the picture in perspective, a task force of the Association of College and Research Libraries (ACRL) identified seven top issues affecting academic libraries.[1] All of these relate to technology, from changes in services and resources, to shifts in administration and funding, to problems of copyright and plagiarism. Four issues relate to education, including the education of new and existing librarians, the role of libraries in the educational process, the development of services for new library users, and funding shortages in higher education. The issue of educating librarians covers the challenge of achieving and maintaining diversity in the profession.

Technically competent librarians are a precious commodity. Another ACRL task force reported on academic library staff recruitment and retention.[2] This report says a major area of concern is competition from the private sector for employees with technology skills, coupled with a concern that academic libraries cannot offer the same level of compensation. To add to the worries, a generation of librarians is retiring, and replacements with master's degrees from ALA-accredited programs are hard to find. On the brighter side, technology positions are increasing, as are salaries for librarians of color. Although the ACRL reports apply to academic libraries, it is fairly safe to say that most of the issues apply to other types of libraries as well.

The transformation of libraries and librarians' roles wrought by new information and communication technologies is well documented. The number and types of resources and tools for accessing them have increased radically. New services, such as web portals and online reference services, have emerged. Professional skills in acquisitions, cataloging, reference, searching, and user education are being ramped up to keep pace with the technologies. In a talk for the International Federation of Library Associations and Institutions (IFLA), Sharp says, "The core skills traditionally associated with information professionals, which include information handling skills, training and facilitating skills, evaluation skills and concern for the customer are still relevant. . . . It is the way in which these values are translated into operations and activities that will undergo substantial change."[3]

Unfortunately, librarianship does not present itself as the most attractive career option. As a whole, it is seen as a primarily white, female-dominated, service-oriented profession that has a stodgy image and pays poorly. At the same time, it requires a graduate education, with a high level of technological competency, for professional status. This combination forebodes a high toll of personal investment for the prospective student. For individuals from underrepresented groups, the situation is compounded by allegations of lower pay, nonpermanent positions, and slower rates of advancement. To overcome these negative perceptions, LIS schools must aggressively recruit and educate students for new high-tech professional roles and do so with the best interests of diversity in mind.

DEFINING TECHNOLOGY SKILLS

Technology skills are integral to the practice of librarianship and therefore to LIS education. The ALA lists the educational policy statements of a dozen major North American library organizations.[4] All of these statements describe professional competencies that require specific technology skills.

What are these skills? First, technology encompasses not only the myriad computer-based applications used in the profession (information retrieval systems, resource management databases, communication networks, technical services tools, educational delivery mechanisms, etc.), but also desktop applications necessary for everyday productivity (word processing, spreadsheet, database, e-mail, etc.).

Second, technology skills are seen as a subset of the competencies that comprise information literacy. In its "Information Literacy Competency Standards for Higher Education," the ACRL states, "Information literacy is related to information technology skills, but has broader implications for the individual, the educational system, and for society. Information technology skills enable an individual to use computers, software applications, databases, and other technologies to achieve a wide variety of academic, work-related, and personal goals. Information literate individuals necessarily develop some technology skills."[5]

As the title indicates, the standards pertain to all of higher education and thus also to librarians in their role as facilitators of education. The five standards address the ability of the information literate student to effectively: (1) articulate information need, (2) access information, (3) evaluate information and information sources, (4) use information purposefully, and (5) understand economic, legal, and social issues of information access and use. The standards are backed by twenty-two performance indicators and eighty-seven learning outcomes for assessing the student's level of information literacy. Every one of the five standards includes technology-oriented outcomes, with a total of about twenty-five, or 29 percent, of the outcomes pointing directly or indirectly to technology skills.

There is nothing simple about these standards. They address a continuum of what the ACRL refers to as higher-order and lower-order thinking skills. The abstract cognitive skills, which are relatively stable, are inextricably linked to concrete technical skills, which are constantly changing with the technologies. As an example, one performance indicator on standard three, the ability to evaluate information and information sources critically, is "synthesizes main ideas to construct new concepts," and one outcome for this indicator is "utilizes computer and other technologies (e.g., spreadsheets, databases, multimedia, and audio or visual equipment) for studying the interaction of ideas and other phenomena."

Similarly, there is nothing simple about the variety of knowledge and skills that LIS schools must convey. These fall into three broad and highly interdependent categories: (1) traditional librarian knowledge and skills for information management and access (cataloging, reference, etc.); (2) language skills for indexing, searching, and communication (reference, management, teaching, writing, etc.); and (3) technology skills for performing the professional tasks above. The only category for which some degree of aptitude is not necessary upon admission to an LIS program is, ironically, the librarian skills.

All technology skills are relevant, dynamic, and transferable throughout the education process. By dint of the constant need to upgrade skills to accommodate changing systems, students must develop the ability to adapt to change and to remain flexible in order to survive in a professional field in flux. For distributed learning alone (or even distributed aspects of classroom learning), new students immediately must cope with electronic communications (e-mail, e-mail attachments, discussion lists, online surveys and tests, assignment drop boxes) and be able to express themselves clearly and courteously in writing.

Students who enter LIS programs with poor basic language and technology skills may start slowly, be unable to catch up, and eventually drop out of the program. When such students are members of historically marginalized groups, the loss to the profession doubles. This is why my emphasis below is on entry-level skills and early identification of students at risk.

IDENTIFYING STUDENTS AT RISK

Students at risk are students who for one reason or another may not perform well academically or even complete an academic program. Traditional admissions criteria, such as Graduate Record Exam scores, help predict academic success, but give no indication of why students might fail.

Entry-level technical proficiency has long been a sticking point for LIS programs. Although the situation is improving, there will always be some older individuals returning to school and individuals with weak academic histories who are unprepared for coursework. Admission requirements and measures for ensuring technical competency vary among schools. Basic skills instruments range from self-tests to formal graded tests and from self-reports to task-based demonstrations. These are typically administered before or during the first term of coursework.

Schools can write their own instruments, based on faculty consensus, surveys of alumni and current students, or performance indicators, as in the ACRL information literacy standards. Or they can adopt or adapt existing instruments. These are widely available, from undergraduate entrance tests at their own universities to publicly available general education tests. One public source is Profiler, a survey library containing more than 1,700 tests used in education at all levels nationwide.[6] It has more than 100 tests for technology skills and four tests for information literacy. Most basic technical skill tests simply list a series of computer tasks, such as copying a file. These instruments may or may not have been validated statistically, but are useful for purely practical purposes. Some may need updating, as specific areas (e.g., ftp) have changed.

Although high-tech distributed learning may add stress for new students, educators have not yet developed a thorough understanding of the risk factors. In an exploratory study, however, Osborn recently developed an instrument to identify at-risk students in distributed courses and tested it with 240 LIS students.[7] The instrument consists of eight indicators of course completion: (1) preparation for the course, (2) study habits, (3) locus of control, (4) enrollment encouragement, (5) tenacity, (6) focus, (7) lack of interest, and (8) need for support. The indicator for preparation for the course contains three items to assess computer confidence. The results of this study found preparation for the course to be one of the strongest predictors of completion, along with educational level, study habits, hours worked per week, and grade point average.

LIS education in general lacks uniform testing instruments that focus on skills or aptitudes specific to librarianship. The distributed learning instrument is significant in that it encompasses an array of factors that affect students at risk. Ideally, LIS entrance tests should cover a variety of factors, including technology and language skills and critical demographic predictors. Education researchers have developed a host of instruments for assessing socioeconomic characteristics that are known to be academically relevant. Such instruments may help LIS educators identify students who come from racial, ethnic, or socioeconomic groups that pose additional considerations. These may be students who, for example, are the first generation in their families to attend college, attended poor-quality undergraduate programs, are financially disadvantaged, or speak English as a second language. The possible factors are many and complex, and I discuss some of the issues in the section on technology and society.

BALANCING THE FIELD

LIS schools are charged with finding qualified people to recruit and then helping these people to succeed academically and professionally. Many innovative strategies for achieving diversity through recruitment, retention, and placement programs are described elsewhere in this book. For purposes of this chapter, my focus is on ways to attract and develop students who are technologically competent. The goal is to find individuals with an interest in and aptitude for, if not experience with, information technologies.

Recruitment

Potential students from underrepresented groups have many reasons for choosing a career in librarianship[8] and can be found in many places. Library paraprofessionals are a rich and often overlooked source of students for professional master's programs. LIS schools should seek them out in libraries that are racially and ethnically diverse and technologically progressive. They can troll for prospective students in historically black colleges and in high schools with strong technology resources and programs. They can recruit master's students from undergraduate and school library certification programs in their own institutions. Technology-savvy individuals who are particularly attractive, for example, are undergraduate majors in LIS and computer science and paraprofessionals in technology-oriented continuing education courses.

Three kinds of incentives may work especially well in a campaign targeting both diversity and technology: one financial and two based on the technologies themselves. The first incentive, financial support, is not always the most important, but it can make the difference to an individual student. Money is short these days, and educators, students, and professionals must pursue it creatively and tenaciously. The ALA's diversity campaign and scholarships are widely publicized. Its Spectrum Initiative suggests numerous ways for individuals, libraries, and organizations to lend support, including raising funds for Spectrum Initiative Scholarships.[9] Since none of these speak to technology, I would add a suggestion to contribute matching funds for technology and technology training. The ALA Scholarship Program lists other opportunities for underrepresented groups. Worth noting are two minority scholarships for library and information technology cosponsored by the Library Information and Technology Association (LITA).[10] Prospective students should check other professional organizations and several LIS schools for financial support programs.

Universities and libraries should constantly be aware of and seek grants. Many government grants encourage partnerships between educational and professional institutions for projects that will improve technology resources and skills. For example, federal grants from the Institute of Museum and Library Services support high-tech collaborative projects for digitization of historical and cultural archives with a variety of themes.[11] A subset of these is devoted to Native American and Hawaiian American projects. The benefits can accrue on all fronts: obtaining state-of-the-art equipment, recruiting and supporting students in high-tech positions, and placing students in multicultural projects in libraries and museums. LIS schools should seek equipment donations, as well as funding, to upgrade their equipment and put students to work helping to maintain it.

The second incentive is distributed learning, which uses information technology to attract students who otherwise would not have access to graduate education for geographical or financial reasons. Distributed learning programs have been shown to significantly increase minority enrollments. As an example, Totten states that the first year that the LIS master's program of the

University of North Texas was delivered via videoconference to Edinburg, near the Mexican border, enrollment there raised the proportion of Hispanic students from 3 percent to 16 percent of the student body.[12] Again, LIS schools should seek grants, internal or external to their institutions, to support faculty and obtain technologies for course development. Additional funds or donations can be solicited to provide or upgrade home hardware/software for distributed learning students.

The third incentive uses technology to recruit for a high-technology field. The websites of LIS schools should present a positive image of librarianship and promote their programs in a way that emphasizes both technology and diversity. At present, most school sites either fail to promote the career (assuming the visitor has already decided) or emphasize one theme strongly (see, for instance, FSU[13] and UK[14] on technology and UCLA[15] and UW[16] on diversity). Two exemplary career pages are by the Central Jersey Regional Library Cooperative[17] and the Medical Library Association (MLA).[18] The MLA offers brochures for adults and teenagers in English and Spanish that demonstrate how just a few words or photos can get both themes across.

To develop career recruitment material, LIS faculty members can ask students and alumni for suggestions and harness their enthusiasm. An excellent example is the comprehensive career site created by a class of Syracuse students.[19] Recruitment planners should bear in mind that people who are using the Internet to explore high-tech service careers encounter an enormous range of options, so a school site must be competitive. They can identify the kinds of institutions (community colleges, libraries, etc.) that career seekers are likely to visit, and then create web pages with reciprocal links to these institutions. Of course the best web design principles apply, such as using terms that will be picked up by search engines.

Retention

Beyond (or within) the more general advice for enhancing diversity through faculty representation, mentoring, and curriculum changes are a couple of strategies for retaining students who are at risk because of poor technical skills. The first is to follow assessment testing quickly with remediation. Even without testing, students may self-identify and voluntarily take action to bring themselves up to speed. They are helped if remedial technical training is accessible and non-threatening. It need not be in the form of full-scale courses, but can be online tutorials (possibly off the shelf), neighborhood programs (e.g., at community colleges), or peer tutoring by other LIS students. Several choices should be available to accommodate students who learn better from self-paced tutorials versus those who learn better from face-to-face guidance.

The tone of instruction is important. Positive and individually supportive instruction can improve students' self-efficacy or "can do" attitude. Students who expect to succeed at technology tasks tend to try harder, perform better, and be motivated to learn more.[20] The confidence to overcome technology hurdles early in their programs can translate into a sense of accomplishment and control that carries over into related academic and professional endeavors. Confidence is further built by the attention of faculty members who mentor students personally or refer them to appropriate campus services and student organizations to help deal with other problems, such as language skills or social isolation.

A second strategy for retaining students at risk is to drive home the importance of technology through example and engagement. Exposure to professional librarians who serve as racial and ethnic role models and who hold high-tech positions is crucial for vesting students in their career tracks. Relationships between local (or not so local) institutions should be developed and exploited. LIS schools can invite librarians to speak on technology topics and librarians can arrange day-on-the-job experiences for new students.

All students should be urged to take advantage of low student fees to join professional organizations and attend conferences. At conferences, they can learn about the latest technological innovations and begin making contacts and building their professional networks. Many local student chapters develop programs and websites related to technical skills and job hunting. Student organization activities can intersect coursework in creative ways. At the University of Washington, for instance, students' papers from a diversity course were published online in a student organization newsletter.[21]

Placement

The most successful programs, in my opinion, are internship and hiring efforts in which universities and libraries cooperate to mutual benefit. Rogers highlights three successful public library recruitment programs with strong ties to universities.[22] Some of the strategies are to offer paid internships, support paraprofessionals in MLS programs, hold open houses with universities, and develop positive career websites.

For students, internships hold the ultimate incentive value of real-world professional involvement. Paid internships are of course most attractive, but unpaid internships deliver just as much practical experience. LIS schools should cultivate internships that require technical expertise at libraries with up-to-date technologies. They should place as many students as possible (not just students with technology specializations) in high-tech positions to gain hands-on experience. In an article on managing change in libraries, Youngman says, "Adding technology-based services usually increases rather than decreases the number of staff hours required to develop and mainstream effective patron services."[23] This presents an opportunity to negotiate project-based positions such as web design at libraries that lack the necessary staff or skills. Paraprofessionals and senior librarians alike need continuing education to stay abreast of change. This brings another opportunity not only for LIS faculty, but also for advanced student interns to deliver technology-oriented workshops.

Libraries need to recruit new employees with tech skills, so technically capable interns are in the perfect spot for hiring to full-time positions. If minority interns enter the field at any stage with technical expertise, they are more likely to land the newer positions. If these positions are strongly technical, the interns are likely to get the higher pay that goes with such positions. "Many recent library school graduates bring to the employment market specific technology skills that did not exist just a few years ago," says Youngman. "These specialized skills can allow an entry-level person to quickly become productive in a new, non-traditional role while taking time to develop expertise in more traditional subject-based tasks. In some cases a synergy may develop where the fresh skills and enthusiasm of a new librarian can catalyze the interest of experienced librarians and help them see the value of acquiring and applying newer skills."[24] He promotes a model for managing change that emphasizes flexibility in staffing and an atmosphere conducive to continuous learning.

UNDERSTANDING TECHNOLOGY AND SOCIETY

Librarians are members of the information and technology elite of society. LIS students are novitiates to this exalted group. In this section I address LIS education and technology from various sociological perspectives, looking at issues in education and society that affect LIS students individually and socially. These issues include the upside and downside of technology skills: the implications of social capital versus the implications of being labeled at-risk. On a larger scale, the issues include roles of libraries and multicultural staffs and the concept of the digital divide with regard to education and the Internet.

Educational Issues

Insofar as lack of technology skills puts new LIS students at risk, improving these skills contributes to their social capital. Social capital is the resource network of human relationships that exist among people in family, school, work, and community groups. From childhood on, social capital shapes individuals' social interactions, behavioral expectations, and communication channels. Basically, it allows them to fit in and to operate smoothly and effectively within the culture of a given social environment. For adults seeking to raise their social capital in the work environment, "workers with solid educational credentials, problem-solving capabilities, and technological expertise are the ones who will likely secure decent jobs with generous and growing compensation," say Beaulieu et al.[25] If the reason some LIS students enter the program with low technology or communication skills is a weakness in social capital, then better skills should significantly boost their chances for academic and professional success.

Agada puts quite a different spin on the idea of students fitting in. In a paper for the ACRL, he criticizes the concept of at-risk itself, calling it a problem of the institution rather than the student. He contends that the at-risk approach focuses on learner deficiencies and assumes a predisposition to failure that results in a self-fulfilling prophecy. It results in lowered expectations for at-risk students, particularly students with certain racial, ethnic, or socioeconomic backgrounds. Perceptions of at-risk factors are socially constructed within the dominant culture, in this case the university, and students are labeled as at risk when they do not fit into that culture. Agada suggests that educators focus less on student deficiencies and more on reducing cultural dissonance—social distance between students and the institution—based on inequities in the learning and social environment. While educators now promote diversity, or providing students with equal opportunities for multicultural study, they should go further to promote pluralism, which requires students to study multicultural perspectives and thus build social equity through understanding.[26]

Libraries are agents of the status quo, and Agada sees a contradiction in their traditional stance as democratic and egalitarian purveyors of knowledge. "Librarian rhetoric," he says, "assumes that information, its technology and market forces are neutral agents."[27] He points out that providing equal physical access to information is not enough, as demonstrated by the serious inequities in access in society. In their educational roles, libraries have the opportunity to choose social responsibility over neutrality by supporting a pluralistic teaching model. They can do so by collecting information on multicultural topics, teaching information literacy in a culturally sensitive fashion, and generally creating non-threatening spaces in which students can affirm and expand their cultural knowledge. Library staffing should support this effort. Agada suggests hiring at-risk students to teach library use to their peers, recruiting minorities to library intern positions, and requiring sensitivity training for all staff. The result would be a library that is better equipped to serve a diverse user community.

Another perspective on at-risk students blames the economic problems of schools and colleges. Carrier notes that budget cuts have forced many institutions to reduce spending for technology. Poorer schools have less equipment and training or get it too late to help prepare students for careers or further education. In a cycle that widens the information gap, students who cannot afford richer schools are further marginalized because they do not get current technology and advanced information skills. At the same time, the information elite have access to the latest technology, use the technology to gain more knowledge, and continue to be better prepared for change. Simple access to technology is insufficient, Carrier says: students need to learn advanced information skills, and beyond that, theoretical and critical thinking skills.[28] Obviously these factors affect LIS students, along with all other students.

Internet Issues

The information gap is part of a larger concept: the digital divide. The digital divide basically means that those with technology skills get ahead and the rest get left behind. Clearly technology access and use reap economic and social benefits for users. The U.S. government has sponsored an enormous amount of research on technology issues and entire conferences on the digital divide. The data on Internet users alone are telling. Carrier cites studies that found Internet users to have higher-than-average incomes, people who used computers at work to have markedly higher incomes, and e-mail use to be the most highly rewarded computer task at work.[29]

Carrier's chapter appears in an excellent book, edited by Ebo, about the social effects of the Internet. This book addresses the paradox of perceptions about this newest and increasingly powerful mass medium. The full scope of implications is as yet unclear. Ebo says, "Proponents believe that the Internet could create a cybertopia because of its potential to generate new egalitarian social networks. But critics argue that the potential for a cyberghetto is real because the Internet will retain vestiges of traditional communities with similar hierarchical social linkages and class-structured relationships."[30]

The proponents' view reflects conventional wisdom, the notion that the Internet is a democratizing force that, by opening the door to incalculable masses of information, empowers its users to learn, use, and enjoy information in an independent, self-directed fashion and to express themselves candidly. In the United States and other countries that provide free public Internet access—much of it in libraries—the Internet is seen as removing the last barriers to open learning and communication based on race, gender, disability, or socioeconomic class. Obvious beneficiaries of this phenomenon are the students who can afford to attend better schools through web-based learning because they can avoid the expense of sacrificing jobs and moving to campus.

From the critics' view, however, the Internet is seen as a tool for the continued exclusion of marginalized groups. Various writers contend that Internet culture is dominated by an affluent, college-educated, white-male establishment, a perception supported by hard data.[31] This elite constituency designs the hardware and software and owns and controls the Internet access providers, thus reifying its own logical, linguistic, and cultural orientation. The result is a medium that is biased by its very structure against non-mainstream groups distinguished by race, ethnicity, class, or gender. If technology conveys only one mainstream cultural identity, then concerns about the cultural content of information in classrooms and libraries, or where education takes place, or how much it costs, are essentially moot.

CONCLUSION

Libraries are technology-intensive institutions. Technology skills are vital to students both entering and exiting LIS master's programs. All students are promising—the challenge is to find ways to enhance the assets they bring with them to higher education and to support them as they develop professional knowledge and skills. Attention to at-risk students not only can improve their retention and academic success, but also can affect their eventual placement and career success. When the students are members of underrepresented groups, these efforts can improve diversity and representation in education and the profession. As they grow and become leaders, they will move the goal of librarianship for equity and diversity closer to reality. These are the people who, as information access providers and educators, hold the power to help close the digital divide.

NOTES

1. Andrew Richard Albanese, "The Top Seven Academic Library Issues," *Library Journal* 128, no. 5 (2003): 43.

2. Association of College and Research Libraries, "Recruitment, Retention & Restructuring: Human Resources In Academic Libraries," 2002). www.ala.org/Content/NavigationMenu/ACRL/Issues_and_Advocacy1/Recruiting_to_the_Profession/Recruitment,_Retention,_and_Restructuring.htm (accessed 15 July 2003).

3. Kate Sharp, "Internet Librarianship: Traditional Roles in a New Environment," *IFLA Journal* 27, no. 2 (2001): 78–79. Available at: www.ifla.org/V/iflaj/art2702.pdf.

4. American Library Association, Office for Accreditation, "Educational Policy Statements." 2003. www.ala.org/Content/NavigationMenu/Our_Association/Offices/Accreditation1/edpol/Educational_Policy_Statements.htm (accessed 15 July 2003).

5. Association of College and Research Libraries, "Information Literacy Competency Standards for Higher Education," 2003. www.ala.org/Content/NavigationMenu/ACRL/Standards_and_Guidelines/Information_Literacy_Competency_Standards_for_Higher_Education.htm (accessed 15 July 2003).

6. High Plains Technology in Education Consortium, "Profiler," 2002. http://profiler.hprtec.org (accessed 15 July 2003).

7. Viola Osborn and Philip Turner, "Identifying At-Risk Students in LIS Distributed Learning Courses," *Journal of Education for Library and Information Science* 43, no. 3 (2002): 205–213; see also Viola Osborn, "Identifying At-Risk Students in Videoconferencing and Web-Based Distance Education," *American Journal of Distance Education,* 15, no. 1 (2001): 41–54.

8. See Mark Winston, "The Role of Recruitment in Achieving Goals Related to Diversity," Paper for the Association of College and Research Libraries, 1997. www.ala.org/Content/ContentGroups/ACRL1/Nashville_1997_Papers/Winston. htm (accessed 15 July 2003).

9. American Library Association, Spectrum Scholarship Initiative, "Spectrum Initiative—New Faces, New Era," 2003. www.ala.org/Content/NavigationMenu/Our_Association/Offices/Diversity3/Spectrum_Initiative/Spectrum_Initiative.htm (accessed 15 July 2003).

10. American Library Association, Scholarships, "ALA Scholarship Program," 2003. www.ala.org/Template.cfm?Section=Scholarships&Template=/TaggedPage/TaggedPageDisplay.cfm&TPLID=18&ContentID=18318 (accessed 15 July 2003).

11. Institute of Museum and Library Services, "All About Grants and Awards," 2003. www.imls.gov/grants/index.htm (accessed 15 July 2003).

12. Herman L. Totten, "Ethnic Diversity in Library Schools: Completing the Education Cycle," *Texas Library Journal* 76, no. 1 (2000): 16–19. Available at: www.txla.org/pubs/tlj76_1/diversity.html

13. Florida State University, School of Information Studies, "Digital Age Info Professions," 2003. www.lis.fsu.edu/Prospects/ssd51_infoprofessions_desc.cfm (accessed 15 July 2003).

14. University of Kentucky, School of Library and Information Science, Information for Prospective LIS Students, "Are You Interested in a Career in Information Technology?" 2001. www.uky.edu/CommInfoStudies/SLIS/prospect.htm (accessed 15 July 2003).

15. University of California, Los Angeles, Department of Information Studies, "Explore Cultural Diversity—An Integral Component of IS," 2000. http://is.gseis.ucla.edu/diversity/index.htm#department (accessed 15 July 2003).

16. University of Washington, Information School, "Diversity Homepage," 2003. www.ischool.washington.edu/services/diversity.htm (accessed 15 July 2003).

17. Central Jersey Regional Library Cooperative, "Become a Librarian!" 2003. www.becomealibrarian.org (accessed 15 July 2003).

18. Medical Library Association, "Careers," 2003. www.mlanet.org/career/index.html (accessed 15 July 2003).

19. Syracuse University, School of Information Studies, "Librarians in the 21st Century," 2000, http://istweb.syr.edu/21stcenlib/ (accessed 15 July 2003).

20. See Diane Nahl, "Affective Monitoring of Internet Learners: Perceived Self-Efficacy and Success," *Proceedings of the 59th Annual Meeting of the American Society for Information Science* 33 (1996): 100–109.

21. University of Washington, Information School, Association of Library and Information Science Students, "Special Issue: Diversity," *Silverfish* (April 2003). http://

students.washington.edu/aliss/Silverfish/archive/april2003/index.shtml (accessed 15 July 2003).

22. Michael Rogers, "Tackling Recruitment," *Library Journal* 128, no. 2 (2003): 40–43.

23. Daryl C. Youngman, "Library Staffing Considerations in the Age of Technology: Basic Elements for Managing Change," *Issues in Science and Technology Librarianship* 24 (Fall 1999). Available at: www.library.ucsb.edu/istl/99-fall/article5.html

24. Youngman, "Library Staffing Considerations in the Age of Technology."

25. Lionel J. Beaulieu, Glenn D. Israel, Glen Hartless, and Patricia Dyk, "For Whom Does the School Bell Toll? Multi-Contextual Presence of Social Capital and Student Educational Achievement," *Journal of Socio-Economics* 30 (2001): 121.

26. John Agada, "Deconstructing the At-Risk Student Phenomenon: Can Librarian Values Salvage Education for the 21st Century?" Paper presented at the ACRL Tenth National Conference, Denver, CO, March 2001. Available at: www.ala.org/Content/NavigationMenu/ACRL/Events_and_Conferences/agada.pdf

27. Agada, "Deconstructing the At-Risk Student Phenomenon," 86.

28. Rebecca Carrier, "On the Electronic Information Frontier: Training the Information-Poor in an Age of Unequal Access," in *Cyberghetto or Cybertopia? Race, Class, and Gender on the Internet*, ed. Bosah Ebo (Westport, CT: Praeger, 1998), 153–168.

29. Carrier, "On the Electronic Information Frontier," 156.

30. Bosah Ebo, "Internet or Outernet?" in *Cyberghetto or Cybertopia? Race, Class, and Gender on the Internet*, ed. Bosah Ebo (Westport, CT: Praeger, 1998), 2.

31. See Alecia Wolf, "Exposing the Great Equalizer: Demythologizing Internet Equity," in *Cyberghetto or Cybertopia? Race, Class, and Gender on the Internet*, ed. Bosah Ebo (Westport, CT: Praeger, 1998), 15–32.

11

Curriculum Reform and Diversity

Lorna Peterson

From the Williamson reports of 1921 and 1923,[1] to the KALIPER Report (Kellogg-ALISE Information Profession and Education Renewal Project) of 2000,[2] library education has been regularly analyzing, critiquing, and updating its curriculum. Similar to other professions and education for its professionals, library and information science experiences tensions between the teaching of theory and practice; debate over the essential elements, or a common core, to be taught; how to distinguish between fads and legitimate new practices for the development of new courses; and demands from practitioners for perfect graduates in little need of on-the-job training. Curriculum reform is a messy business in higher education and library education is no exception. Practitioners may be frustrated with why changes are always so slow or professors seem so resistant. Professors may be bored with practitioner insinuations that the academy doesn't know what it is doing. Acknowledging this, a reality check on the efforts toward and the challenges to incorporating race and equity issues in the library and information science (LIS) curriculum might be helpful in advancing discussion of the LIS curriculum. What follows is a discussion of work in the area of folding race and equity issues into the LIS curriculum. Multiculturalism will be used interchangeably when discussing race and equity because multiculturalism is the term more generally used in librarianship when discussing race, ethnicity, and equity issues.

REVIEW OF THE LITERATURE

Clara Chu provides a thorough investigation of multicultural, race, and ethnicity issues in LIS education from the 1970s to the 1990s. She traces and summarizes the literature on services to the disadvantaged. United States federal efforts to increase the number of minority librarians, surveys by LIS educators on minority student experiences, and professional organization activities.[3] She concludes with an optimistic and positive view and provides evidence that there has been progress, but acknowledges that there is certainly more that can be done.[4] Dennis East and Errol Lam surveyed schools of LIS on multiculturalism as an issue and plans for curriculum modification or revision regarding multiculturalism.[5] Thirty-seven usable questionnaires, out of fifty-nine mailed, were analyzed. Results indicated a positive environment for multiculturalism in LIS education, with sixty-five percent of respondents stating that some modification to include multiculturalism had taken place.[6] Winston (2001) covers the challenges of discussing diversity or multiculturalism in the LIS classroom.[7] Criticism of multiculturalism as an important topic in the LIS curriculum is represented by Saracevic and Cronin. Saracevic characterizes multiculturalism as an insignificant concern given the problems programs and schools of LIS were facing in the 1990s.[8] LIS education had just experienced a series of closings; 25 percent of LIS programs closed between 1978 and 1993. His point was that given the overall problems with the LIS curriculum, research output, cost of the degree, and overall health of the programs, the focus on diversity was the least of LIS education's problems.[9] Cronin provides an analysis of LIS education beset by the malaise of social activism and multicultural mania.[10]

STRUCTURAL BARRIERS TO CURRICULUM REFORM

National Opposition

It is important to note that curricular changes in higher education result in heated debates at the national level, and the issue of multiculturalism in the higher education curriculum provided an arena for a hotly contested battle. Where there was enthusiasm for multiculturalism in the 1990s, there was also well-organized, serious opposition. This national, general opposition influenced LIS education and educators as well. Discussions of race, gender, and equity issues were decried as examples of political correctness. Organizations such as the National Association of Scholars defended western civilization, and, by defending it, viewed attempts to critique, expand or re-examine scholarship through the lens of race or gender as a denigration of Western European and Anglo-American values. Efforts at bringing race, equity, and multicultural issues into the curriculum were also seen as a politicization of scholarship and teaching, a decline in academic standards, a denouncement of American society, and suppression of free speech. Founded in 1985, the National Association of Scholars has 4,400 members and an operating budget of $1 million.[11] Its members believe strongly that there are deleterious effects to incorporating race, equity, and multiculturalism into the curriculum.[12] They assert their beliefs just as strongly as those who desire increasing multiculturalism in the curriculum. Incorporating race, gender, and equity issues—usually under the rubric of multiculturalism—in the LIS curriculum, unlike some other curricular issues, does not benefit from a general agreement that the curriculum is broken and needs fixing. Those in the field who think that LIS education does not do enough for multiculturalism may need to remember that there is a sizeable group that feels it does too much.

Association Considerations

The ALA's *Standards for Accreditation of Master's Programs in Library & Information Studies 1992*[13] added multiculturalism to the mission, curriculum, and student standards. From the standards:

I. Mission, Goals, and Objectives: Program objectives are stated in terms of educational results to be achieved and reflect . . .
    "the role of library and information services in a rapidly changing, multicultural, multiethnic, multilingual society, including the role of serving the needs of underserved groups."[14]
II. Curriculum:
    "responds to the needs of a rapidly changing multicultural, multiethnic, multilingual society including the needs of underserved groups."[15]
III. Students:
    "The school has policies to recruit and retain a multicultural, multiethnic, and multilingual student body from a variety of backgrounds."[16]

The standards describe essential features and are indicative, not prescriptive.[17] Programs seeking accreditation from the ALA are expected to show evidence in compliance with these standards. The accreditation standards provide a framework for influencing curriculum reform regarding multiculturalism. In some cases, these standards have influenced curriculum reform regarding multicultural issues in the LIS program of study.

Professional Considerations

What is it a graduate should be able to do upon earning the MLS? What are the core courses that bestow and distinguish the expertise that a librarian has and no other profession has? Although there might be general, broad-based agreement that reference, cataloging, and collection development are the broad skills of the librarian, intellectual freedom is one of the profession's values and serving a variety of people from diverse backgrounds, representing multiple roles in institutions is primarily what we do. But even this statement would generate controversy. The unbridled enthusiasm for information technology in the late 1990s saw the profession question its direction, values, and essential elements. In 1999, a Congress on Professional Education was held in Washington, DC. Its purpose was "to reach consensus among stakeholder groups on the values and core competencies of the profession and on strategies for action to address common issues and concerns. The impetus for the congress arose from changes in name of some programs of graduate education, the seeming lack of attention to core competencies, and the national shortage of professionals to work with young people and diverse and underserved populations.[18] From its recommendations, the following is stated concerning multiculturalism:

"4.6. give particular attention to diversity, including multilingual, multiethnic and/or multicultural considerations, programs and services and support for special needs and the underserved, in the context of these recommendations

- this particular recommendation appears throughout these suggested strategies as it needs to be made visible and pervasive in the profession and its institutions."[19]

The profession has shown a commitment to multiculturalism in the LIS curriculum through its reports and recommendations as written by special task forces of the ALA.

Student Concerns

Students are concerned about job readiness and placement and must be judicious in course selection in constructing their plans of study. Should they do a practicum? Should they take all the computer courses, or, at the very least, as many as possible? For those in certain specializations that have certification requirements, there is often little room left over for electives. With this situation, even if a student wanted to take a separate course on multiculturalism, would her plan of study accommodate it? Most MLS programs are thirty-six semester hours, with several at the thirty-nine or four-two hour level. With required courses (which can range from three to six or nine to eighteen semester hours), employers desiring to see that the student has had a practical experience, a majority of students commuting and part-time, which can restrict course taking opportunities, there is the likelihood that even if a student is willing, they may not be able to take newly created multiculturalism courses in the numbers that will justify having them in the course catalog. Courses require someone to teach them and enough students to register for them to make the course a go. New course development can be an expensive and timely proposition for a program, which results in caution by schools before developing courses and adding them to the curriculum. There are programs with multicultural courses (examples include Queens, Rhode Island, Rutgers, UCLA, University of Texas, University of Arizona, and others), but it cannot and should not be expected by the profession that all LIS programs will have such courses. Other institutions incorporate multiculturalism into course content by special lectures, readings, use of examples for reference questions or cataloging exercises, seminars, and symposia. The lack of a special course on multiculturalism does not mean that the issue isn't covered in some way. Chu found that in forty out of forty-eight surveyed schools, "[t]hirteen schools stated that their philosophy was to integrate diversity in LIS education. Of these, nine integrated diversity throughout the curriculum and four integrated diversity in the core curriculum and in some courses where appropriate or as students' needs arose."[20]

Faculty Culture

Faculty protect their subject expertise, and one way to control this is through teaching. Because faculty value ideas and contribute to the knowledge base through research, scholarship, and publication, the marking off of subject expertise is a territorial and protective reflex. Rarely does anyone successfully tell a faculty member what or how to teach.

Who will teach such courses? Does a multicultural course necessarily fall upon a racial or ethnic minority to teach? If so, does it strengthen hostility against the message (and the faculty member) or does it strengthen the legitimacy of the delivery and content? Race or ethnicity certainly does not by itself qualify a person to teach regarding matters of race. In the development of new courses, there is not always a faculty member interested or inclined to take on a topic that is outside their area of expertise. Practitioners should not be disappointed when a faculty member will not develop or take on a new course—instead, practitioners should applaud a faculty member for knowing what she cannot teach.

RECOMMENDATIONS

Practitioners interested in curriculum reform should:

- Stay abreast of changes in higher education curricular reform;
- Be knowledgeable about the positions contrary to curricular reform;
- Serve on advisory boards to LIS programs or somehow participate in LIS education;
- Be willing to teach; and

- Provide financial support to programs for special lectures, visiting professors to teach a course, conferences, etc.

Incorporating multiculturalism courses in the LIS curriculum is curricular addition and not reform. Practitioners who desire new courses to be offered must acknowledge that delivering courses is an expensive proposition. It should also be acknowledged that compromise might be needed. Most significantly, the importance to professional practice must be clear. Students, administrators, faculty, and employers all have a stake in the curriculum, and curricular reform requires that each stakeholder group be consulted. If the stakeholders do not have a commitment to the cause, or they do not see a need for investment, multicultural courses will come and go without affecting the professional practice at the level expected by proponents.

NOTES

1. Charles C. Williamson, *The Williamson Reports of 1921 and 1923,* including *Training for Library Work* (1921) and *Training for Library Service* (1923) (Metuchen, NJ: Scarecrow Flew, 1971).

2. KALIPER Project final report (special issue), *Journal of Education for Library and Information Science* 42, no. 3 (2001): 170–247.

3. Clara M. Chu, "Education for Multicultural Librarianship," in *Multiculturalism in Libraries,* ed. Rosemary Ruhig Du Mont, Lois Buttiar, and William Caynon (Westport, CT: Greenwood Press, 1994): 127–56.

4. Chu, "Education for Multicultural Librarianship," 149.

5. Dennis East and Errol Lam, "In Search of Multiculturalism in the Library Science Curriculum." *Journal of Education for Library and Information Science* 36, no. 3 (1995): 199–216.

6. East and Lam, "In Search of Multiculturalism," 204.

7. Mark D. Winston, "Communication and Teaching: Education about Diversity in the US Classroom," in *Diversity Now: People, Collections, and Services in Academic Libraries,* ed. Teresa Y. Neely and Kuang-Hwri (Janet) Lee-Smdtzer (New York: Haworth Press, 2001): 199–212.

8. Tefko Saracevic, "Closing of Library Schools in North America: What Role Accreditation?'" *Libri* 44, no. 3 (1994): 190–200.

9. Blaise Cronin, "Shibboleth and Substance in North American Library and Information Science Education," *Libri* 45, no. 1 (1995): 45–63.

10. Saracevic, "Closing of Library Schools," 192.

11. Cronin, "Shibboleth and Substance," 45, abstract.

12. American Library Association, *Standards for Accreditation of Master's Programs in Library & Information Studies* (Chicago: American Library Association, 1992, reprinted March 1999).

13. *Standards,* 10.

14. *Standards,* 11.

15. *Standards*, 15.

16. *Standards*, 3.

17. American Library Association, Press Release, May 3, 1999. www.ala.org/congress/pressrelease.html (accessed 1 March 2003).

18. American Library Association, Press Release, May 3, 1999. www.ala.org/congress/press release.html (accessed February 27, 2003).

19. Associations Unlimited, *Encyclopedia of Associations Online* (Detroit, MI: Gale Research, 1996).

20. Chu, "Education for Multicultural Librarianship," 146.

12

Communication and Difficult Topics in LIS Education: Teaching and Learning about Diversity in the Classroom

Mark Winston

With regard to the issue of public discourse related to diversity, topics include diversity dialogues, diversity education and training and sensitivity training, town hall meetings and other discussions of race, gender, orientation, racism, sexism, etc. in the workplace, professional and scholarly meetings and in the classroom. The importance of these types of discussions and exchanges has been highlighted in the literature; however, the success of such discussions in increasing awareness and improving relations and organizational climates is debatable. One of the reasons for the difficulty in ensuring the success of diversity education, training, and discussions is the nature of what communication scholars describe as "taboo topics." The research about communication related to these topics can assist us in enhancing the effectiveness of education in academia, as well as other settings, by better understanding why people have difficulty discussing issues of race, gender, orientation, and ability, among others. The research also reveals how to make these discussions more productive.

Diversity is and has been one of the most perplexing and substantive issues that society has faced and that librarians, administrators, and educators have encountered in the library and information science profession, as well as in higher education generally. In considering issues of diversity in organizations, we generally focus on the concepts of staffing with regard to recruitment, retention, and underrepresentation; services for diverse populations; collections; and organizational climate for employees and library users.

In organizations in general there are organizational, social, interpersonal, and client-related issues that relate to the need for an understanding and appreciation of issues of diversity. Clearly, issues of organizational climate and interpersonal communication among employees and between employees and clients, as well as concerns about equity and fairness, are concerns in terms of understanding of race, gender, and so on.

Certainly there is a need for continuing a substantive exploration of issues related to diversity. Success in achieving goals related to diversity and equity is far more likely to be achieved when the issues are well defined through reasoned debate, scholarly discourse, and practical discussion in a number of settings, including the classroom, as individuals are prepared to work in and contribute to organizations. It should be noted, however, that initiating and facilitating the discussion of these issues and placing the diversity discussion in context are tasks that are not easily accomplished considering the nature and complexity of the issues. The efforts to educate and inform are represented by the public discourse related to diversity. Certainly if those who are in higher education, including those in library and information science education, do not initiate these discussions, we are not fulfilling our responsibility and we are not creating the type of learning environment that is necessary to prepare professionals to be successful and to contribute in the larger profession.

In order to make diversity a priority in libraries, and in the information professions more broadly, it seems that the consideration of issues of diversity should focus on specific topics. Such topics might include defining what is meant by diversity, clarifying the goals and priorities that are to be achieved, and exploring issues related to the political and societal factors that affect diversity efforts. Others to consider are underrepresentation and recruitment, as well as the role of library and information science education in preparing professionals to be successful in a multicultural society. Thus, there is the need to place the diversity discussion in context with regard to the larger societal, organizational, and interpersonal environments of which we are a part.

DIVERSITY IN ORGANIZATIONS

It must be noted that in many organizations, and certainly in the private sector, there is generally the realization among managers and researchers that the reasons organizations should promote diversity go beyond the fact that it is a good thing to do. In the 1999 *Fortune* magazine article identifying "America's Best Companies For Minorities," the researchers report that the "companies that pursue diversity outperform the S&P 500."[1] Specifically, the companies that are the most diverse as measured by factors such as minority representation among senior administrators, middle managers, staff, and the board of directors, as well as spending with minority suppliers and underwriting business that goes to minority-owned investment banks, have also been identified as more successful on the basis of stock performance.

Generally, stock performance reflects the strength of the company, organizational performance, and investor confidence, among other factors. Thus, the benefits of having a diverse organization appear to be: better performance related to making better decisions with more perspectives represented, better understanding of the diverse customer base, and an enhanced ability to market on the basis of a good record as a socially responsible company. While there is the need for further research to identify a causal relationship between investment in diversity and organizational performance, a number of hypotheses become apparent in terms of the measures of performance and diversity-related indicators that are appropriate in the context of libraries. While there is the age-old argument regarding the dissimilarities between private- and public-sector organizations, the correlation between successful performance and the identification of diversity as a priority does, at the very least, indicate that there are substantive reasons for library and information services organizations to promote diversity. Those reasons extend as well with regard to applicable criteria, such as minority representation among library faculty and staff and on library boards and the ability to market to and provide services for a diverse user population.

Talking about Diversity in Organizations

The approaches taken in talking about diversity in organizations include diversity dialogues and diversity education and training, as well as discussions in the workplace that arise as staff and administrators address specific issues in relation to human resources, customer service, and client relations.

A number of challenges are associated with diversity education or training, which is designed to increase awareness, facilitate communication, and enhance the likelihood of addressing organizational issues related to diversity. Specifically, it is difficult to create an environment in which individuals are comfortable in discussing issues such as race and gender, as well as see the discussion of diversity as relevant to them, if they are not members of minority groups or not women. Certainly, the representation of diversity as being synonymous with affirmative action appears to have led to a perception that diversity as an issue is relevant only to those who are women and minorities.

The Association of Research Libraries (ARL), a membership organization of the largest academic and research libraries in the United States and Canada, employs a program officer for diversity whose responsibilities include providing consulting services and offering diversity training for member organizations and others. While it is the organization's philosophy that issues of equity and underrepresentation are quite important, techniques such as the use of a broad definition of diversity are employed to facilitate the learning and communication processes that are a part of diversity training. According to

DeEtta Jones, former ARL senior program officer for diversity, the organization "embraces a broad definition of diversity with the belief that diversity is an important—indeed, key—issue to every member of a library staff, a campus community, and a global society. Further, a broad definition allows multiple access points to the discussion of diversity, from race to spirituality to communication styles. In other words, a greater number of individuals will see the relevance and personal connection to this issue and will then have access to points in the discussion and implementation." [2]

Another aspect of the process of encouraging discussion and learning about issues of diversity is the use of diversity dialogue groups. According to Barbara Walker in *Diversity 101,* the dialogue group is a small group of people (seven to nine) who come together voluntarily on an ongoing basis to learn about issues created by differences. Through a series of structured and unstructured activities and exercises, they learn to identify and strip away stereotypes, examine differences in their assumptions, raise their level of personal efficacy, and build authentic relationships with people they regard as different.[3]

Diversity dialogue groups have been employed in a number of institutions, including the University of Iowa. Janice Simmons-Welburn has indicated that "Collaborative learning is requisite to success in study circles and dialogue groups. It is the responsibility of every member to become engaged in a small group process of personal growth and learning."[4]

The Difficulty of Discussing Diversity

While many scholars and practitioners have addressed in the literature the importance of the above-mentioned types of discussions and exchanges, it is not clear that such approaches have proven successful with regard to increasing awareness and improving relations and organizational climates. What the research tells us about interpersonal communication related to these topics can assist us in enhancing the effectiveness of education in the classroom and the effectiveness of other diversity initiatives. Communication scholars refer to issues that are identified as taboo topics and describe the nature of the difficulties associated with communication about such topics in a variety of settings, including the classroom. In addition, there are historical issues related to the topics that are not appropriately discussed in public or in polite society, race and related issues being among those topics. By providing a better understanding of why people have difficulty discussing issues of race, racism, gender, and sexism, among others, it appears possible to identify approaches that will make lectures and discussions more productive in preparing graduates in terms of awareness and sensitivity and to take on leadership roles in organizations, the profession, and in an increasingly diverse society.

Polite Society and Taboo Topics

According to Elizabeth Arveda Kissling, "Like other communication norms and rules, communication taboos and the social phenomenon of embarrassment work to preserve the expressive order."[5] Thus, there seems to be a motivation among individuals to avoid the discussion of difficult topics to avoid embarrassment and to maintain propriety. The issue of taboo or sensitive topics relates not only to classroom discussion and lectures, but to research that requires the posing of questions to study participants and discussions in various types of interpersonal relationships. Kissling states that such topics "are generally regarded as unpleasant conversational fodder that polite people avoid."[6] The topics that might be considered taboo include "illegal or embarrassing activities, such as drug use and sexual behavior,"[7] including HIV risk factors and birth control;[8] alcohol use; incest; menstruation;[9] death and illness;[10] as well as issues of race, gender, sexual orientation, sexism, and racism, among others.[11]

In the context of survey research, "A question is sensitive if it raises concerns about disapproval or other consequences (such as legal sanctions) for reporting truthfully or if the question itself is seen as an invasion of privacy."[12] Thus, researchers have attempted to identify ways to encourage truthful and complete disclosure by those who are participating in research studies. A significant body of research has revealed that "self-administration of sensitive questions increases levels of reporting relative to administration of the same questions by an interviewer."[13]

In terms of interpersonal relationships, it appears that individuals identify other communication approaches if there is a need to address difficult topics. Kissling indicates that

> although girls frequently recognize a need to talk about menstruation and to share information about it with each other, they are usually embarrassed to talk about menstruation with adults. To avoid and prevent the embarrassment of violating menstrual taboos, girls creatively use such linguistic strategies as slang terms, circumlocutions, pronouns, and euphemistic deixis to find ways to talk about something they are uncomfortable talking about or believe they shouldn't talk about.[14]

In addition, "modern medical training includes instruction in sensitive discussion of terminal illness with patients and their families."[15] As a result, it appears that professionals receive educational training with regard to how to address sensitive issues with their clients and patients, and individuals develop ways to approach these issues in their interpersonal communication.

More generally, the concept of diversity might be in and of itself a representation of this idea of attempting to facilitate communication about difficult subjects in a more benign, less direct way. In this regard, it might be posited that the word diversity is a euphemism and that the concept has been watered down as it relates to the idea of valuing differences of many types in order to make the concepts of racism, sexism, race, and ethnicity, among others, more palatable. The word diversity, which came into common usage in this context only as recently as the *Bakke* case in the late 1970s, might be viewed as an all-encompassing term and as representation of a less direct way of communicating ideas that are uncomfortable to discuss.

In this regard, Edna Andrews addresses the potential relationship between political correctness in speech and the nature of taboo topics in "Cultural Sensitivity and Political Correctness: The Linguistic Problem of Naming."[16] In addition, Loma Peterson cites the work of other researchers and incorporates her own analysis in indicating that "[c]ritics of the diversity movement commonly point out that the concept of diversity includes so many groups that the terminology is rendered meaningless."[17] In addressing the fact that issues of equity and discrimination have been overshadowed by the focus on diversity, Peterson goes on to suggest that

> diversity is a term that is used widely, often without consideration for its meaning and roots. Scholars have analyzed the diversity movement, its definition, and the detriment that it has caused to the goal of the achievement of equity. Equity issues have become clouded by a "me too" claim to victim status, thereby diminishing the possibility of achieving equity. Diversity defaults to little progress and substantial rhetoric that many can join in on without sacrifice or regulation that the promise of equity will be fulfilled.[18]

Thus, if the concept of diversity itself is viewed by some to be a component of the process of avoiding communicating about and possibly addressing issues of race, gender, orientation, and ability, facilitating direct communication in the context of the discussion of diversity is not likely to be easily accomplished.

LIBRARY AND INFORMATION SCIENCE EDUCATION

In library and information science education, issues of diversity and multiculturalism are expected to be a part of the curricula of ALA-accredited master's programs. However, according to Peterson, "[T]he interpretation of this is left up to the individual library and information science school. A school can design a curriculum that does not address issues of equity, justice, and the historical difference in treatment of particular groups; a school can define diversity simply as the quality of being different and state that their graduates are prepared to work in a multicultural environment."[19] The literature related to diversity and LIS education, while focusing mainly on issues of underrepresentation among students and faculty and the importance of fostering diversity in terms of recruitment of students and faculty,[20] offers some discussion of issues of the inclusion of diversity in the curricula and in class lectures and discussions. Welburn addresses the factors to be considered in the development of a course in cultural diversity as a part of the process of incorporating diversity into the curriculum.

First, such a course would have to be considered an intermediate step or transitional step toward rethinking the curriculum at large. Second, a separate course should "revolve around the trifold concept of linkages between the multicultural contexts of information, its users, and information providers. Third, distinctions should be drawn between diversity as a workplace issue and diversity as a service issue. In my opinion, workplace concerns are more appropriately presented within the context of teaching management."[21]

Welburn and Jeng decry the limited amount of library and information science research literature on diversity, with few exceptions.

> We lack a body of knowledge and a critical mass of scholars engaged in the kind of research that can be used in effecting a shift in pedagogy. There is a paucity of scholarship on racial or ethnic perspectives in information and library science. Contrast our predicament with law, where a body of literature has emerged in the areas of critical race theory and feminist scholarship.[22]

Also, with regard to the issue of content, Jeng refers to the need to relate "diversity as an academic topic on the one hand, and the real life of library and information services and its people, both providers and the users, on the other."[23] She goes on to indicate that "[d]iversity education without a concrete connection to LIS services and people inevitably provides students with nice concepts, but with no context in which to apply them."[24] She suggests that "good pedagogy to establish the missing link in the classroom between diversity lectures and the LIS life is the 'scenario' approach: to present specific scenarios that could happen to individual librarians in real libraries."[25] To address one of the communication issues related to such discussions, "The instructor needs to explain that, at times, potentially offensive words and descriptions are used to present the scenarios. This is done with the sole intention of eliciting classroom discussion on diversity."[26]

In the article "Teaching the Practitioners: One Professor's Attempt at Library Education and Sensitivity to Multicultural Diversity," Peterson describes her attempts to foster learning about issues of race and gender through the use of "a questioning context, by creating curricular activities, and responding to student curricular resistance."[27] According to Peterson, her "role is to encourage analytic questioning by students."[28] For example, as a basis for analysis, discussion, and learning she presents to students one of the often mentioned quotes related to the substantial increase in the minority population in the United States and the effect that this population shift will have on higher education. "As a slogan, 'one-third of a nation' makes an excellent classroom example to question the context of multiculturalism and librarianship."[29]

Peterson also makes use of guest lecturers who are members of minority groups, lecture topics that include global perspectives, and the use of a broad array of examples in assignments to enhance the learning process. With regard to the issue of resistance to instruction about issues of race and gender, Peterson observes the following:

> Teaching involves the liberation of students' minds, not indoctrination. Students rarely view teaching this way and believe they must parrot teacher views in order to be successful. When the perceived "indoctrination" is threatening to their power, one can expect resistance in some form. This is especially true for the professor who happens to be a minority male, minority female or white female. Unfortunately, the exploration or inclusion of multicultural diversity in the curriculum, especially if it is taught by a "diversifier," is often considered mind control and indoctrination by some students. When unpopular views or new perspectives are explored in the classroom, one must be prepared for threats to the professor's authority and hostile reactions by students.
> . . . It is important to have rational arguments at hand when resistance to lectures occurs.[30]

With regard to concerns about broader dimensions of diversity, Belay addresses the need for instructors to have an understanding of the "cognitive styles" and approaches to learning and engagement in the classroom that are based on culture and country of origin[31] to increase the likelihood of success for students. Thus, the library and information science education literature does address some considerations and approaches related to instruction about diversity.

CONCLUSION

It appears to be the case that the discussion of diversity, race, gender, and related issues requires trained facilitators and instructors. In a context in which the students, training participants, employees, or others are apprehensive and reluctant to be involved in the discussion, it is clear that the facilitators must create an environment in which participants are able to communicate openly and respectfully. However, it seems that a key issue relates to the facilitator's or instructor's ability to communicate clearly and directly with regard to issues that are difficult to discuss.

Managers and researchers in the area of organizational theory have begun to document the relationship between the fostering of diversity in organizations and the overall success of organizations. In consideration of the importance of fostering diversity in organizations generally, and in the library and information science profession, which has responsibility for documenting much of recorded human history, instructing users and facilitating access to that information, we are compelled to facilitate and engage in discussions of the complex issues related to diversity. Understanding of diversity should be of paramount importance to create organizational climates that promote equity and enhance the likelihood of success of all employees and users. Thus, we must identify the most effective ways to instruct students in a learning environment in which the difficult issues are discussed, focusing on the research and theoretical literature that underlie graduate and professional education for individuals who will not only work with diverse populations, but who will serve as professionals and administrators.

The shortage of library and information science research literature on diversity is a concern and a call to action for researchers. However, the literature in other professions, particularly education, other service professions, and business, which has begun to focus on the connection between diversity and organizational success, is equally relevant for inclusion as readings for graduate students in library and information science programs. The shortage of published literature that focuses on libraries exclusively does not justify a lack of effective instruction for students. In addition, the organizations in which they are employed should be such that communication is encouraged in ways that promote best practices in the provision of information services and in which diversity is valued, supported, and rewarded.

Certainly professionals whose educational experiences have included education and learning about issues of race, gender, ability, orientation, the "isms," and diversity are more likely to be in a position to apply their knowledge in the performance of their responsibilities and more likely to contribute to environments that foster diversity. In addition, professionals whose educational experiences include discussions of traditionally "taboo" topics are more likely to be open to participating in discussions of similar issues in the workplace.

NOTES

1. Geoffrey Colvin "The 50 Best Companies for Asians, Blacks and Hispanics: Companies that Pursue Diversity Outperform the S&P 500. Coincidence?" *Fortune,* July 19, 1999, 3.

2. DeEtta Jones, "The Definition of Diversity: Two Views: A More Inclusive Definition," *Journal of Library Administration* 27, no. 1/2 (1999): 8.

3. Barbara Walker, "Learning about Differences . . . through Dialogue," *Diversity 101* (January/February 1994): 1.

4. Janice Simmons-Welburn, "Diversity Dialogue Groups: A Model for Enhancing Work Place Diversity," *Journal of Library Administration* 27, no. 1/2 (1999): 114.

5. Elizabeth Arveda Kissling, "That's Just a Basic Teen-Age Rule: Girls' Linguistic Strategies for Managing the Menstrual Communication Taboo," *Journal of Applied Communication Research* 24 (December 1996): 292.

6. Kissling, "That's Just a Basic Teen-Age Rule," 293.

7. Roger Tourangeau and Tom W. Smith, "Asking Sensitive Questions: The Impact of Data Collection Mode, Question Format, and Question Context," *Public Opinion Quarterly* 60, no. 2 (1996): 276.

8. Tourangeau and Smith, "Asking Sensitive Questions," 278–279.

9. Kissling, "That's Just a Basic Teen-Age Rule," 292–294.

10. Kissling, "That's Just a Basic Teen-Age Rule," 293.

11. Malcolm Gladwell, "The Sports Taboo: Why Blacks are Like Boys and Whites are Like Girls," *The New Yorker*, May 1997, 50–55.

12. Tourangeau and Smith, "Asking Sensitive Questions," 276.

13. Tourangeau and Smith, "Asking Sensitive Questions," 277.

14. Kissling, "That's Just a Basic Teen-Age Rule," 292–293.

15. Kissling, "That's Just a Basic Teen-Age Rule," 293.

16. Edna Andrews, "Cultural Sensitivity and Political Correctness: The Linguistic Problem of Naming," *American Speech* 71, no. 4 (1996): 389–404.

17. Lorna Peterson, "The Definition of Diversity: Two Views: A More Specific Definition," *Journal of Library Administration* 27, no. 1/2 (1999): 20.

18. Peterson, "The Definition of Diversity," 21.

19. Peterson, "The Definition of Diversity," 23.

20. E. J. Josey, "The Challenges of Cultural Diversity in the Recruitment of Faculty and Students from Diverse Backgrounds," *Journal of Education for Library and Information Science* 34, no. 4 (1993): 302–311.

21. William Welburn, "Do We Really Need Cultural Diversity in the Library and Information Science Curriculum," *Journal of Education for Library and Information Science* 35, no. 4 (1994): 329.

22. Welburn, "Do We Really Need Cultural Diversity in the Library and Information Science Curriculum," 329.

23. Ling Hwey Jeng, "Facilitating Classroom Discussion on Diversity," *Journal of Education for Library and Information Science* 38, no. 4 (1997): 334.

24. Jeng, "Facilitating Classroom Discussion on Diversity," 335.

25. Jeng, "Facilitating Classroom Discussion on Diversity," 335.

26. Jeng, "Facilitating Classroom Discussion on Diversity," 335.

27. Loma Peterson, "Teaching the Practitioners: One Professor's Attempt at Library Education and Sensitivity to Multicultural Diversity," *The Reference Librarian* 45/46 (1994): 24.

28. Peterson, "Teaching the Practitioners," 25.

29. Peterson, "Teaching the Practitioners," 29.

30. Peterson, "Teaching the Practitioners," 33.

31. Getinet Belay, "Conceptual Strategies for Operationalizing Multicultural Curricula," 33 (Fall 1992): 299.

13

Faculty Development and Cultural Diversity in Teaching: LIS Education's Last Frontier

Maurice B. Wheeler

Back in the late 1980s, while discussing our profession's response to diversity with a colleague, I made an observation on the lack of cultural diversity in the curricula of most LIS programs of the time. My colleague, a black female LIS faculty who was an outspoken proponent of cultural diversity in the profession, passionately protested the notion of anyone "telling" her what or how to teach. Although her response was shocking to me, it served as a real eye-opener. Because of my strong belief that no individual, at any level, should be allowed to opt out when diversity initiatives are established, I was extremely uncomfortable with her position. However, as a librarian with only a few years of experience and someone who had given little thought to faculty rights, I chose not to pursue the issue further. I knew that championing diversity in the profession was an important part of my colleague's professional activities. Yet, her willingness to allow "faculty issues" to override her position on diversity was a disquieting discovery for me.

Since that time, I have held several faculty and administrative positions and participated in countless discussions on the topic of diversity in academia. These experiences have provided me with a deeper understanding of the possible responses and perspectives on the topic in academia. My initial position on the subject, rather than having changed drastically, is now tempered by an awareness of how political realities and organizational culture affect individual and collective responses.

Throughout America's history, issues of race, ethnicity, and other "differences" have affected not only society and culture but politics and legislation. What's more, it is likely that these topics will continue to generate widescale political activity in American society. Prime examples are recent U.S. Supreme

181

Court decisions relating to the unconstitutionality of sodomy laws and the use of race as a factor in university recruitment.

The *Brown v. Board of Education* decision of 1954 and the Civil Rights Act of 1964 legitimized the struggle for equality in education. Subsequent legislation laid a foundation for the principle of equal access that is, at least in theory, standard practice in higher education today. In the past several decades, not only have more African Americans sought degrees in higher education, but on many campuses, classrooms are "populated by more women, students of color, older, part-time, international students, as well as students with various disabilities and a range of sexual orientations."[1] The latest U.S. Department of Education student statistics indicate that U.S. colleges and universities are composed of 68.3 percent whites, 11.3 percent blacks, 9.5 percent Hispanics, 6.4 percent Asians, and 1 percent Native Americans.[2]

These figures indicate that there are far more students of color than before the Civil Rights Act of 1964, yet student statistics are still not representative of society as a whole. For example, while the groundbreaking predictions of *Workforce 2000*[3] are now a reality, with Hispanics exceeding the African American population, current U.S. Census figures show that the Hispanic presence on campus in the form of students and faculty falls far short of national norms. The racial demographics for faculty are considerably out-of-sync with the general population. Of the nearly one million men and women who comprise U.S. faculty, 86 percent are white, 5.5 percent are African American, 3 percent are Hispanic, 5 percent are Asian/Pacific Islanders, and 0.5 percent are American Indian/Alaskan Natives.[4]

The demographics of the library and information science profession are even more troubling. Clearly, we are faced with a crisis regarding recruitment of librarians of color. The most recent statistics show that 84.2 percent of LIS students are of European ancestry, with only 6.7 percent African American students, 4.7 percent Asian students, 3.9 percent Hispanic students, and 0.48 percent Native American students.[5] The most disturbing aspect of the demographics shifts in the United States is that the growing number of people of color in the population will not see themselves reflected in this profession. They will be served by people who they can only hope have been educated appropriately to address their information needs with cultural awareness and sensitivity.

In 2000, Wallace posed the question of how to best prepare students for the realities of the new millennium. She states an option in the form of a question: "Should we systematically review our curriculum and establish the goal of infusing multicultural content across all course work, ensuring it is relevant to the particular course's content?"[6] Considering the tremendous range of cultural, ethnic, and other types of visible and invisible diversity present in our lives, it might appear to some that the answer would be an easy "yes." Yet opponents of diversity initiatives often characterize such approaches as indoctrination.[7]

This chapter explores both the variety of organizational and personal challenges that arise and the forms of support essential to the establishment of faculty development diversity initiatives. In addition, it will present and discuss components of a model faculty development initiative.

THE "WHY" FACTOR OF DIVERSITY

Even in the best of circumstances, little collective effort is made to assure that PhD students who choose to teach are equipped with the basic pedagogical tools and experience to ensure their success in the classroom. At present, one is even less likely to find graduate-level teachers with knowledge and expertise in diversity issues, unless that topic happens to be their academic specialty. Without having a little insight about their teaching styles and the effect of their approaches and methods, faculty are unable to provide a learning experience in which cultural and ethnic diversity are acknowledged assets.

Many universities have been incorporating diversity initiatives in student educational activities since the 1980s. This is particularly true for undergraduate programs. For those students who have moved on to graduate schools during this time, diversity is an integral part of the curriculum and the overall academic experience. However, the same cannot be said for faculty who have been teaching for more than twenty years and for practicing professionals returning to school as students. These older faculty and students, and perhaps others, are more prone to question why diversity is a worthy and important topic for staff. Some may wonder why the administrative goal of increasing the number of underrepresented students is not sufficient.

If, as Banks proposes, "people's way of thinking, behaving, and being are deeply influenced by race, ethnicity, social class, and language,"[8] then it could be reasoned that teaching and interactions with students are also influenced by the same factors. Wallace asserts that "what passes as knowledge may actually reflect unconscious attitudes and erroneous beliefs."[9]

Setting aside for a moment the issues of race and diversity, the fact remains that classrooms are not socially and politically neutral learning environments. But should they be? This is an important question when considering the process by which future librarians are educated and, one hopes, prepared to work in a diverse local and global society. According to Bossman,[10] the notion of a value-free education has been a mere pretense for the sake of public relations rather than an actual goal. The educational process must provide ways for both scholars and students to "examine and understand the range of values implicit in a core curriculum." Building on that thought, Torrey[11] states that effective teachers should be expected to reflect a range of social and cultural perspectives in their teaching.

In terms of how subject material is presented, areas that may need revision and improvement can be identified by posing two simple questions: "In what ways do our curriculum and instructional material exclude the experiences of women, people of color, and lesbian and gay people? In what ways do they address issues of racism, sexism, ethnocentrism, and homophobia?"[12]

Torrey believes that one purpose of higher education is to "prepare today's students to shoulder their moral and ethical responsibility to confront and wrestle with the complex problems they will encounter."[13] It is essential that librarians be prepared not only to work with people from diverse backgrounds, but also to pursue multiple and divergent perspectives, even when their own opinions, personal boundaries, or beliefs are not validated or affirmed.

In many ways, the library and information science profession is a reflection of the society it serves. Therefore, library education programs must accept responsibility for populating the profession with a new generation of culturally competent librarians. That task falls squarely on the shoulders of faculty and their success will be determined by how well their teaching reflects the evolution of both society and the profession. This can best be achieved by providing future librarians with broad and expansive exposure to the history and practices of the profession and its effect on all of society.

REALISTIC EXPECTATIONS OF FACULTY DEVELOPMENT

Because of the limited opportunities for financial gain and a paucity of perks, academicians' professional activities can in some respects be considered a labor of love. For that reason, faculty autonomy in teaching how and what they please is widely regarded as a "right." Indeed, with the possible exception of freedom of speech, no other "right" in academia is guarded as passionately. As researchers observed at State University of New York, Buffalo, "Collegial examination of syllabi, curriculum and pedagogy rarely occurs."[14] Consequently, regardless of what other faculty responsibilities may be discussed or incorporated into a development program, curriculum and classroom activities have remained sacrosanct and off limits.

In approaching the issue of faculty development, particularly regarding curriculum and course content, it is important not to challenge the subject expertise of faculty. In some circumstances, it can be incendiary even to suggest that teaching skills could be enhanced. It has been pointed out that often the real challenge involves "distinguishing the expert teacher from the content expert."[15] In any case, making teaching and curricula culturally relevant is often a risky business since it requires a fundamental change in what and how we teach future information professionals.

As noted earlier, faculty development programs "usually distinguish or focus on the individual faculty member as a teacher, scholar, professional, and as a person . . . rather than focusing specifically on the course, curriculum or student learning."[16] The challenge for development programs emphasizing diversity and multiculturalism is to focus specifically on areas that have previously been avoided: teaching methods and course content.

According to Adams and Marchesani,[17] graduate schools have ill-prepared their students to teach in the social and cultural climate found on most campuses. As they observe, "For faculty socialized within another historical and cultural situation, the understandable difficulty is to know how best to facilitate diverse student learning within an increasingly multicultural context." Another often overlooked reason for resistance to faculty development is that "advancement is seldom based on an evaluation of teaching skills; research and publication are paramount."[18] Thus, faculty may view any improvements to teaching in strictly practical terms, believing that their time, energy, and resources are better spent on efforts to help them achieve tenure and promotion.

A recent analysis of data based on research conducted at Macalester College and University of Maryland, College Park, supports the need for addressing diversity both systemically and systematically. According to the findings, "The vast majority of faculty members reported that student diversity did not lead them to make significant changes in their classroom practices. Slightly less than one-third of faculty respondents said that the presence of racially diverse students led them to adjust their course syllabus."[19] Furthermore, the research revealed that "full professors and faculty with more years of teaching have less positive views of benefits of diversity than respondents generally."[20] The latter findings seem to support the premise that faculty who need the development most are those least likely to take advantage of it. The research also provides a possible explanation for the marked increase over the past twenty years in students charging faculty with classroom discrimination.[21] In essence, student awareness and expectations have risen regarding diversity, but faculty classroom behavior has not changed significantly to meet and match those expectations.

Clearly, leadership and support regarding diversity must come from outside the faculty ranks. Equally important is the need for a critical mass of individuals throughout the organization, with varying degrees of political power, to initiate discussion and action. Confronted with the prospect of tackling issues that are hotly and very emotionally debated—issues such as evaluation and development of faculty, curriculum revision and reform, and diversity and multiculturalism—it comes as no great surprise that many university administrations have only addressed this issue in a broad and non-prescriptive manner.

ADMINISTRATIVE ENCOURAGEMENT AND LEADERSHIP

Wallace challenges academic administrators to consider their faculty's development regarding multiculturalism, how the level of development is reflected in the curriculum, and lastly, what support is available to "stimulate individual faculty members' professional development in the area of diversity."[22] An additional question for consideration is whether participation in diversity programming should be voluntary or mandated and whether staff participation should be required as a means of addressing diversity. From a legal perspective, there are aspects of diversity and race relations within organizations that are certainly not voluntary. Still, handling issues of both diversity and faculty development requires skill and finesse, as each is deeply embedded in the culture, character, and identity of the faculty members themselves and the organization. Part of the difficulty for administrators stems from the age-old practice of treating faculty as "independent practitioners with few lines of connection" to institutional initiatives or leadership from central administration.[23]

On the departmental level, regardless of whether diversity is presented as a university mandate or a departmental initiative, it is the dean's responsibility to establish the rationale, connect it with the values of the school, and ensure that diversity is reflected in all relevant documents and practices. The school's mission, vision statement, strategic plan, policy statements, curriculum, and student and faculty recruitment must all be aligned in support of the initiative.

Perhaps the most challenging role for an administrator is establishing an institutional climate supportive of diversity initiatives while simultaneously championing the faculty development activities that will make the diversity initiatives a reality. The ultimate goal is to create an environment in which faculty are open to discussions about diversity, have a clear understanding of institutional expectations, and are given opportunities to participate in the process.

It is important that faculty are encouraged to explore new approaches to teaching through incentives rather than directives. Developmental activities that are outcome- or product-based allow faculty to focus on the ultimate benefits rather than the process itself. Also important is the recognition of faculty commitment in the form of appropriate compensation. Rather than money, this could take the form of travel funds, classroom or office equipment, reduced teaching loads, and additional teaching or research assistant hours.

Certainly, compensation for participating in diversity development can be negotiated between individual faculty members and the dean. Faculty development can also be made a departmental expectation reflected in and integrated with the annual performance evaluation process.

The inherently onerous nature of curriculum revision and development can require incentives to stimulate energy and excitement and to encourage faculty to complete the task. Over time, such incentives can become part of the ongoing employment process, institutionalized in the evaluation and reward systems. When significant curricular changes are taking place, as is the case with diversity initiatives, participation in developmental activities is more likely to occur when involvement is tracked for inclusion in periodic performance reviews. To encourage even more consistent participation, it has been suggested that faculty efforts be reflected in the tenure review process.[24] In the absence of such formalized structures, faculty who naturally incorporate diversity in their teaching should be publicly recognized and rewarded, commensurate with their level of participation.

An appropriate level of institutional resources must always be made available to support any venture in which people are prone to look for excuses not to participate. For example, many universities are now offering grants to help faculty integrate technology into their courses. Similar grants could also be offered in those settings where incorporating diversity into the curriculum has been identified as an institution-wide goal.

In most colleges and universities, the faculty assume ownership of the curriculum. Therefore, it is important that any initiatives not faculty-generated are framed in terms of student learning and preparation, rather than as specific to course content. Once diversity has been identified administratively as an area of concentration or emphasis, the faculty must be empowered to determine the degree and manner of response to the administrative directives. In all but the most difficult of circumstances, the administration's responsibility at that point will be to make support and incentives accessible, relevant, and appropriately scaled.

Creating optimal circumstances for the success of faculty development is an elusive venture. However, to improve the likelihood of success, two factors are paramount: the encouragement and support of university and departmental administration and the philosophical position that continued growth and development is not an option. Many universities spend tremendous amounts of money providing faculty with development opportunities, yet seem to be indifferent as to whether or not the services are utilized. If universities cannot persuade faculty to accept development and continued growth as a basic requirement for ongoing appointment, at least through the associate professor level, the effort to incorporate diversity as an aspect of faculty development could be futile.

Nevertheless, the incremental cultural shift in academic institutions regarding both diversity and faculty development continues to evolve. In most institutions, that cultural shift is reflected eventually in promotional materials and policy statements, such as professional standards.

PROFESSIONAL STANDARDS

Professional associations have long struggled with the issue of diversity and equality. For example, the ALA, which initially excluded women from participation in its conference proceedings, has wrestled with racism and diversity in a manner that closely mirrors the struggles of American society. Although many associations have stopped short of taking prescriptive positions, several have issued standards that reflect their position on racial and cultural diversity. The standards set forth by two professional associations are particularly relevant to this discussion: the ALA and the National Education Association (NEA).

The most recent version of the "Standards for Accreditation of Master's Programs in Library and Information Studies" was adopted by the council of ALA on January 28, 1992, and became effective January 1, 1993. The standards identify diversity as being important because of the changing racial and cultural composition of society. Relevant passages are presented below in italicized print.

ALA Standards

I: Mission, Goals, and Objectives

A school's mission and program goals are pursued, and its program objectives achieved, through implementation of a broad-based planning process that involves the constituency that a program seeks to serve. Consistent with the values of the parent institution and the culture and mission of the school, program goals and objectives foster quality education. Program objectives are stated in terms of educational results to be achieved and reflect *the role of library and information services in a rapidly changing multicultural, multiethnic, multilingual society, including the role of serving the needs of underserved groups*

Within the context of these Standards each program is judged on the degree to which it attains its objectives. In accord with the mission of the school, clearly defined, publicly stated, and regularly reviewed program goals and objectives form the essential frame of reference for meaningful external and internal evaluation. The evaluation of program goals and objectives involves those served: students, faculty, employers, alumni, and other constituents.

II: Curriculum

The curriculum of library and information studies encompasses information and knowledge creation, communication, identification, selection, acquisition, organization and description, storage and retrieval, preservation, analysis, interpretation, evaluation, synthesis, dissemination, and management.

The curriculum *responds to the needs of a rapidly changing multicultural, multiethnic, multilingual society including the needs of underserved groups.*

III: Faculty

The school has a faculty capable of accomplishing program objectives. Full-time faculty members are qualified for appointment to the graduate faculty within the parent institution and are sufficient in number and in diversity of specialties to carry out the major share of the teaching, research, and service activities required for a program, wherever and however delivered.

The school has policies to recruit and retain faculty from multicultural, multiethnic, and multilingual backgrounds.

Afterword

The "multicultural, multiethnic, and multilingual" nature of society is referenced throughout the Standards because of the desire to recognize diversity when framing goals and objectives, designing curricula, and selecting and retaining faculty and students.

The most important issues at the time of the revision (1989–1992) were these: action orientation; definition of the field; *discrimination*; distance education; *diversity*; excellence; future focus; globalization; innovation; interaction with other fields of study and other campus units; management; multiple degree programs; ongoing evaluation processes; philosophy, principles and ethics; research; specialization; technology; users.[25]

While the inclusion of four references to diversity in the accreditation standards of the ALA is certainly no small feat, in reality they lack the necessary level of detail to command action or response. The mere presence of the topic in the standards can provide support for schools that want to address diversity. However, the statements are sufficiently weak that schools and programs with no interest in the topic can easily point to half-hearted or marginally related activities in attempts to show their diligence. The standards conclude by stating that there is a "desire" to include diversity. If a reader was uncertain about whether the references to diversity were intended as regulatory, the inclusion of the "desire" in the afterword makes it clear: No, it is not.

In contrast, the NEA takes a much stronger position in its policy statements. While still avoiding heavy-handed prescriptive measures, the standards provide a clear articulation of the association's position and state it with some degree of specificity. In the policy section on curriculum reform, two important areas of expectation are highlighted: the needs of a diverse student population and preparation for students' effective participation in a multicultural society by exposing students to various traditions and realities.

NEA Policy Statements

IV. Curriculum Reform

Efforts at curriculum reform which involve changes in the shape and nature of the baccalaureate degree must incorporate standards of excellence and skills, knowledge, and understanding to help students prepare for the future. No effort at reform can succeed without adequate support for the faculty who have primary responsibility for the curriculum, *nor can it succeed unless it addresses the needs of a diverse student population.*

The goals of higher education curricula should include mastery of basic skills, active participation in the learning process, in-depth study, critical thinking, understanding of a discipline's characteristic methods, and a coherent and relevant course of study. The goals should also be consistent with NEA principles such as faculty control, equal access to quality education for all students, and *multicultural understanding.*

Any effort at curriculum revision should be designed to prepare all students for effective citizenship and participation in an increasingly diverse multicultural and multiracial society. A common body of intellectual reference must be inclusive of all traditions and realities. A diverse student population enriches the knowledge base of all students.

NEA recommends the following:

Curricula must express the goals and mission of individual institutions and address the needs of students.

In designing the college's curriculum and schedule, the faculty should take the responsibility to ensure that it is suited to the needs of a multiethnic, multicultural society, and that it is flexible enough to allow access for different kinds of students (adult learners, students who work, part-time students, transfers, and other nontraditional students).[26]

Policy statements and standards can be effective tools in support of faculty development programs. The above statements are worded such that they provide strong support for not only curricula reform and revision, but also for reviewing other aspects of the educational process from a multicultural perceptive. These and other policy statements and professional standards can be useful in helping administrators make the case that an education inclusive of cultural and racial diversity is a clearly stated expectation.

CREATING A USEFUL MODEL

In order to have skills and abilities that are professionally relevant, librarians must possess a level of cultural competency that enables them to function successfully and provide effective information services within a racially and culturally diverse society. The goal in establishing a diversity or multicultural initiative for faculty development is to infuse the educational process with the structure and components necessary to produce such librarians. Meeting the information service needs of a culturally diverse population will require continuous assessment and reorganization of information and expansion of cultural knowledge. That cannot be accomplished without consideration for what and how we teach.

No effort of this magnitude can be considered without extensive preparation and planning. That preparation must include an institutional audit or assessment of issues related to diversity, including the current climate, levels of support and resistance, and the real or perceived need for change. The sometimes difficult and lengthy process of comprehensive, campus-wide discussions among faculty, staff, and administration must also be incorporated in the planning process.

If a decision is made to move forward with establishing such an initiative, the following suggestions are offered for consideration:

- Establish diversity as an ongoing initiative rather than a program with an expected timeframe or culminating event or goal;
- Include faculty in the creation of development programs to the greatest extent possible;
- Recognize that relegating diversity issues to separate or peripheral courses "ghettoizes" them, minimizing their importance and giving faculty the ability to opt out of participation;
- Make diversity a responsibility for everyone, not just interested parties and faculty of color;
- Establish an institutional expectation of continuous faculty growth and development and tie that expectation to tangible faculty benefits and compensation;
- Link diversity-related faculty development to institutional goals expressed through mission and vision statements, strategic plans and other official documents;
- Reach an appropriate level of recognition for improvement in teaching, such as incorporation of aspects of new educational theory and practice;

- Encourage and support participation in professional associations, particularly those in which diversity is part of an ongoing dialogue, such as the Association of Library and Information Science Education (ALISE) and ALA.

CONCLUSION

Stated simply, diversity initiatives on college and university campuses are about reexamining and refocusing educational processes through a multicultural lens. However, assuring that educational processes are not only socially responsible but also pedagogically sound and theoretically grounded is a tremendous challenge.

Prior to the advancement of multiculturalism in the late 1980s, expertise in a particular discipline, demonstrated through possession of the terminal degree, was the primary requirement for teaching in higher education. The last several decades, however, have witnessed significant increases in the number of people of color and students with other forms of "differences" who have matriculated into mainstream higher education. In addition, the sometimes startling and continuous advances in educational technology have placed new expectations on faculty. In addition to creating a need for new faculty with special skills and pedagogical approaches, these changes have provided the justification for also outfitting existing faculty with new skills and teaching approaches. Faculty development programs offer the administrative support and resources, as well as the social support of peers, to address a variety of developmental issues, including the incorporation of multiculturalism or diversity into teaching. The primary reasons why faculty don't take advantage of these developmental opportunities can be found in the culture of academia and individual university units, as well as the expectations and support of university administration.

When a concerted effort is made to change faculty perceptions about both developmental activities and the incorporation of diversity in the classroom, initiatives can be effective in ensuring that students receive significant and meaningful exposure to different cultures, perspectives, values, and ways of living.

NOTES

1. Maurianne Adams and Linda Marchesani, "A Multidimensional Approach to Faculty development: Understanding the Teaching-learning Process," *Diversity Digest,* 1999. www.diversityweb.org/Digest/W99/multidimensional.html (accessed 15 March 2003).

2. National Center for Educational Statistics, *Digest of Education Statistics 2002*. http://nces.ed.gov/programs/digest/d02/tables/dt206.asp (accessed 16 March 2003).

3. William B. Johnston and Arnold E. Packer, *Workforce 2000: Work and Workers for the 21st Century* (Indianapolis, IN: The Hudson Institute,1987).

4. National Center for Educational Statistics, *Digest of Education Statistics 2002*.

5. Association of Library and Information Science Education, *Library and Information Science Statistical Report 2002.* http://ils.unc.edu/ALISE/2002/Students/Table%20II-4-a.htm (accessed 16 March 2003).

6. Barbara C. Wallace, "A Call for Change in Multicultural Training at Graduate Schools of Education: Educating to End Oppression and for Social Justice," *Teachers College Record* 102, no. 6 (2000): 1086–1111.

7. Troy Duster, "They're Taking Over! and Other Myths About Race on Campus," *Mother Jones*, Sept./Oct. 1991, 30–35; Jon Avery, "Plato's Republic in the Core Curriculum: Multiculturalism and the Canon Debate," *The Journal of General Education* 44, no. 4 (1995): 234–255.

8. James A. Banks, "The Historical Reconstruction of Knowledge about Race: Implications for Transformative Teaching," in *Multicultural Education, Transformative Knowledge, and Action: Historical and Contemporary Perspectives*, ed. James A. Banks (New York: Teachers College Press, 1996).

9. Wallace, "A Call for Change."

10. David M. Bossman, "Cross-Cultural Values for a Pluralistic Core Curriculum," *Journal of Higher Education* 62, no. 6 (1991): 661–681.

11. Evelyn Jeanne Torrey, "Faculty Development Centers in Higher Education: Incorporating Diversity and Technology." Ed.D. dissertation, Florida Atlantic University, 2002.

12. Estela M. Bensimon and William G. Tierney, "Shaping the Multicultural College Campus," *Education Digest* 59, no. 3 (1993): 67–71.

13. Torrey, "Faculty Development Centers."

14. Peter Gold, "Faculty Collaboration for a New Curriculum," *Liberal Education* 83, no. 1 (1997): 46–49.

15. Torrey, "Faculty Development Centers."

16. Professional and Organizational Network in Higher Education. "What is Faculty Development? Faculty Development Definitions 2000." http://lamar.colostate.edu/~ckfgill/facd/definit.html (accessed 16 March 2003).

17. Maurianne Adams and Linda Marchesani, "Dynamics of Diversity in the Teaching-learning Process: A Faculty Development Model for Analysis and Action," in *Promoting Diversity in College Classrooms: Innovative Responses for the Curriculum, Faculty, and Institutions*, ed. Maurianne Adams (San Francisco, CA: Jossey-Bass, 1992).

18. Paul Berman, Jo-Ann Intili, and Daniel Weiler, "Exploring Faculty Development in California Higher Education," California State Postsecondary Education Commission 1988. www.cpec.ca.gov/CompleteReports/1988Reports/88-20.pdf (accessed 15 March 2003).

19. American Association of University Professors, "Does Diversity Make a Difference?" *Academe* 86, no. 5 (2000): 54–57.

20. American Association of University Professors, "Does Diversity Make a Difference?"

21. Wallace, "A Call for Change."

22. Sylvia Hurtado, "The Campus Racial Climate," *Journal of Higher Education* 63, no. 5 (1992): 539–569.

23. William Toombs, "Faculty Vitality: The Professional Context," in *Incentives for Faculty Vitality*, ed. Roger J. Baldwin (San Francisco, CA: Jossey-Bass, 1985).

24. Bensimon and Tierney, "Shaping the Multicultural College Campus."

25. American Library Association Committee on Accreditation. *Standards for Accreditation of Master's Programs in Library and Information Studies* (Chicago: American Library Association, 1992).

26. National Education Association. NEA Policy Statements 2003. www.nea.org/he/policy4.html (accessed 16 March 2003).

Index

195

About the Contributors

Susan Webreck Alman is director, distance education services, and adjunct faculty at the University of Pittsburgh, School of Information Sciences. Dr. Alman has a BA degree in history and education from Washington and Jefferson College and MLS and PhD degrees from the University of Pittsburgh, School of Library and Information Science (SIS). She has held several administrative positions at SIS since joining the staff in 1987, including assistant to the dean and coordinator of professional development. Dr. Alman also served as coordinator of graduate student research at the University of Michigan, School of Information.

Laurie Bonnici joined the College of Information Science and Technology at Drexel University as an assistant professor in 2004. She received her PhD in information studies at Florida State University. Dr. Bonnici previously worked at College of Information Technology at Georgia Southern University, the School of Library and Information Studies at Texas Woman's University, and the School of Information Studies at Florida State University. Her current research includes the "Impact of Interactive Technologies on Satisfaction and Performance in Collaborative Learning." Dr. Bonnici has been awarded several national-level grants to aid her research projects.

Marva J. Bryant is a young adult librarian at the Bordeaux Branch Library of the Nashville Public Library (NPL). Marva joined the staff of the NPL in 2002. She has a BS degree in elementary education from Alabama A&M University and an MLIS from the University of Pittsburgh. While a student a Pitt, Marva was instrumental in reestablishing the Minority Resource Office at the School of Information Sciences.

Kathleen Burnett is associate dean for technology and instructional development and associate professor at Florida State University School of Information Studies. She earned a BA degree in German literature from the University of California, San Diego and an MLS and PhD in the history of printing and publishing from the University of California, Berkeley. Dr. Burnett was previously a member of the faculty of the School of Communication, Information and Library Studies at Rutgers University in New Jersey and has also taught at the University of California, Berkeley, and San Jose State University. She has worked as a rare books cataloger, women's studies librarian, children's librarian, reference librarian, and, briefly, as a business librarian.

Cora P. Dunkley is an assistant professor at the University of South Florida. Dr. Dunkley has a BS degree in English from Fort Valley State College, an MA in library science from Atlanta University, and a PhD from Florida State University (FSU). Before joining the faculty at USF, Dr. Dunkley was an adjunct reference librarian at Albany State University, adjunct faculty member at La-Grange College at Albany, and a practicing media specialist at Merry Acres Middle School in Albany, Georgia (south of Macon). She has worked as a school media specialist in various capacities for more than twenty-five years, primarily in public middle schools.

Elizabeth Figa is assistant professor in the School of Library and Information Sciences at the University of North Texas (UNT). She has held administrative positions in the health care industry and in medical libraries. Prior to joining the faculty at UNT in 2000, she was an administrator in the Graduate College at the University of Illinois at Urbana-Champaign. Dr. Figa has a BS in nursing from DePauw University, an MS in community health education from Illinois State University, and an MS and PhD in library and information science from the University of Illinois at Urbana-Champaign. Dr. Figa's professional activities and publications are focused on information access and retrieval, the ethnography of information systems, and storytelling as information science. http://www.unt.edu/slis/people/faculty/figa.htm.

Trina Holloway is a student in the master's of library science program at Clarke Atlanta University. She is an ALA Spectrum Scholar and works in the Price Gilbert Memorial Library.

DeEtta Jones is director of organizational learning services at the Association of Research Libraries (ARL). In that capacity, she manages the portfolio of programs in the Office of Leadership and Management Services. She piloted the ARL Leadership and Career Development Program, a program to prepare mid-career librarians from underrepresented groups for top-level leadership positions, and the Initiative to Recruit a Diverse Workforce, an effort to recruit new talent to academic and research librarianship. Ms. Jones's experiences include human rights advocacy and education and multicultural awareness and skill training. Ms. Jones has an MBA from Johns Hopkins University, an MS in higher education administration, and a BS in psychology from Colorado State University.

Em Claire Knowles is assistant dean of the Graduate School of Library and Information Science at Simmons College. Before going to Simmons in 1988, she was coordinator of bibliographic instruction at Shields Library at the University of California, Davis. Dr. Knowles has a BA degree from the University of California, Davis, an MLS from the University of California, Berkeley, an MPA from California State University, Sacramento, and a DA from Simmons College, Graduate School of Library and Information Science. She is an active member of several professional organizations, and is a past board member of the Black Caucus of ALA.

Janet Macpherson is a doctoral student and clinical faculty in the School of Library and Information Sciences at the University of North Texas. Prior to pursuing her PhD, she worked for more than seventeen years in various positions related to information access and retrieval in several corporations. Macpherson has a BS in education from Bowling Green State University, an MS in special education from the University of North Texas, and an MS in mathematics from Texas Woman's University. Her teaching and research interests relate to the social interaction and stories involved in the use of information systems in diverse environments.

Kathleen de la Peña McCook is distinguished university professor at the University of South Florida (USF). Dr. McCook has a BA degree in English from the University of Illinois, an MA in English from Marquette University, an MA in library science from the University of Chicago, and a PhD in library and information studies from the University of Wisconsin at Madison. Prior to joining the faculty at USF, she held a variety of faculty and administrative positions, including a position at Louisiana State University School of Library and Information Science. She was named the Arnulfo Trejo Latino Librarian of the Year in 2002 by REFORMA. Dr. McCook has chaired the ALA Advisory Committee for the Office for Literacy and Outreach Services and written broadly on the topic of diversity. She is editor of *Women of Color in Librarianship* and received the ALA Equality Award in 1987.

Teresa Y. Neely is the head of reference at the Albin O. Kuhn Library and Gallery, University of Maryland in Baltimore County, Maryland. Most recently, she was assistant professor and reference librarian at Colorado State University Libraries, Fort Collins, Colorado, where she held several positions.

Dr. Neely holds a BS degree in accounting from South Carolina State College (now University) and received her MLS and PhD degrees from the School of Information Sciences, University of Pittsburgh. Dr. Neely was co-chair of the first Diversity Leadership Institute sponsored by the ALA Office of Diversity.

Lorna Peterson is associate professor of library and information science at the University of Buffalo, School of Informatics. Dr. Peterson has a BA from Dickinson College, an MSLS from Case Western Reserve University, and a PhD from Iowa State University. Having spent a significant portion of her career as a bibliographic instruction librarian, Dr. Peterson has focused her research and publications on issues related to teaching people how to use the library and multiculturalism and diversity in the profession.

Loriene Roy is a professor in the School of Information at the University of Texas (UT). Prior to joining the faculty at UT in 1987, she was a research associate in the Library Research Center at the University of Illinois, Urbana. Dr. Roy has a BT degree from the Oregon Institute of Technology, an MLS from the University of Arizona, and a PhD in library and information science from the University of Illinois. Dr. Roy has twice received the Excellence in Advising Award and received the Texas Excellence in Teaching Award. Among her research interests are public library history and services and services for Native Americans.

Linda Schamber is associate professor in the University of North Texas (UNT) School of Library and Information Sciences. Prior to joining the faculty at UNT in 1991, she taught in the field of communications at two other universities and worked as a newspaper editor and freelanced as a copyeditor. Dr. Schamber has a BS degree in education and a MA in journalism, both from Ohio State University, and a PhD in information science from Syracuse University. Her research interests include information and communication theory, information seeking and use behavior and information skills development. Dr. Schamber is active in the American Society for Information Science and Technology.

Anne Steffans is a reference librarian at the Gumberg Library, Duquesne University. She graduated with the MLIS degree from the University of Pittsburgh in 2003.

Maurice B. Wheeler is associate professor in the School of Library and Information Sciences at the University of North Texas. He has held administrative positions in both academic and public libraries. Prior to joining the faculty at UNT in 2001, he was director of the Detroit Public Library. Dr. Wheeler has a BMus degree from Shorter College, and MMus and MLS from the University of Michigan, and a PhD in library and information science from the University of Pittsburgh. An active member of ALA, Dr. Wheeler's professional activities and publications have focused primarily on issues related to diversity in library and information science.

Mark Winston joined the faculty of the School of Communication, Information and Library Science at Rutgers University as an assistant professor in 1998. He received a BS degree from Hampton University and an MLS and PhD from the School of Information at the University of Pittsburgh. Prior to joining the faculty at Rutgers, Dr. Winston served as assistant university librarian and assistant professor at Valdosta State University Library. His research and extensive publications focus on management and organizational behavior, leadership development, diversity, and recruitment.